Social Work Practice with Latinos

Also available from Lyceum Books, Inc.

Essential Skills of Social Work Practice:
Assessment, Intervention, and Evaluation
by Thomas O'Hare

Diversity, Oppression, and Change: Culturally Grounded Social Work
by Flavio Fransisco Marsiglia and Stephen Kulis

Complex Systems and Human Behavior
by Christopher G. Hudson

Community Health Care in Cuba
by Susan E. Mason, David L. Strug, and Joan Beder

Critical Multicultural Social Work
by Jose Sisneros, Catherine Stakeman, Mildred C. Joyner,
and Cathryne L. Schmitz

Cross-Cultural Practice: Social Work with Diverse Populations
by Karen V. Harper and Jim Lantz

Women in Social Work Who Have Changed the World
by Alice Lieberman

Mindfulness and Social Work
by Steven F. Hick

Social Work Practice with Latinos
Key Issues and Emerging Themes

Editors

Rich Furman
University of Washington, Tacoma

Nalini Junko Negi
University of Maryland, Baltimore

LYCEUM
BOOKS, INC.

Chicago, Illinois

© 2010 by Lyceum Books, Inc.

Published by
LYCEUM BOOKS, INC.
5758 S. Blackstone Avenue
Chicago, Illinois 60637
773-643-1903 fax
773-643-1902 phone
lyceum@lyceumbooks.com
www.lyceumbooks.com

6   5   4   3   2   1   10   11   12   13

ISBN 978-1-933478-57-9

Printed in the United States of America.

Library of Congress Cataloging-in-Publication Data

Social work practice with Latinos : key issues and emerging themes / editors, Rich Furman, Nalini Negi.
    p.   cm.
Includes bibliographical references and index.
ISBN 978-1-933478-57-9 (pbk. : alk. paper)
1. Hispanic Americans—Services for—United States.   2. Hispanic American families—United States.   3. Social work with minorities—United States.   4. Hispanic Americans—Social conditions.   I. Furman, Rich.   II. Negi, Nalini.
HV3187.A2.S63   2010
362.84'68073—dc22

                                                                    2009033350

Contents

Part II: Strengths and Vulnerabilities

Part III: Interventions, Programs, and Methods

CHAPTER ONE

Introduction

Rich Furman
Nalini Junko Negi
Melody Loya

The profession of social work has a long and time-honored history of providing services to populations that have been placed at risk by social factors that rest outside of the control of individuals, families, and communities. This social justice orientation has led to the promotion of services to the persistently mentally ill, the developmentally disabled, substance abusers, at-risk children, and ethnically diverse communities. But social work as a profession has yet to step up to the challenge of providing culturally responsive and effective interventions and community-based programming for the diverse needs of Latinos. Perhaps this has echoed the general ambivalence that many sectors of U.S. society have felt toward Latinos. Such sentiments are typified by the current immigration debates and the negative perceptions of some people about the contributions and roles of Latinos in the United States. Many Latinos still encounter a good deal of misunderstanding at best, and, at worst, prejudice and discrimination. Latinos continue to be asked questions about when they came to this country, when in fact their ancestors may have been living in the territories of Texas and Arizona for a great deal longer than most Americans (Furman, Langer, Sanchez, & Negi, 2007).

Overall, Latinos represent the largest ethnic minority population in the United States, and their numbers are increasing rapidly (Pew

Hispanic Center, 2005). Currently, Latinos account for more than 15 percent of the population in the United States. Owing to the difficulty of counting migrant populations, which traditionally do not make themselves available for census counts, the population of Latinos is in all likelihood much higher than current estimates reflect. While estimates vary, it is thought that by 2025 approximately one in four people living in the United States will be Latino (U.S. Census Bureau, 2006).

In many parts of the country, Latino populations are increasing. For instance, while not viewed as a traditional receiving state for Latino immigrants, North Carolina currently has one of the fastest-growing Latino populations in the United States: In 1990, Latinos constituted just over 1 percent of the total population of the state, but by the year 2000, they made up 4.7 percent of the population (U.S. Census Bureau, 2005a). Similarly, in Mecklenburg County, which contains the city of Charlotte, the largest city in the state, Latinos constituted 6.5 percent of the population in the year 2000 (U.S. Census Bureau, 2005b). Advocates now estimate that the Latino population in Charlotte is currently approaching 10 percent of the overall population. The trend continues in other states such as Nebraska and Washington, which are also experiencing enormous growth in their Latino population due to the influx of Latinos arriving from elsewhere in the United States, as well as new immigrants from Mexico and Central and South America.

As with other historically marginalized populations, Latinos often experience a disproportionate number of psychosocial problems due to discrimination, among other factors. Many of these psychosocial issues are explored in great detail in subsequent chapters. Latinos are at risk for various psychosocial maladies, including poverty (Prelow & Loukas, 2003), low educational attainment (Prelow & Loukas, 2003), mental health concerns (McGowan 1988; Padilla, Ruiz, & Alvarez, 1989; Vega & Amaro, 1998), substance abuse (Hernandez & Lucero, 1996), ill health (Fiscella, Franks, Doescher, & Saver, 2002; Grantmakers in Health, 2003), and exposure to violence (Peacock, McClure, & Agars, 2003).

Research, however, also indicates that Latino cultural values can serve as protective factors or buffers against both physical and mental health problems. In fact, studies show that first-generation Latinos have better health statuses when compared to second, third, and subsequent generations. It has been found that the following health indicators worsen with increased acculturation: rates of infant mortality, low birth weight, overall cancer rates, high blood pressure, and adolescent pregnancy, as well as increased alcohol use rates, illicit drug use, and depressive symptomology (Vega & Amaro, 1998). This so-called health paradox necessitates increased social work research that examines the role of protective factors in ameliorating problems and asks why these protective factors may deteriorate over time.

In terms of social work practice, social workers need to be equipped with the knowledge of how to conduct culturally responsive practice that leverages existing protective factors while diminishing the effects of modifiable risk factors. Unfortunately, while the Latino population has been growing, the number of social workers able to respond to their needs has not kept pace.

Providing services to Latinos not only requires an ability to provide culturally responsive practice, but also, in the case of monolingual first-generation Latinos, the ability to speak Spanish with near-native fluency. There are several reasons why a disparity exists between the availability of social workers who can effectively work with Latinos and the number and needs of this population. First, the number of Latino students entering the social work profession is not keeping pace with the Latino population's growing numbers. In 1998 only about 3 percent of MSW graduates were Latinos (Council on Social Work Education, 1998). Not only does the Latino population lag behind the white population in graduation rates from colleges, but Latinos who do graduate from college tend to choose to serve their communities by going into helping professions other than social work, such as law, medicine, nursing, or education. (And even if there were more Latino MSWs, they would not necessarily have the language skills to provide services in Spanish, or even the cultural competency skills to work with Latino clients.)

Second, while the number of social workers who are interested in working with Latinos seems to be growing, non-Latinos are even less likely to speak Spanish well enough to engage in advanced practice with monolingual first-generation Latinos. The development of language fluency is difficult and demands many years of study. In the program in which the first author teaches, the majority of students who are committed to Latino issues speak Spanish only marginally. This has also been the case at the two other universities at which he has worked. While this often means that these students have gone on to practice with second-generation (and beyond) Latinos, some research has indicated that many graduates with social work degrees may not be prepared for culturally sensitive social work practice with Latinos. In a 2002 study, only 40 percent of social work faculty believed that their students were prepared for culturally sensitive practice with Latinos (Furman, Bender, Shears, & Lewis, 2006). This contrasted with the fact that 90 percent of these faculty members stated that preparing students for practice with Latinos is very important.

The discrepancy between the growing populations and psychosocial needs of Latinos, and the lack of culturally competent and bilingual social workers provides an important rationale for improving the education of social workers working with Latinos. However, there are several other important reasons why social workers should develop the skills and competencies to work with Latinos. First, the NASW Code of Ethics (1999) requires social workers to work with diverse populations and calls upon social workers to work toward the amelioration of discrimination and social disparity. While Latinos have always been subject to linguistic, racial, and ethnic discrimination, recent anti-immigration sentiments have led to an increase in this discrimination for many. Additionally, social workers who can work effectively and competently with Latinos will be more likely to match the future workforce needs of the profession, thereby maximizing the resources of the profession as well as their own employability.

When social workers and social work educators identify gaps between the populations we serve and our capacity to provide services, historically, the profession has risen enthusiastically to the challenge. For instance, over the last decade the profession has responded in a variety of ways to the growing need for gerontological social workers. Grants have been created to support the infusion of social work content regarding aging into the curriculum of MSW programs. Emerging social work educators have been provided with support and resources to train the next generation of gerontological social workers. In a similar way, the profession, including social work educators, must respond to the needs of the growing Latino population. The current need includes new research, teaching, and practice initiatives to expand and improve our ability to serve Latino communities.

Perhaps the best rationale for being a social worker serving Latino communities is not what we give, but what we receive. The editors of this book have worked in Latino communities in the United States, Mexico, and Central and South America for nearly three decades, combined. It has been our experience that when we entered these communities humbly, with a desire to learn, share, and work collaboratively, we received nothing but warmth, kindness, and compassion. It is with gratitude that, over the years, we have learned to love Nicaraguan poetry, Mexican murals, Peruvian *cebiche* (raw fish), Cuban rum, and have enjoyed much Latino *cariños* (warmth) and *abrazos* (hugs). Our lives have been deeply enriched through the relationships of friends, colleagues, and clients from Latino communities. We hope your experiences are equally as rich and full.

Why an Edited Book?

The advantage of an edited book lies in the diversity of experiences and perspectives of the different authors. In this book, you will read chapters by practitioners and scholars from many disciplines, including social work, sociology, Latin American studies, family therapy, and anthropology. The majority of the authors are Latino, including Mexicans, Cubans, Peruvians, Puerto Ricans, and others. Some of these authors were born in the United States, while others are immigrants. Some of the authors are not Latinos, but are scholars who have dedicated their personal and professional lives to practice, service, and research with various Latino populations. This diverse group of authors provides a wealth of insights that transcend what one author would be able to offer. An edited text also allows for the engagement of authors who are internationally recognized as experts in their substantive areas. We are humbled by the talent that is represented here.

While it may be true that a range of perspectives is a valuable aspect of any edited volume, this may be particularly true for a text on Latinos, a population as diverse as any other. It is unlikely that any one perspective, theoretical orientation, or set of experiences will be sufficient to understand who Latinos are, or how to provide services to them. Because of this diversity, the various perspectives provided here are not always congruent. Ideas presented by one author may challenge the perspectives of another. In this sense, this volume can be viewed as an opportunity for dialogue between the various authors and the social work students and practitioners who will read this book. We encourage you to engage in dialogue, discussion, and debate around the ideas presented here. We hope that they will stimulate future practice innovation and subsequent research and evaluation. Because social work practice with Latinos is an evolving area, and practice models and scholarship are in their adolescence, there is much room for dialogue with and learning from one another.

Organization of This Book

When editing this text, we had to make difficult decisions about the degree to which chapters should function as stand-alone entities versus as components of a highly integrated book. It is our hope that this book be used in classes on culturally competent practice with Latinos, but since very few classes as such exist, we believe it will more frequently be used in practice courses concerned with diverse populations in general; and many instructors may assign some chapters and not others. Therefore, we decided that each chapter should be able to stand by itself, to some degree, and so allowed key practices and valuable principles to be reiterated somewhat throughout the book. We also believe that some of these concepts are so powerful and important—for example those of *personalismo* and *familismo*—that addressing them through the lenses of different authors and work with different Latino populations can help social work students and social workers develop deeper levels of understanding.

This book is organized into three sections. Part I, Chapters Two through Four, The Context of Practice with Latinos, provides a context to the macro social issues that frame social work practice with Latinos. Part II, Strengths and Vulnerabilities, is comprised of Chapters Five through Nine and examines both aspects of Latino culture. Finally, Part III, Chapters Ten through Seventeen, looks at specific programs and methods that may be helpful when serving Latino clients. The following is a brief overview of each chapter:

In Chapter Two, "The Social Welfare of Latino Transmigrants: Implications for Social Work Practice," Nalini Negi and Dennis Poole explore key concepts related to globalization, migration, and practice. Through their chapter, you will develop an understanding of the interconnectedness of globalized social and economic issues, and the relationship between these factors and providing social services to Latino transmigrants. For example, economic conditions in Latin America affect the manner and type of migration to the United States and will often dictate the social service needs of new immigrants. Economic and social transformations within these countries also affect the manner in which the lives of people have become increasingly transnational, whereby financial and personal resources are shared across nation and state boundaries.

Thomas Sanchez and Susanna Jones's Chapter Three, "The Diversity and Commonalities of Latinos in the United States," explores both differences and similarities among Latinos. Although Latinos in the United States share many historical similarities, there are many differences that distinguish each group as well. For example, those who trace their ancestral roots to the countries of Latin America and the Caribbean do not all speak the same language, with more than a hundred thousand Brazilians speaking Portuguese and many indigenous people speaking ancient, native dialects. As you shall come to understand, the majority of Latinos identify more by their country of origin than by the general terms *Latino* or *Hispanic*.

The quest to provide for their families has always been the primary reason that immigrants have come to the United States from their countries of origin, and Latinos are no exception. In Chapter Four, "*¡Sí, Se Puede!* Revisited: Latina/o Workers in the United States," Paul Ortiz traces the history of work and labor issues vis-à-vis Latinos. In this chapter, he tells the stories of Latinos in the United States fighting for the right to dignified, meaningful work. His chapter deftly shows the interrelationship between migration, social justice, labor, national identity, and even language.

The next section, Strengths and Vulnerabilities, begins with Chapter Five, "Family and Community as Strengths in Latino Communities," in which Sandra Magaña and Marci Ybarra explore how to leverage existing strengths inherent within Latino families and communities to ameliorate social problems. They examine how social workers can utilize micro and macro practice methods for helping Latinos capitalize on their cultural strengths expressed within their families and communities, which have long been recognized as important protective factors among Latinos. Latino values often endorse a communal sense of self that views the self as an integral part of the family—so core to existence is the family that it is truly the lens through which all of life is viewed. Latino cultural values also endorse a strong sense of community, as it is within communities that families meet their various needs. Research and a case study are presented, demonstrating how community networking and family practice were used in providing services to a Latino family of an autistic young adult who was placed in residential treatment. It powerfully explores how services that were originally conceptualized based upon an individualistic paradigm can be altered to meet the needs of Latinos who endorse Latino cultural values. The chapter highlights a key concept that is woven throughout this book. At times social workers will not be able to find services that are culturally sensitive to the needs of Latinos but will need to find ways of altering available services to meet the needs of their clients. This type of environmental systems change work is a key to social work practice with Latinos.

Spirituality and religion are important in all human communities. In the Latino community, spirituality and religion serve as strengths and resources that have helped various Latino populations survive numerous hardships. In Chapter Six, "Spirituality as a Strength in the Latino Community," Clay Shorkey and colleagues explore the complexity and vitality of spirituality in the Latino community. They skillfully resist the temptation to view spirituality and religion as synonymous and demonstrate how diverse Latino spirituality truly is. They explore how traditional Catholic practice has mixed with indigenous religions and belief systems to form truly unique, culturally relevant religious expressions. This blending of identity in terms of religion, culture, geography, and so forth lies at the very heart of what it means to be Latino. The authors provide excellent advice for how social workers can explore spiritual and religious issues in their work with Latino clients.

Too frequently, the profession of social work has neglected the importance of art as a vehicle of growth and renewal. Art and artistic expression are invaluable means by which people create meaning out of their own experiences, and in the process create rich culture for others to experience and share. George Rivera, in Chapter Seven, "Art as a

Source of Strength in the Latino Community," explores art through the lens of a Latino scholar, artist, and activist. Professor Rivera views the arts not through a Eurocentric, individualistic perspective, but through the lens of community and collective values that lie at the heart of the Latino worldview. His essay is both personal and archetypal, and challenges the more detached, positivistic way of exploring the arts. The images that he presents are powerful and evocative, demonstrating Latino youth's exploration of HIV/AIDS-related themes, the importance of spiritual imagery in the arts, and the centrality of the mural and antiwar images in Latino activism.

The next chapter, Chapter Eight, is "Barrier to Health Care Utilization among Latinos in the United States: Recommendations for Social Workers," in which Marcia Shobe and Maren Coffman explore the staggering health disparities that exist in the Latino community. Latinos face numerous barriers in receiving quality health care, including cultural differences that are not taken into account by health care providers, the lack of Spanish-speaking health care providers, and fear and distrust of mainstream institutions. They explore the "Latino health paradox," which notes that in some health indicators, Latino immigrants fare better than whites and African Americans. Exploring the reason for this phenomenon is an important aspect of a strengths-based approach to practice, in which social workers can help Latinos maximize the cultural factors that positively influence their health. The chapter also explores key policy considerations and their impact on the health of Latinos and social work practice. Finally, the authors provide recommendations for social work practitioners who work with Latinos within and outside of health care settings.

In Chapter Nine, "Violence and Latino Communities," Reba Brown and her colleagues explore the complex phenomenon of violence in the Latino community. Intimate-partner violence, gang violence, and other types of violence impact many new and vulnerable communities. It is essential that social workers who encounter the victims and perpetrators of violence respond in a culturally competent manner. Too frequently, social workers neglect important cultural values when advocating for victims' rights. This "color blind" position often leads to clients not following safety or treatment plans and can put victims at further risk. Additionally, victims may feel misunderstood and alienated from service providers, making it less likely that they will seek help in the future.

In Part III, the final section of the book, we explore social work methods for working with Latinos. Chapter Ten, "Culturally Competent Assessment of Latinos," contributed by Luis Torres and his colleagues, explores the multiplicity of factors that social workers must consider when conducting an assessment of Latino clients. In many ways, this chapter serves as an overview or introduction to the topic of service provision to Latinos; many of the factors explored within this chapter are considered in subsequent chapters as they pertain to specific Latino populations. This chapter briefly addresses many of the issues that are explored in depth in other chapters and demonstrate how these factors become part of a comprehensive assessment.

It can be argued that all social work practice with Latinos is family practice. As previously mentioned, so central is the institution of family to Latinos that viewing the self as separate from the family may be problematic. However, family practice has long been viewed as a method of social work practice and frequently shapes the context of service provision. Jason Platt's outstanding Chapter Eleven, "Direct Practice with Latino Families," provides a model of family practice based upon constructivist, systemic, and liberational perspectives. He demonstrates the importance of understanding the Latino construction of family, and how integral this construction is to providing family therapy. He explores how perspectives rooted in liberational thought bridge the too-often arbitrary divide between micro and macro practice. He guides practitioners through the necessary skills and perspectives to help social workers of various skill levels develop new ways of providing family services.

The child welfare system has long struggled to provide culturally competent services to Latinos and other diverse communities. Too often, workers are not trained to understand the family values that influence how they should address sensitive family matters. Throughout Chapter Twelve, "Child Welfare Practice and the Use of Family Group Conferencing: A Culturally Responsive Intervention with Hispanic Children and Families," Maria Puig, Jim Drendel, and Deb Deluca present a model that engages Latino families with a culturally competent, strengths-based approach. The authors begin with a discussion of the importance of considering the diverse needs of Latinos in relation to child welfare issues, and they provide a solid discussion of the history of child welfare as it relates to Latinos. The authors then present the family conferencing model and demonstrate the strengths inherent in this model for working with Latinos. An excellent case example brings the model to life.

In Chapter Thirteen, "Substance Abuse Prevention and Latino Youth," Guillermo Prado and colleagues explore substance abuse among Latinos, particularly among Latino youth. As Latinos are one of the youngest ethnic groups, the psychosocial needs of Latino children and teenagers are of the utmost importance. The chapter deftly describes the prevalence and causes of substance-abuse problems in the population. It provides an in-depth description of the prevention literature and the importance of prevention as a paradigm for working with this and other Latino groups. The case study demonstrates the importance of integrating prevention and intervention throughout social work practice.

In Chapter Fourteen, "Social Work Practice with Older Latino Adults," Blanca Ramos and Gary Wright explore the needs of a growing and neglected population, older Latinos. Traditionally, older Latinos have predominantly relied on their families and religious organizations to provide the care they need. However, the complexities of modern life, varied medical and psychosocial conditions, a growing acceptance of professional helpers within Latino communities, and changes due to acculturation have increased the need and desire for social work services with older Latinos. The authors explore a life-course perspective along with the cultural norms and practices that are essential to consider when working with older Latinos. They delve into how social workers can engage with a client's support systems and caregivers to help meet the needs of this diverse and often misunderstood population.

It would seem apparent, given the nature of Latino collectivist values, that group work practice with Latinos would be common and well developed. However, a review of the literature indicates that this is not the case. In Chapter Fifteen, "A Tale of Two Groups: Culturally Sensitive Group Therapy for Latinos," Margarita Leonor Díaz fills an important gap in the practice literature. As with other chapters in this book, the differences between Latino and Eurocentric values are deconstructed, and Díaz then explores the implications of these values for group work practice. She writes her chapter as a practitioner, sensitive to the needs of clients and to the importance of helping group workers understand the day-to-day realities of practice. She provides a case example of group work with Latinos that strongly suggests the importance of paying careful attention to all aspects of group design, from recruitment to subsequent intervention strategies. She candidly presents a discussion of the obstacles that even she, an experienced group worker with Latinos, can face.

As has previously been noted, far too few social workers are able to fully provide services to monolingual first-generation Latinos in Spanish. In Chapter Sixteen, "Latinos and Spanish: The Awkwardness of Language in Social Work Practice," Lissette Piedra explores political, social, and practice issues related to language, immigration, and Latino life. Her discussion deftly explores the relationship between language, identity, and social service provision. She examines what social workers need to know when they engage clients who are linguistically different.

Our book concludes with a thought-provoking and innovative chapter by Dawn Belkin-Martinez that approaches community work from the eyes of a radical social worker. Chapter Seventeen, "'*Solidaridad Y*

Justicia: Latinas, Community Organizing, and Empowerment,'' challenges the medical model's blaming of social problems on Latinos, Latino immigrants, and other at-risk groups. It also calls into question the
artificial split between micro and macro practice. We believe that this
challenge, of bridging micro and macro levels of social work practice, is
an essential task for those wishing to provide services to Latinos. Few
problems that Latinos face do not have powerful implications for all
levels of social work practice. Even those who provide clinical services
will be called upon to engage in social change and advocacy activities.

Self-Awareness, Self-Reflection, and Cross-Cultural Practice

The chapters described are designed to challenge your understanding,
enhance your skills and knowledge, and to encourage new insights into
your work with Latino clients. While the development of self-awareness
is an essential skill for social workers, it is especially crucial for those
engaging in cross-cultural practice. As you read through this book, you
will discover a wealth of diversity within the Latino community, and,
hopefully, some preconceived notions will be questioned. The commitment to the development of culturally sensitive practice is a lifelong
one. It is a journey that should be consciously embarked upon by all in
the helping professions. Cultural competence is not an end-point or a
fixed place where one can say that he or she has "arrived." It is a continuum, and movement along the continuum is born of self-awareness
and self-reflection, along with the active pursuit of knowledge. Developing your capacity for self-awareness and self-reflection is as important as developing a cognitive understanding of Latinos. It would be
impossible for anyone to become totally "culturally competent" in
working with any one Latino group, let alone with all Latinos as there
is much diversity among them. By developing the capacity to reflect
upon your own cultural experience, behaviors, and practice, you can
become aware of what you bring to cross-cultural helping situations.

Self-reflection is the means by which we think about and make sense
of our personal and social worlds. In a sense, it is the capacity to think
about one's cognitions, feelings, and behaviors. Being self-reflective is
to be able to witness oneself with some degree of objectivity or critical
analysis. Furman, Coyne, and Negi (2008) observed that:

> In the process of self-reflection, individuals' cognitive medi-
> ating mechanisms allow them to connect to and interpret
> their social world. Through self-reflection, people may

develop the capacity to understand their own biases in relation to their present life and personal history; thereby developing the capacity to understand their social conditioning
in a critical, potentially transformational way. Self-reflection
helps develop critical consciousness through reflecting upon
class status, privilege, internalized oppression, and other
structural barriers, which then becomes internalized, allowing an individual to transcend, or be liberated from, oppressive environments and social contexts. Self-reflection is the
mechanism that leads to epiphany, moments of clarity, and
existential realizations that can lead to life-altering change.

Many authors have noted the importance of self-reflection for cross-
cultural practice (Lee & Greene, 1999; Schwartz, Fluckiger, & Weisman,
1977). Each stresses that the practitioner is the vehicle through which
interventions are conducted, and that practitioners must learn to assess
their own behaviors while they are occurring. As you read this book, we
hope you stop and reflect upon your own responses to the materials.
What thoughts and feelings arise for you? How are your own behaviors
or attitudes enhancing or inhibiting your practice? What assumptions
do you bring to the helping relationship? Each of us carries with us
assumptions and prejudices based upon our upbringing and education
and by being raised in a society with a historical legacy of racism.
Admitting to having our own baggage and biases is an essential part of
becoming a good social worker. Being able to identify these within
yourself is an important step to developing critical self-reflection.

   At the end of many chapters, you will find questions designed for
personal or group reflection. Please use these to begin to develop your
self-reflective skills and to enhance your self-awareness about your personal culture as well as your understanding of the culture of others. Our
hope is that, as you read this book, you find a way to step beyond your
personal worldview and try to view the world as others might see it. It
is important to remember that each chapter in this book was contributed by persons with unique circumstances, experiences, and their own
worldview. Their experiences may not be your experiences, and their
understanding of how to best engage in culturally sensitive practice
with Latinos may not match yours. It is important, however, for each of
us to open ourselves up to a deeper understanding of sociopolitical and
cultural contexts, to consistently engage in self-reflection and self-
awareness, and to be willing to risk feeling uncomfortable or to have
feelings of dissonance in order to encourage growth. An unfolding journey of self-discovery awaits you.

References

Council on Social Work Education. (1998). *Statistics on social work education: 1998.* Alexandria, VA: Author.

Fiscella, K., Franks, P., Doescher, M. P., & Saver, B. G. (2002). Disparities in health care by race, ethnicity, and language among the uninsured. *Medical Care, 40*(1), 52–59.

Furman, R., Bender, K., Shears, J., & Lewis, C. W. (2006). Faculty perceptions regarding MSW curricular deficits for educating students for practice with Latinos. *Advances in Social Work, 7*(1), 36–48.

Furman, R., Coyne, A., & Negi, N. (2008). An international experience for social work students: Self-reflection through poetry and journal writing exercises. *Journal of Teaching in Social Work, 28*(1–2), 78–86.

Furman, R., Langer, C. L., Sanchez, T. W., & Negi, N. J. (2007). A qualitative study of immigration policy and practice dilemmas for social work students. *Journal of Social Work Education, 43*(1), 133–146.

Grantmakers in Health. (2003). In the right words: Addressing language and culture in providing health care. Issue brief no. 18. San Francisco: Author.

Hernandez, L. P., & Lucero, E. (1996). DAYS La Familia community drug and alcohol prevention program: Family-centered model for working with inner-city Hispanic families. *The Journal of Primary Prevention, 16*(3), 255–272.

Lee, M. Y., & Greene, G. J. (1999). A social constructivist framework for integrating cross cultural issues in teaching clinical social work. *Journal of Social Work Education, 35*(1), 21–37.

McGowan, B. G. (1988). Helping Puerto Rican families at risk: Responsive use of time, space, and relationships. In C. Jacobs & D. D. Bowles (Eds.), *Ethnicity and race: Critical concepts in social work* (pp. 48–70). Silver Spring, MD: National Association of Social Workers. National Association of Social Workers (1997). *Code of ethics.* Washington, DC: Author.

Padilla, A. M., Ruiz, R. A., & Alvarez, R. (1989). Community mental health services for the Spanish speaking/surname populations. In. D. R. Atkinson, G. Morten, & D. W. Sue (Eds.), *Counseling American minorities: A cross-cultural perspective.* (167–198) Dubuque, IA: Wm. C. Brown.

Peacock, M. J., McClure, F., & Agars, M. D. (2003). Predictors of delinquent behaviors among Latino youth. *The Urban Review, 35*(1), 59–72.

Pew Hispanic Center (2005). The new Latino south: The context and consequences of rapid population growth. Retrieved October 5, 2007, from http://pew hispanic.org/files/reports

Prelow, H. M., & Loukas, A. (2003). The role of resource, protective and risk factors on academic achievement-related outcomes of economically disadvantaged Latino youth. *Journal of Community Psychology, 31*(5), 513–529.

Schwartz, F., Fluckiger, F. A., & Weisman, I. (1977). A cross cultural encounter: A non-traditional approach to social work education. San Francisco: R & E Research Associates.

U.S. Census Bureau (2005a). North Carolina quick facts form the U.S. Census Bureau. Retrieved May 21, 2007, from http://quickfacts.census.gov/qfd/states/37000.html

U.S. Census Bureau (2005b). Mecklenburg county quick facts from the U.S. Census Bureau. Retrieved May 21, 2007, from http://quickfacts.census.gov/qfd/states/37/37119.html

U.S. Census Bureau. (2006). *Hispanic Heritage Month 2005: September 15–October 15.* (Internet Release). Retrieved June 4, 2007, from http://www.census.gov/PressRelease/www/releases/archives/facts_for_features_special_editions/005338.html

Vega, W., & Amaro, H. (1998). Lifetime prevalence of DSM III-R psychiatric disorders among rural and urban Mexican Americans in California. *Archives of General Psychiatry 55*(2), 771–782.

PART I

The Context of Practice with Latinos

CHAPTER TWO

The Social Welfare of Latino Transmigrants

Implications for Social Work Practice

Nalini Junko Negi
Dennis Poole

The phenomenon of globalization has altered the lives of people forever through the dramatic advancement of technologies that have allowed faster access to global networks, opportunities, and activities. A considerable focus on the business and political aspects of globalization has been developed (Adler & Bartholomew, 1992; Homburg, Krohmer, Cannon, & Kiedaisch, 2002; Jones, 2002; Kastoryano, 2000), but surprisingly little has been written about its effects on social welfare, social policy, and the experiences of people (Jones, 2002; Ley, 2004; Wilding, 1997). This paucity of research is especially glaring as the global scope of social problems becomes increasingly recognized (Link, Ramanathan, & Asamoah, 1999; Stoesz, Guzzetta, & Lusk, 1999). One such aspect of social globalization can be evidenced in the mass migration of people around the world, which has led sociologists and other scholars to redefine nation-state borders from rigid boundaries to intersocietal and supraterritorial spaces (Sassen, 2002). This symbolic de-territorialization of borders has led to the development of a transnational space—a particularly high-risk social welfare area, as the often poor and undocumented migrants are rendered socially and politically vulnerable (Sassen, 2002).

The U.S.-Mexico border is a particularly relevant site of analysis regarding transmigrants, or migrants who continuously move back and forth between borders. This is due to the existence of large-scale migrations coupled with a border both symbolic and physical that separates a developing country (Mexico) from the only hegemony in the world (the United States). This disparity of wealth between the two nation-states makes the U.S.-Mexico border or transnational space a particularly high-risk social welfare area, as the often poor and undocumented migrants are rendered socially and politically vulnerable (Sassen, 2002). Among this migrant population, transmigrants can be distinguished from traditional migrants whereby their back and forth activities between borders renders them vulnerable to different sources of distress (Pries, 2004). Transmigrants are exposed to high antecedents of distress through potential isolation and problems associated with immigration, as well as problems with depression, health, poverty, and anxiety (Latapi, 1999; Lopez & Salgado De Snyder, 2001; Poole, 1996; Rousse, 1989; Salgado De Snyder, 1993; Sassen, 2002).

While there is a body of research on the social welfare needs of Latino migrants, relatively little is known about the social welfare of Latino transmigrants. Theoretical studies have indicated the positive effects of immigrant transnational networks and activities on political and social empowerment movements, but little is known about transmigrants' involvement in similar transnational activities or networks. This article explores the social welfare of Latino transmigrants and the potential ameliorative effects of transnational networks upon their well-being.

The literature review that follows provides a theoretical background regarding globalization and the emergence of transnational spaces and transmigrants, with a specific focus on Latino transmigrants. The transnational activities and the often-difficult life conditions of Latino transmigrants are discussed in an attempt to explore their social welfare.

Globalization and Transnational Spaces

The conceptualization of globalization has been generally restricted to economic and political domains. Globalization has thus been generally described as changes in the economic and political structures, trends and processes on a transnational and international scale (Yeates, 1999). Economic globalization is defined by shifts in capital flows, production systems, markets, and trade of goods and services. Transnational business enterprises provide relevant examples of this process (Hamm, 2003; Homburg et al., 2002), as they have received considerable attention from scholars and practitioners regarding the development of new organizational structures, technology, communication patterns, resource exchanges, personnel, and customer service to manage enterprises whose identity transcends national boundaries (Adler & Bartholomew, 1992; Mauri & Phatak, 2001). Political globalization, in turn, comprises changes in the global context of political processes and activities as well as awareness. Bretherton (1996) defines political globalization as "a growing tendency for issues to be perceived as global in scope, and hence requiring global solutions; and the development of international organizations and global institutions to address such issues" (p. 8). There is a burgeoning body of research that examines political globalization via the development of global civil society and bi-national political alliances. However, the bulk of globalization studies have generally had a disproportionate focus on the mechanisms of this phenomenon via its economic tendencies, and as a result have neglected the study of human agency (Ley, 2004). Despite the paucity of research on the social aspects of globalization and its impact on the individual, it is apparent that the lives of common people have been forever altered as a direct result of globalization (Appadurai, 2000).

Economic and political globalization has changed social life through the development of technologies that have facilitated an intense level of contact, communication, and social interaction over long distances. These processes have rendered borders as more porous, less insulated, and permeable to global influences. Subsequently, national borders have shifted from localized spaces to transnational spaces. The emergence of these transnational spaces has led to the development of intersocietal and supraterritorial spaces, transnational networks of relationships and activities (Sassen, 2002) that span local boundaries and borders to encompass bi-national (or more) states. Transmigrants are one such population that exists within these transnational spaces.

Transmigrants

Transmigration can be conceptualized as a unique feature of globalization because it represents an altered condition of migration that is distinguished from traditional migration. According to Pries (2004), immigrants and traditional migrants discontinue their movement across boundaries over time, while transmigrants continuously engage in lives in different places, countries, and cultures for economic reasons. The transmigratory lifestyle can then lead to multiple crossings of nation-state boundaries and a lack of a long-term residential base.

Although, transmigration is not a new phenomenon, with precedents extending back as far as trading diasporas of the Middle Ages, or farther (Foner, 1997), it is unique today because of the advances in technology and electronic communication, as well as fast and cheap transportation. This process has allowed many transmigrants to develop transnational identities, transnational relationships, and to engage in transnational activities. The involvement of transmigrants in transnational networks and activities is particularly relevant because they challenge traditional localized conceptions of a single allegiance to a nation-state and expand it to more globalized and transnational ways of being (Kastoryano, 2000).

Transmigrant Activity and Networks

A myriad of factors influence the nature and structure of transnational activity. These include geographic proximity and historical ties between sending and receiving countries, and economic and political opportunity structures in the host country. Literature documents the involvement of immigrants in transnational activities, but scant literature indicates if transmigrants are also engaging in similar activities.

According to Portes, Haller and Guarnizo (2001) the transnational activities of immigrants encompass: *economic activity* (via transnational enterprise), *political activity* (via membership in home-country political parties or participation in hometown civic committees and political campaigns), and *socio-cultural activity* (via regular performance by home-country artistic groups or participation in hometown cultural festivities and civic celebrations). Although this conceptualization illustrates the broad range of transnational activities, it is unclear if this range of activities cut across migratory status and, more specifically, if transmigrants are engaged in these activities.

According to the work of Ireland (1994), immigrants' political behavior is contingent upon the host society's institutional framework of opportunity structure, which includes immigrants' legal status, host-society citizenship laws and welfare policies as determinants that shape migrants' collective action (Ireland, 1994). However, transmigrants often operate outside this "opportunity structure" since they are generally unauthorized migrants and "are often treated as a reserve of flexible labor, outside the protection of work safety, health, and minimum wage and other standards, and easily deportable" (Taran, 2000, p. 7). Transmigrants, then, function within the shadows of marginalization and uncertainty, even when compared to immigrants who may have more stability owing to a consistent stable residential base, citizenship, and access to resources. Consequently, the application of transnational activities as developed by Portes, Haller, & Guarnizo (2001) to transmigrants does not seem likely for this population. In fact, Pries states that "transmigrants are not the new sovereign cosmopolitans who move freely and voluntarily between different locales, places, and opportunities without problems. Transmigrants adapt themselves to uncertain and unpredictable situations, learn to manage risks and live with them, accumulate cultural and social capital." The social welfare of transmigrants is therefore especially relevant to social work practice.

Mexican transmigrants are of particular interest because of the mass migration from Mexico to the United States and back (Kelly, 2003; Massey, Durand, & Gonzalez, 1991). High levels of poverty and prevalent drug trafficking are harsh realities within the border cities where many Latino transmigrants work and live (Wallisch, 1996). The difficult conditions of life for transmigrants in border cities are often compounded by the physical nature of their employment: most Mexican transmigrants are employed in industrial sectors that require great physical strength and long hours of work away from family support systems and so may suffer physical, psychological, and social problems. These problems often surface as social welfare issues (in either their home or host communities, or both) in the form of substance abuse, domestic violence, divorce, or crime (Lopez & Salgado de Snyder, 2001; Poole & Salgado de Snyder, 2002).

The Social Welfare of Latino Transmigrants

Although Latino transmigrants are able to adapt to uncertain and unpredictable living and occupational situations, this population faces an insurmountable amount of psychological distress. Most Latino transmigrants are employed in industrial sectors that entail grueling work conditions, intensive physical labor, and long work hours. The often difficult work conditions of transmigrants may also impede their social welfare by affecting their health. Long hours of physical labor can ill-dispose transmigrants to good physical health. These health problems can be especially distressing to transmigrants as they may interfere with their ability to work and earn money, as well as cause direct expense through hospital bills. Furthermore, lack of access to health care may often have disastrous long-term health care consequences. This is particularly relevant as the Latino transmigrant population is an economically vulnerable and "hidden" population (Sassen, 2002) that has to struggle to financially maintain day-to-day survival.

LACK OF SOCIAL AND EMOTIONAL SUPPORT

The high potential for social isolation in Latino transmigrants is a potential antecedent to distress. Transmigrants' lack of a long-term residential base and their back and forth activities across countries may prevent them from creating positive social support networks, which serve to ameliorate distress. This lack of social and emotional support may result in transmigrants relying solely on themselves to take care and manage their well-being. Consequently, the accumulation of stressors associated with constantly having to adapt to unfamiliar environments, work-related stress, and the lack of social and emotional support may take a psychological and physical toll on many transmigrant individuals. This toll experienced by Mexico-U.S. transmigrants has been shown to surface as social welfare issues such as an increased likelihood of experiencing physical health problems, substance abuse, domestic violence, divorce, crime, high poverty rates, social isolation, depression, and anxiety (Lopez & Salgado de Snyder, 2001; Poole & Salgado De Snyder, 2002; Sassen, 2002; Rousse, 1989).

IMMIGRATION POLICIES

Immigration policies potentially have a direct effect on transmigrants' feelings of distress. Undocumented transmigrants may experience fear and insecurity regarding their legal status in their receiving country. Negative interaction with border officials may further exacerbate distress. For example, Mexican migrants have been reported to experience negative altercations and discrimination from U.S. and Mexican border officials (Latapi, 1999). This negative interchange with border officials may be a stronger concern to Latino transmigrants because of the back and forth nature (across nation-state borders) of their migratory activities.

These difficult circumstances that transmigrants live in may lead to increased levels of anxiety. All of these examples highlight how transmigrants are a marginalized population that potentially faces a myriad of conditions that place them at risk for lack of psychosocial well-being. Therefore, there is a pressing need for the development of focused studies that indicate the social welfare conditions of transmigrants, their coping strategies, and how specific stressors affect their psychological well-being.

The Social Welfare of Transmigrants: A Call for Research and Development

Absent from the discussion of Latino transmigrants is the need for social work research and development on maintaining this population's well-being and that of their families. Perhaps this omission is due to the inattention to the impacts of globalization on the dynamics of social welfare (Wilding, 1997; Yeates, 1999), or perhaps it reflects the paucity of social work research on global issues. Regardless of what the roots of this gap in research might be, it is clear that the social work perspective can add a unique contribution to the body of literature on transmigration. A key tenet of social work practice is social justice (*Social Work Code of Ethics*); the social work profession is in fact one of very few professions that explicitly bases its identity on restoring and enabling social justice. This specialized focus on social justice issues places social work in a position to meet the challenges of a growing diverse client population with specialized needs. According to Antle and Regehr (2003), social work research can utilize the justice principle of representing the interests of oppressed people with research methodology that attempts to legitimize the experiences of historically unheard, misunderstood, or misrepresented populations. Social work research and practice development on the social welfare of transmigrants is relevant to the profession of social work in that it can inform practice with this vulnerable population, and the profession has a very relevant contribution to make in the area of transmigration and social globalization. Social work research and practice involvement can occur at the local as well as the global level.

At the local level, social service providers are increasingly encountering clients who lead a transmigratory lifestyle, and it may often be difficult to provide them with consistent and stable services. Social service providers in Austin, Texas, developed an innovative strategy that has helped to alleviate this problem. They formulated an online community of Spanish-speaking counselors in order to provide support, information, and resources to their mainly Spanish-speaking clients. The online postings include job listings, resources, and ideas relevant to clients. The online community members have also been able to cut across transnational spaces via transnational referrals. For example, a social worker whose client was moving to Mexico posted a query asking if anyone within the online community could recommend a social service provider in the city to which her client was moving. Another online community member responded to her query by recommending an agency and the name of a provider in that city. Thus the social worker was able to provide a transnational referral to her client. The utility of such an online community or network to develop transnational referrals, information, and resources is invaluable. Online communities, such as the one developed in Austin, can be easily developed and maintained with relatively little or no cost. This type of online network is also time expedient, as it reduces the time that might be normally spent identifying and gathering relevant sources of information.

Although membership in the Austin online community of Spanish-speaking counselors is limited to local service providers, further development of such a network could include bi-national membership. In this case, since most of the Spanish-speaking clients (and transmigrants) in Texas are from Mexico, Mexican social service providers could be invited to become members. The inclusion of Mexican service providers would add more depth to the information, resources, and referrals for clients who lead a transmigratory lifestyle.

A qualitative study regarding the online community's development and facilitation of transnational referrals for the social welfare of transmigrants would also be beneficial. Such a study could inform future practice and development of these networks across national borders. It could also add to the body of research recommending the development of transnational strategies for the well-being of transmigrant clients.

Transnational Alliances

On a global level, the social work profession can also facilitate the development of global civil society by becoming involved in transnational alliances that improve the social welfare of transmigrants. The traditional conception of civil society can be described as facilitating citizens' rights and democracy (Halpern & Laxer, 2003). Transnational or global civil society applies this basic concept beyond the local boundaries to a larger transnational context. The development of global civil society can be traced to the 1990s with the emergence of a supranational sphere of social and political participation, wherein citizen's groups, social movements, and individuals engaged in dialogue and negotiation with each other and with various international and national governmental and local players, as well as with the business world (Anheier & Themudo, 2002). The creation of such a network has enabled individuals and organizations to exchange information, form transnational alliances, and respond to challenges and developments (Batliwala, 2002). Global civil society is then a highly complex ensemble of structured civil action (Keane, 2003) and is aligned to the social work ethic of social justice. Transnational social movements (TSMOs) and international nongovernmental organizations (INGOs) are two avenues of involvement in global civil society.

TSMOs are efforts by marginalized people to promote social or political change (Smith, Chatfield, & Pagnucco, 1997), whose membership exerts public pressure toward that end. According to Alger (1997), TSMOs are involved in creating and mobilizing global networks, participating in multilateral political arenas, facilitating interstate cooperation, acting within states, and enhancing public participation. Social work practitioners can support TSMOs by assisting in the promotion of their social welfare activities. For example, social workers can utilize their fund-raising skills to support these activities, raise awareness regarding the often-depressed conditions that transmigrants live in, become involved in community-building efforts, and facilitate access to health care and education about rights regarding policies. Such a grassroots effort to facilitate the well-being of this group is rooted in a rich and long history of activism for the development of socially just conditions for vulnerable peoples.

Furthermore, social workers can increase their participation in international INGOs. According to Brown & Moore (2001), INGOs are important actors in two interconnected realms, the national realm and the international one. At the national level, INGOs promote the social, economic, and political development of the country of operation. At the international level, they create global civil society and influence the practices and policies of international institutions (Brown & Moore, 2001). Social work practitioners can utilize their skills to build transnational coalitions and facilitate transnational collaborations between INGOs. Relevant examples of effective transnational collaborations between INGOs that promote the international social welfare of transmigrants are those of Comite Fronterizo de Obreras, the Frente, and La Mujer Obrera.

COMITE FRONTERIZO DE OBRERAS

Comite Fronterizo de Obreras (Border Committee of Women Workers, or CFO) (http://www.cfomaquiladoras.org) seeks to improve the condition of women workers in the *maquiladoras* (factories that are located near boarders that utlize inexpensive labor) and to protect their health, life, and welfare. Their tactics are both local and global: at the local level, they encourage women to organize and report abuses. At the global level, they have created transnational alliances with the American Friends Service Committee and have developed networks with U.S. trade unions (e.g., the United Steelworkers of America and the United Auto Workers). The CFO has been actively involved with the Human Rights Watch (HRW) campaign to stop pregnancy testing in the *maquiladoras* and has been an active contributor of a HRW report on sex discrimination in the *maquiladora* sector. The CFO's report contributed to a formalized complaint and investigation by the Mexican Asociacion de Abogados Democraticos (National Association of Democratic Lawyers) and the International Labor Rights Funds. The U.S. Department of Labor also conducted an independent investigation as a direct consequence of CFO's investigations and found lack of clarity in Mexican law regarding the legality of hiring processes and pregnancy screening. As a result, tri-national meetings between Mexico, Canada, and the United States were held to discuss how to proceed and remedy the problems.

THE FRENTE

The Frente (http://www.redindigena.net/organinteg/1fiob.html) is composed of communities and organizations of Mixteco, Zapoteco, and Trique peoples who have migrated temporarily or permanently from Oaxaca to other Mexican states and to the United States for their economic survival. Members of this group are located in Oaxaca, Baja California Norte, California, Oregon, and Washington. Frente was established in 1991 after a meeting of five indigenous Mexicans who had migrated to California to work; within three years it developed a larger membership and became known as the Frente Indigena Oaxaqueno Binacional. Currently, there are approximately two thousand members actively involved in Frente. The mission of this organization is to promote and defend human rights of indigenous Mexican migrants, as well as to improve their living conditions on both sides of the border. Frente's transnational orientation is evidenced by its work in labor and human rights in both the migrants' communities of origin and the United States. Its transnational activism is through involvement in members' community-of-origin local politics from across the border (from the United States). Members' political involvement strengthens and transforms their communities' cultural and social resources.

LA MUJER OBRERA

La Mujer Obrera (http://www.mujerobrera.org) is a grassroots organization that seeks to defend the dignity of immigrant women workers. Their mission is to create a sustainable community to obtain basic necessities such as education, housing, and health, among others. They work in a transnational space at the U.S.-Mexico border in El Paso. La Mujer Obrera has worked against discrimination and the exploitation of workers in the manufacturing industry for more than twenty-three years. Their focus is on basic needs such as jobs, education, housing, health, and political liberty.

The three INGOs highlighted above, Comite Fronterizo de Obreras, the Frente, and La Mujer Obrera, are prime examples of how effective INGOs can promote the social welfare of transmigrants on both national and international levels through the development of transnational alliances. Social work practitioners, trained to empower groups and communities, can then make a significant contribution to the development of global civil society. They can utilize their considerable skills to build transnational networks and achieve buy-in from community members or policy makers, and lead educational efforts to increase awareness regarding the often-adverse social conditions that transmigrants live in. Social work research can further highlight effective strategies to build transnational networks and alliances. Such an under-standing can provide a significant contribution to the field of international social work as social problems are becoming increasingly global in nature (Link et al., 1999).

Conclusion

The scope of social problems is becoming increasingly global in nature, which requires a focused attention on international social welfare issues. The case of Latino transmigrants is one such international social welfare issue. The social work profession, with its strong roots in social justice work, has an important contribution to make in the development of an understanding of the impact of globalization on people, particularly transmigrants. Thus, the development of a focused attention and study on transmigrants offers an important opportunity to provide a significant contribution to the field of international social work. Moreover, as the population of Latino transmigrants continues to grow, social service providers must be prepared to meet the rising challenges of service provision.

Social work practitioners and researchers can become involved on both local and international levels to promote the social welfare of transmigrants. Social work practitioners, much like social service providers in Austin, Texas, can create local or international Internet communities to facilitate collaboration between social service providers and to foster strategies to ensure the well-being of their transmigrant clients. Furthermore, social work practitioners can support TSMOs by assisting in the promotion of transmigrants' social welfare activities by utilizing their community-building and empowerment skills. Social work practitioners can also become involved in building global civil society by assisting in the development of transnational alliances across INGOs. In addition, focused research on the social welfare of transmigrants is vital to develop an understanding that elucidates salient strategies for effective social service provision with this population. Thus, the role of social work research and practice is crucial in ensuring the psychosocial and health-related well-being of Latino transmigrants and their families on both sides of the border.

In this chapter, we explored issues related to migration and transmigration. These dynamics shape the composition of Latinos in the United States. The similarities and differences between Latino groups are often influenced by a confluence of many forces that are implicated in transmigration: levels of assimilation and acculturation, capacity to maintain transnational relationships, political and social relationships between countries of origin, among other factors. The following chapter explores the commonalities and differences among and between Latinos in the United States, an important topic that highlights how transnational forces influence the lives of Latinos.

References

Adler, N. J., & Bartholomew, S. (1992). Managing globally competent people. *Academy of Management Executive, 6*(3), 52–65.

Alger, C. F. (1997). Transnational social movements, world politics and global governance, in J. Smith, C. Chatfield and R. Pagnucco (eds), *Transnational Social Movements and Global Politics.* (pp. 260–75) Syracuse: Syracuse University Press.

Anheier, H., & Themudo, N. (2002). Organisational forms of global civil society: Implications of going global. In M. K. M. Glasius & A. Helmut (Eds.), *Global Civil Society, 2002* (pp.191–262). Oxford, England: Oxford University Press.

Antle, B. J., & Regehr, C. (2003). Beyond individual rights and freedoms: Metaethics in social work research. *Social Work, 48*(1), p.135–150.

Appadurai, A. (2000). Grassroots globalization and the research imagination. *Public Culture, 12*(1), 1–19.

Batliwala, S. (2002). Grassroots movements as transnational actors:Implications for global civil society. *International Journal of Voluntary and Non-profit Organizations, 13*(4), 393–410.

Bretherton, C. (1996). Introduction: Global politics in the 1990s. In C. B. a. G. Porton (Ed.), *Global politics: An introduction.* Oxford, England: Blackwell.

Brown, L. D., & Moore, M. H. (2001). Symposium: New roles and challenges for NGOs: Accountability, strategy, and international nongovernmental organizations. *Nonprofit and Voluntary Sector Quarterly, 30*(3), 569–587.

Foner, N. (1997). What's new about transnationalism? New York immigrants today and at the turn of the century. *Disapora, 6*, 355–375.

Halpern, S., & Laxer, G. (2003). Effective resistance to corporate globalization. In G. L. S. Halperin (Ed.), *Global civil society and its limits* (pp. 1–21). New York: Palgrave Macmillan.

Hamm, S. (2003, 9/22/2003). Borders are so 20th century. *Business Week*, 68–71.

Homburg, C., Krohmer, H., Cannon, J. P., & Kiedaisch, I. (2002). Consumer satisfaction in transnational buyer-supplier relationships. *Journal of International Marketing, 10*(4), 1–29.

Ireland, P. (1994). *The policy challenge of ethnic diversity.* Cambridge, MA: Harvard University Press.

Jones, A. (2002). The "global city" misconceived: The myth of "global management" in transnational service firms. *Geoforum, 33*(3), 335–350.

Kastoryano, R. (2000). *Settlement, transnational communities and citizenship.* New York: United Nations Educational, Scientific and Cultural Organization (UNESCO).

Keane, J. (2003). *Global civil society?* Cambridge, England: Cambridge University Press.

Kelly, P. (2003). Canadian-Asian transnationalism. *The Canadian Geographer, 47*(3), 209–218.

Latapi, A. E. (1999). Low skill emigration from Mexico to the United States. Current situation, prospects and government policy. *International Migration, 37*(1).

Ley, D. (2004). Transnational spaces and everyday lives. *The Institute of British Geographers-CHECK, 29*(1), 151–164.

Link, R. J., Ramanathan, C. S., & Asamoah, Y. (1999). *All our futures: Principles and resources for social work practice in a global era.* Pacific Grove, CA: Brooks and Cole.

Lopez, S., & Salgado De Snyder, V. N. (2001). El funcionamente psicosocial de los migrantes de retorno de origen rural. *Instituto Nacional de Psiquiatria/ Instituto Nacional de Salud Publica, Mexico.*

Massey, D., Alarcon, R., Durand, J., & Gonzalez, H. (1991). Los Ausentes: El proceso social de la migracion internacional en el occidente de Mexico. *Mexico: Alianza editorial y Consijo Mexicano para le Cultura y las Artes.*

Mauri, A. J., & Phatak, A. V. (2001). Global integration as inter-area product flows: The internalization of ownership and location factors influencing product flows across MNC units. *Management International Review, 41*(3), 233–250.

National Association of Social Workers (1997). *Code of ethics.* Washington, DC: Author.

Poole, D. L. (1996). NAFTA, Mexican health, and American health: They tie together. *Health & Social Work, 21*, 3–7.

Poole, D. L., & Salgado De Snyder, V. N. (2002). Pathways to health and mental health care: Guidelines for culturally competent practice. In A. R. R. G. J. Greene (Ed.), *Social Workers' Desk Reference* (pp. 51–56). New York: Oxford University Press.

Portes, A., Haller, W., & Guarnizo, L. E. (2001). *Transnational entrepreneurs: The emergence and determinants of an alternative form of immigrant economic adaptation.* Unpublished manuscript, Princeton University.

Pries, L. (2004). Determining the causes and durability of transnacional labour migration of transnacional labour migration between Mexico and the United Status: Some empirical findings. *International Migration, 42*(2).

Rousse, R. (1989). *Mexican migration to the United Status: Family relations in the development of a transnational migrant circuit.* Unpublished manuscript, Stanford University.

Salgado De Snyder, V. N. (1993). Family life across the border: Mexican wives left behind. *Hispanic Journal of Behavioral Sciences, 9*, 287–298.

Sassen, S. (2002). Global cities and diasporic networks: Microsites in global civil society. In M. K. M. Glasius & A. Helmut (Eds.), *Global Civil Society, 2002* (pp.217–238). Oxford, England: Oxford University Press.

Smith, J. C., Chatfield, C., & Pagnucco, R. (1997). *Transnational social movements and global politics: Solidarity beyond the state.* Syracuse, NY: Syracuse University Press.

Stoesz, D., Guzzetta, C., & Lusk, M. (1999). *International development.* Boston: Allyn & Bacon.

Taran, P. A. (2000). Human rights of migrants: Challenges of the new decade. *International Migration, 38*(6).

Wallisch, L. S., & Spence, R. T. (2006). Alcohol and drug use, abuse and dependence in urban areas and colonias of the Texas-Mexico border. *Hispanic Journal of Behavioral Sciences, 28*(2), 286–307.

Wilding, P. (1997). Globalization, regionalism and social policy. *Social Policy and Administration, 31*(4), 410–428.

Yeates, N. (1999). Social politics and policy in an era of globalization: Critical reflections. Social Policy and Administration, 33(4), 372–393.

CHAPTER THREE

The Diversity and Commonalities of Latinos in the United States

Thomas Wayne Sanchez

Susanna Jones

Introduction

A core value of social work practice is to work with oppressed and marginalized populations. According to many indicators, Latinos in the United States qualify as such a group. Twenty-one percent of Latinos experience poverty and, consequently, high rates of food insecurity; roughly 20 percent of Latinos do not have enough food to meet their dietary needs (Ng'andu & Gianfortoni, 2006). Inequalities do not end there. Rios-Ellis (2005) reports that Latinos are at a disproportionately higher risk of experiencing mental illness, in particular depression, and they do not access mental health services as readily as other ethnic groups (González & González-Ramos, 2007). It is imperative for social workers to adopt the skills necessary to engage in culturally competent practice that takes into account "differences that exist in social class, level of education, degrees of acculturation, citizenship or resident status, nationality, and worldview between and within Hispanic groups" (González & González-Ramos, 2007, p. 12).

The Latino population is a highly diverse group and the designation can be quite complicated. There are many different ideas about who is, and who is not, Latino. The term *Latino*, which is often used synonymously with *Hispanic*, has only existed since the 1970s, before which time Latinos were not discussed as a significant U.S. minority group. In 1976, after much political struggle, the designation of "non-white Hispanic" was developed to help the U.S. Census Bureau determine how many Hispanics were in the United States. This new racial category also allowed Hispanics to be included in affirmative action laws and has had implications for policies. Education, health benefits, and citizenship, for instance, are connected to and determined by one's racial classification. Latinos comprise different national groups coming from Puerto Rico, Mexico, Cuba, and Central and South America as well as various other Spanish cultures, although the designation most commonly refers to people of Mexican, Cuban, or Puerto Rican origin (many race-relations textbooks still cover only those three nationalities in the *Latino* chapter). Additionally, Hispanics/Latinos self-identify as belonging to various racial identities, including, but not limited to, black, white, Asian, Pacific Islander, or a combination of several racial groups. The Latino reality has grown with its proportion of the U.S. Census and currently counts increasing numbers of Central and South Americans.

The following experience helps illustrate a Latino reality. On a trip to New York two Latinos are sitting in a Dominican restaurant situated in a Puerto Rican neighborhood and listening to Mexican norteña music on the jukebox while drinking Mexican beer. The next night they go around the corner to a Brazilian steakhouse, and the table shares Chilean wine and Guatemalan beer while enjoying the Colombian music. Of course it could just as easily be some Mexican Americans eating at a Salvadoran pupuseria (pupusas are a Salvadoran food, and a pupuseria is where they are made and consumed), drinking Miller Lite, and not understanding the indigenous language spoken by the three Guatemalans at the next table. It is a reality that oftentimes raises more questions than it answers and begs the questions: What terminology is appropriate and when? And, how does language shape identity, or not? This chapter describes the differences and commonalities among and between various Latino groups in an attempt to offer a solid grounding for quality social work practice with diverse Latino populations.

Latinos came to the United States before there even was an established United States of America. The Spanish established a settlement in present-day Santa Fe, New Mexico, in 1609, years before the English settlement of Jamestown was established in 1622, and Santa Fe remains the oldest state capital in the United States (Gonzales, 1999, p. 33). Since that time, Latinos have gone from a small and largely neglected minority to the largest minority group, comprising 42.7 million, the equivalent of 14 percent, of the U.S. population in 2005 (this estimate excludes the 3.9 million residents of Puerto Rico) (http://www.census.gov/Press-Release / www / releases / archives / population / 006808.html). Debates, ostensibly on immigration in general but where Latino immigration is the focus, rage on in Congress and in the streets, town halls, and any-where Americans gather. *Latino, Spanish, Mexican,* and *American* are, at times, used to describe the same ethnic group, and most designations can be legitimately claimed by any individual in that group, depending on where they situate themselves. So who are these people, and how should they be described? What is their preferred racial/ethnic identity term? Where are they from, and why are they in the United States? Any answer to these questions will contain caveats, exceptions, and qualifications. Latinos or Hispanics[1], Mexicans, Cubans, Puerto Ricans, Guatemalans, or Americans (and depending on the specific situation many combinations thereof) have light skin and dark. They speak Spanish, English, or both, Portuguese or indigenous languages (with large numbers being bi- and trilingual). They are Catholics, Protestants, Muslims, Jews, and atheists. They are very rich, very poor, and everything in-between. Most are natural-born citizens, although many of the foreign born are naturalized citizens or permanent residents. Some are undocumented and some have been citizens for generations. The following descriptions and definitions are generalizations, and as such they should not be used to define and describe every person who claims Latino descent.

A proper understanding of Latinos in the twenty-first century requires an understanding of the U.S. laws and treaties that often served as de facto certificates of belonging. A brief history of selected Latino groups and their relationship to the United States follows.

The first Latinos were actually Mexicans, who became Mexican Americans when the Treaty of Guadalupe Hidalgo was signed in 1848, ending the U.S.–Mexican War. The defeated Mexicans were forced to cede almost half their territory, and more than a hundred thousand Mexicans became U.S. residents and citizens. These new Americans were still a very small percentage of the overall population, especially as Anglo-Americans flooded the land in the last half of the nineteenth century. Beginning in the first half of the twentieth century and continuing to this day, Mexicans began migrating north to fill U.S. labor needs.

The island of Puerto Rico has been under direct U.S. control since the end of the Spanish-American war in 1898. Puerto Ricans were granted U.S. citizenship with the Jones Act of 1917 but did not come to the mainland in large numbers until after 1952, when cheaper airfares brought larger numbers to the East Coast of the United States—places like New York, Philadelphia, and New Jersey—to fill industrial labor

---

1. This chapter will use the term *Latino* except where *Hispanic* had been specified by data cited. For example, the U.S. Census uses *Hispanic*, so that term will be used when describing census numbers.

needs. Although still concentrated on the East Coast, Puerto Ricans are now found throughout the United States with a large community in Chicago, among other cities.

Cuban contact with the United States began in the 1850s, when revolutionaries seeking independence from Spain began to congregate in New York and Florida to plan their revolution. While Cuban contact with the United States is old and storied, the Cuban population did not become numerically significant until Fidel Castro took control of Cuba in 1959. As a result, for more than fifteen years, hundreds of thousands fearing economic and political persecution fled Cuba. The Cuban immigrants who followed beginning in the 1980s—starting with the so-called *Marielitos*, immigrants who took part in the Mariel Boatlift—were mostly white, wealthy, politically conservative, and vehemently anticommunist. This group of immigrants received support, both in the form of in-kind aid as well as financial assistance, from the U.S. government. Cubans were, and still are, welcome in the United States in the form of preferential immigration policies and entitlements to social welfare benefits. Mexicans, on the other hand, were and continue to be desired for their labor yet denied entitlement to many social welfare benefits.

When the term *Latino* is used, it typically refers to a member of one of the three groups mentioned above: Mexicans, Puerto Ricans, or Cubans. To reduce Latinos to these three groups is highly problematic, as there are numerous other nationalities that fit within this U.S.-imposed construct. The story of Guatemalans in the United States highlights some of these differences.

Guatemalans are present in significant numbers in numerous places in the United States, places like Jupiter, near Palm Beach, Florida; Canton, Georgia; and Schuyler, Nebraska. There are two key differences between Guatemalans and other Latinos. Most of the Guatemalans in the United States are indigenous peoples in their country of origin, and while indigenous Mexicans come to the United States, they represent a small percentage of all Mexicans in the country. The second key difference is asylum status, which many Guatemalans (and even more Salvadorans) are granted as the result of their fleeing civil wars during the 1980s.

According to the U.S. Census estimate of July 1, 2005, Hispanics make up 14 percent of the nation's population, with 42.7 million people (this does not include the almost 4 million residents of Puerto Rico). Latinos are the largest minority group, and while Asians are a faster growing one, Latinos contributed to half of the country's population growth from July 1, 2004 to July 1, 2005, growing nationwide by 3.3 percent. Since the 1970s, Mexicans have continued to comprise roughly two-thirds of the total U.S. Hispanic population. Puerto Ricans comprise approximately 10 percent, while Cubans, Salvadorans, and Dominicans make up 3 percent each. The rest of the Latino population is from Central or South America.

Latino is an umbrella term that designates people with origins south of the U.S.-Mexican border and much of the Caribbean residing in or having direct contact with the United States; that is, the term *becomes relevant only through U.S. contact*[2] (although U.S. exclusiveness is starting to change with an increasingly globalized culture). *Latino* includes all races and people of every shade from more than twenty-two countries including Mexico, and Central America, South America, and much of the Caribbean. So every Mexican-American is a Latino but not every Latino is a Mexican-American. *Hispanic* and *Latino* are identity terms and as such are self-chosen. They refer, more or less, to the same group of people. Individuals and groups can choose either term and be correct most of the time. Why the confusion and why the difference? *Hispanic* can be a misnomer because it implies Spanish origin or at the very least the Spanish language, and not all Latinos have Spanish origin; there are large numbers of indigenous peoples for whom Spanish is not their first language. This also eliminates the Portuguese-speaking Brazilians. *Latino*, on the other hand, can be a misnomer because it could include the Spanish, French, and Italians, and they are not Latino. (Europeans should not be included in the designation because they are not usually concerned with the same issues or problems associated with being Latino in the United States, including economic and education issues, but most important, the struggle for first-class citizenship or to be treated and thought of as first-class citizens by U.S. society.) *Hispanic* can also be seen as an imposed term (Oboler, 1995), whereas *Latino* is more often seen as one that people chose for themselves.

Geography: Latinos Are Everywhere!

Latinos in the United States reside mostly in the three "gateway" areas, where the three most common groups—Mexicans, Puerto Ricans, and Cubans—enter the country. Those with Mexican origins are concentrated in the Southwest. Puerto Ricans are concentrated in New York and the Northeast, and Cubans in South Florida. Although these generalizations remain true in the twenty-first century, there are also large concentrations of Latinos in other parts of the country. Chicago has large numbers of all three groups and has been called the original Latino city (Padilla, 1985). Today's reality finds Latinos in every part of the

---

2. Even though U.S. Latinos are not technically and do not consider themselves Latino in their home country, they become Latino once they arrive in the United States.

United States, including, but not limited to, new and unprecedented locations such as the Southeast and Midwest.

It is not a coincidence that immigrants of Mexican origin overwhelmingly reside in the Southwest; it is, after all, for many their ancestral homeland. As noted above, the first Latinos were actually Mexicans who were forcefully annexed with the signing of the Treaty of Guadalupe Hidalgo, which ended the U.S.–Mexican War (1846–1848). This history coincides with insatiable labor needs of the United States, particularly for agriculture and other related industries in California. In 2007 alone, Latinos made up 24.3 percent of the total population in the Southwest, with the vast majority being of Mexican descent. Almost half of the total U.S. Latino population lives in California or Texas. California has more than 12.4 million Latinos and Texas has 7.8 million, comprising roughly 35 percent of the total population of both those states. New Mexico has the highest percentage of Latinos, who make up 43 percent of the state's population. Mexican migration to the Southwest continues to account for most of total U.S. immigration, a stream that has flowed, mostly uninterrupted, for more than a hundred years.

Puerto Ricans contribute to Latino culture, and Dominicans add Caribbean flavor to the Northeast region. Almost half of all Dominicans living in the United States reside in New York City. The majority of Puerto Ricans live in New York, but there are also large communities in New Jersey, Connecticut, Rhode Island, and Philadelphia, Pennsylvania. Cubans have one of the highest regional concentrations of all U.S. minority groups, "with 67 percent of all Cuban Americans residing in Florida and 52 percents in the Miami area alone" (Healey, 2007, p. 184).

As noted, the still-typical destinations for different Latino national groups are the Southwest for Mexicans, New York and the Northeast more generally for Puerto Ricans, and South Florida for Cubans. There are, however, new destinations as a result of growing numbers of other national groups, such as Guatemalans, coming to the United States. Those new destinations, places where there is not a history of large concentrations of Latinos, are the Southeast, Georgia, North Carolina, Arkansas, and the Midwest, including Iowa, Minnesota, and Nebraska.

URBAN/RURAL DIFFERENCES

Latinos are one of the most urban groups in the United States, with 94 percent living in metropolitan areas in 2000. While they constituted only 6 percent of the total non-metropolitan population, they were 25 percent of the non-metropolitan population growth. Although there have always been large percentages of rural Latinos in California, the new growth is largely in places where there is no history of Latino settlement and, until recently, few Latino residents. Marrow (2005) highlights that Latinos are settling in places outside of the five previously common southwestern states of Arizona, California, Colorado, New Mexico, and Texas. Thus, while the overwhelming majority of Latinos live in urban areas, they have made significant inroads to rural areas and are poised to change the face of the rural United States in degrees comparable to urban communities.

Similarities and Differences among Latinos

IMMIGRATION AND CITIZENSHIP

Of the about 45 million Latinos in the United States, 26.6 million, or 9 percent of the total population and 60 percent of the Hispanic population, are U.S. born. Meanwhile, 17.7 million, or 6 percent of the total population and 40 percent of the Hispanics population, are foreign born (http://pewhispanic.org/factsheets/factsheet.php?FactsheetID=35). Although the majority of Latinos are natural-born U.S. citizens, immigration continues to play a vital role in their lives; and despite the fact that 60 percent are U.S. citizens, there is still stigma associated with being Latino. Some Mexicans have been citizens since 1848, and all Puerto Ricans are born citizens. (Whether citizenship for Puerto Ricans is equal to citizenship for others is questionable—they are not allowed to pay federal taxes or vote for president and have no voting representative in Congress.) Although most Latinos are born in the United States, the majority of the estimated 12 million undocumented persons in the United States are also Latino. It is estimated that Mexicans make up 60 percent of the total undocumented population of the United States (Eitzen & Baca Zinn, 2007). Many immigrant scholars (Hayduk, 2006) argue that the rise in numbers of Latino immigrants partially explains the contentious and fierce nature of the current immigration debate.

Even with the advantageous position of Puerto Ricans vis-à-vis U.S. citizenship, Cuban immigrants, the most recent of the three major Latino groups, gain from the most immigration-friendly policies. The end of the cold war did not stop the benefits and entitlements afforded to Cuban immigrants, and many Cuban immigrants are provided with programs such as bilingual education and small-business loans. Cubans also brought more capital with them when they came, and, due to their close relationship with the United States, cultural knowledge of how to thrive in the country. Officially, the Cuban Adjustment Act (1966) allows Cubans the immediate right to legal residency, a work permit, and citizenship after one year. Contrast this to the reality of many Mexican immigrants who wait an estimated eight to ten years for citizenship (Hayduk, 2006).

LANGUAGE

Most Latinos speak English or a combination of English and Spanish. This makes sense considering that the majority of Latinos are born in the United States but is contrary to the common assumption that all Latinos speak primarily Spanish. Many Latinos speak both Spanish and English, and some Brazilians and groups indigenous to their countries of origin speak neither as their primary language.

The reality is that most Latinos speak some Spanish. In fact, there are 31 million U.S. households where primarily Spanish is spoken at home. That is the equivalent of 10 percent of all households, and, further, more than half of Latinos say that they also speak English "very well" (U. S. Census Bureau, 2003). In terms of intra-Latino differences, Puerto Ricans are the most bilingual Spanish/English-speaking group among Latinos. Brazilians, who make up a small proportion of Latinos, speak Portuguese. Indigenous Guatemalan and indigenous Mexican immigrants to the United States are examples of groups that are often trilingual. They were taught Spanish at school in their home country, they learn English as an immigrant, and they continue to speak their native language.

As with other elements of *Latinidad* (Latino-ness), there is wide variation among English and Spanish speakers, revolving mostly around generational differences. The percentage of Spanish- and English-language dominance practically reverses for first- and third-generation Latinos. Seventy-three percent of first-generation Latinos report their language as Spanish-only or Spanish-dominant, while 78 percent of third-generation Latinos report using English-only or English-dominant language (Aguirre & Turner, 1998). This parallels previous sociological findings, which showed that most immigrant families are monolingual-English or English-dominant by the third generation. There are areas, however, where this picture does not apply. For example, there are seven counties in South Texas where more than 80 percent of residents reported speaking primarily Spanish in the home. In addition, there were two metropolitan areas of more than a hundred thousand people where 90 percent of residents reported speaking Spanish primarily in the home: Hialeah, Florida, and Laredo, Texas, places where Cuban Americans and Mexican Americans, respectively, predominate (U.S. Census Bureau, 2005).

While many Latinos speak Spanish, and the language and culture continues to heavily influence Latinos historically, culturally, and economically, it is far from the only language they speak, particularly for the minority born outside of the United States. The prevalence of Spanish depends on many things, including national origin, generation, and, equally important, area of residence.

GENDER

One of the most ignored variables among Latinos, as it often is among other U.S. racial/ethnic groups, is gender. In all modern societies women are marginalized, to varying degrees, from positions of power. Power is sometimes determined, but not single-handedly, by sheer numbers. In 2005, there were 107 Latino males for every 100 Latino females. Conversely, there are 97 males for every 100 females in the overall population (http://www.census.gov/Press-Release/www/releases/archives/population/006808.html). Female marginalization among Latinos is further exacerbated by both traditions of machismo and low socioeconomic status. *Machismo* is derived from the Latin word for male. In Spanish and Portuguese, *machismo* means "sexism" or "male chauvinism." It has an overt negative connotation and too often translates into a misuse or abuse of power on the part of men. Oboler (1995) argues that the very existence of today's Hispanic—a mix of European and indigenous biology and culture—is the embodiment of a history of European men historically conquering native women (p. 21).

The level of male privilege enjoyed by many men in Latin America, especially those from working-class communities, is diminished, though not eliminated, for immigrant groups in the United States. Men who previously made money and nominally made economic decisions are now forced to deal with wives and daughters who, in the model of late-twentieth-century U.S. feminism and global labor markets, want and are forced by economic conditions to work. In some instances, Latino women workers make comparable, or better, wages than Latino males. In 2002, Latino males made 63 percent of what white males made. Latina females did slightly better, making 73 percent of the dollar earned by white females (Aguirre & Turner, 1998, p. 177). While Latinas as a whole do better relative to their Latino male counterparts as compared to whites overall, Mexican American females remain the lowest-paid racial/ethnic group.

On average, Latinas with a bachelor's degree make less than white males with a high school diploma. The resulting income differences are magnified when looking at Latinas who are single parents. While less than 20 percent of white households headed by a single female live below the poverty line, that number rises to 40 percent for Mexican Americans and 44 percent for Puerto Ricans (Healey, 2007).

RELIGION

Just as Spanish is the dominant language among Latinos in the United States, Catholicism is the dominant religion, although there are small but growing numbers of Latinos who practice other religions. Catholicism for most Latinos takes on cultural significance, so while they may not attend Mass, many are likely to be baptized and buried under the auspices of the Catholic faith. Latino national groups sometimes practice Catholicism differently from each other and from white ethnic groups (e.g., the Irish or the Italians). As far as differences among Latino groups, Portes and Rumbaut (2006) found that Cubans, unlike Mexican Americans, were better able to leverage their Catholicism to increase their socioeconomic status. This was in part a result of the assistance provided by the Catholic Church to Cuban immigrants.

> [Mexicans], the largest immigrant group in the nation and the one that comprises, along with its descendants, the fastest-growing component of the American Catholic population has not had access, *yesterday or today*, to the mobility escalator that served other Catholic groups in the past . . . [in] contrast with that of Cuban exiles arriving in South Florida in the 1960s and 1970s. Cuban parishes were promptly established in the archdiocese of Miami, and Cuban priests and bishops quickly found their way into the U.S. Catholic hierarchy. (p. 334)

AGE

Latinos are a considerably younger population than other racial/ethnic groups, with a median age of 27.2 years compared to 36.2 years for the entire U.S. population (http://www.census.gov/Press-Release/www/releases/archives/population/006808.html). As of July 1, 2005, 22 percent of the total U.S. population under the age of five was Latino. The implications of a young Latino population are many. First, Latinos already have a higher proportion of school-age children than the general population. This can become problematic, as older whites may vote to withhold taxes used to support education on the grounds that their children have already grown, resulting in fewer tax dollars for public education. Second, with the baby boom generation nearing retirement, it will increasingly fall to Latino workers to meet the demand for labor, and, therefore, to contribute to social security. Finally, age differentials can impact formal positions and degrees of power. Young people are less likely to vote, and Latinos will continue to disproportionately comprise the young (Healy, 2007, p. 191).

INCOME AND EDUCATION

Latinos are overrepresented in poverty statistics and underrepresented in educational statistics relative to their proportion of the overall U.S. population. Latino household income equaled 72 percent of white household income in 2002, a decline from 76 percent in 2000. The percentage of those living in poverty ranged from a high of 26.1 percent for Puerto Ricans to a low of 16.5 percent for Cubans compared to 8 percent for whites (Aguirre & Turner, 1998, p. 174).

The overall Latino poverty rate was 21.9 percent in 2004 (http://www .census.gov/Press-Release/archives/income_wealth/005647.html). Not all Latinos are equally poor. Cubans had the lowest poverty rates (12 percent), comparable to whites (13 percent), in 2007s (Healey, 2007, p. 194). Cuban American income and education is close to and at times higher than the national average, with that of Mexican Americans and Puerto Ricans being much lower than national averages. It is no coincidence that poverty among Latinos relates to their relative lack of formal education. Fifty-eight percent of Latinos over the age of twenty-five have at least a high school diploma compared to 87 percent of those who are non-Latino. Latinos, who make up 14 percent of the population, are only 11 percent of those attending college.

FAMILIES

Latinos are more "family oriented" than many groups, one of the few positive associations that the mainstream affords them. In fact, 67 percent of Latino families consist of a married couple, and 65 percent of Latino children reside with two parents (http://www.census.gov/population/www/socdemo/hh-fam.html).

Latino Exclusion and the Complexity of the Ambivalent Reception

There is no such thing as a Latino culture. There is no Latino food or Latino music. Latinos do not all speak Spanish, and they are not all Catholics. Latinos have more differences than commonalities. One element that Latinos share is the ambivalent reception they receive in the United States forging their struggle for citizenship. Whether annexed forcefully, as with early Mexicans and Puerto Ricans, or migrating later, Latinos have been denied, formally and informally, legally and illegally, the rights long overdue as longtime citizens of the United States. They have been welcomed and shunned by employers of all kinds and sizes, and they are themselves employers of all kinds and sizes. Many Latinos receive an ambivalent reception, whether they are citizens or immigrants. The story that follows helps to illustrate this point.

While traveling back and forth between research sites in northeastern Nebraska, I had car trouble and went to a nearby farmhouse for help. I managed to buy a battery from the owner and even had help transporting it up the road and installing it. When the time came to make payment, the older gentleman who had sold me the battery looked at the name on the check and said, "Hmm . . . Sanchez . . . you speak pretty good English." I replied, "I better, it is the only language I speak" (which was not entirely true, but I did grow up as a monolingual English speaker). He said, "No, but where are you from?" I replied, "Scottsbluff, right here in Nebraska." He said, "No, I know you're *from* here, but where were you born?" I said, "I was born in Scottsbluff," and he said, "But where is your dad from?" and I said, "He is from Texas." Eventually we arrived at my grandfather being from Mexico; the point being that I could not be from the United States and have a name like Sanchez.

To further illustrate the point of identity, and Latino identity specifically, one must look at what it means to people in the United States versus what it means to those outside the country. Oliva Espín (1997) writes about the difficulties encountered by newly arrived immigrants because they are forced to decide on new identities, including racial/ethnic ones. Adding to this dilemma is the fact that racial/ethnic identities are constructed differently in different countries. Identity is a combination or a dialectic between self-identity and societal identity. Societal identity is geographically specific. The following short vignette highlights some of the differences. During research interviews with Latino immigrants, when asked the question, "How do you self-identify?" most participants gave answers like, "I am a good person" or "I am a hard worker," or even, "I am average." Very few identified with ethnic/racial terms like *Latino* or *Hispanic* or *Mexican*. Even after prompting and asking about ethnic identity, few knew or had an answer that related to the way they are identified by U.S. society. All answered readily, however, when asked about nationality, and all persons interviewed were proud of their previous home country. These individuals had been forced to think about nationality in a way that was not authentic to them. The respondents were people from a small town, from at least eleven different countries grouped together as *Latinos* by white hegemonic constructs, which did not fit into their worldview. Identity constructs were and continue to be imposed upon many minority groups.

In sum, Latinos are assumed to be from somewhere other than the United States. Latino immigrants must negotiate between their ethnic identity and the one that society imposes. They must make a decision about who they are with little knowledge of the system they inhabit. In many ways, Latinos do not neatly fit into the social or cultural system of the United States, yet they have made significant progress and gains in multiple spheres. While Cubans came to the United States with the advantage of being given many of the tools and capital needed to be economically successful, many other Latino groups have also made economic, political, and social strides. Henry Cisneros, for example, a Mexican American from Texas, was the mayor of San Antonio and a member of the Clinton cabinet. He is currently the president of the most-watched television network in the United States, Univision. The tremendous leverage of Latino purchasing power is evident in the bilingual ads and ad campaigns specifically targeting Latinos. While some in the country are upset that customer service centers and ATMs offer multilingual options, the financial sector recognizes the power of the Latino consumer.

Latinos occupy a precarious position: they are as American as apple pie and foreign at the same time. Latinos are native-born and simultaneously the largest immigrant group. They can be found at every level and in every region of the United States. Latinos have various nationalities, speak many languages, practice many religions, and come from many different countries. They are not a monolithic group of people, so when encountering Latinos, in whichever sphere, avoid making sweeping generalizations about their histories and social needs.

In this chapter, we explored the complex diversity within the Latino community. Inherent within this discussion are numerous complexities, paradoxes, and unresolved issues. One of the key ways in which the diversity and commonalities of this community are expressed is through work and employment. In the following chapter, you will come to understand the central role that work has played in the development of unity and difference within the Latino community, and the importance of solidarity, advocacy, and organizing within the realm of employment.

References

Aguirre, A., Jr., & Turner, J. H. (1998). *American ethnicity: The dynamics and consequences of discrimination* (2nd ed.). NY: McGraw-Hill.

Eitzen, S. D., & Baca Zinn, M.(2007). *In conflict and order: Understanding society.* Boston, MA: Allyn & Bacon.

Espín, O. M. (1997). *Latina realities: Essays on healing, migration and sexuality.* Boulder, CO: Westview Press.

García, M. C. (1996). *Havana USA.* Berkeley, CA: University of California Press.

Gonzales, M. G. (1999). *Mexicanos: A history of Mexicans in the United States.* Bloomington, IN: University of Indiana Press.

González, M. J., & González-Ramos, G. (2007). Hispanics in the 21st century: A mental health perspective. *Current, 51,* 6, 1–12.

Hayduk, R. (2006). *Democracy for all: Restoring immigrant voting rights in the United States.* NY: Routledge.

Healey, J. F. (2007). *Diversity and society: Race, ethnicity, and gender.* (2nd ed.). Thousand Oaks, CA: Pine Forge Press.

Marrow, H. B. (2005). New destinations and immigrant incorporation. *Perspectives in Politics*, 3, 781–799.

Ng'andu, J., & Gianfortoni, E.M.L. (2006). Sin provecho: Latinos and food insecurity. National Council of La Raza Report.

Oboler, S. (1995). *Ethnic labels, Latino lives: Identity and the politics of (re)presentation in the United States.* Minneapolis, MN: University of Minnesota Press.

Padilla, F. (1985). *Latino ethnic consciousness: The case of Mexican Americans and Puerto Ricans in Chicago.* University of Notre Dame Press.

Portes, A., & Rumbaut, R. G. (2006). *Immigrant America: A portrait.* Berkeley, CA: University of California Press.

Rios-Ellis, B. (2005). *Critical disparities in Latino mental health: Transforming research into action.* Report by National Council of La Raza and California University of Long Beach.

Statistical Portrait of Hispanics in the United States, 2006. Pew Hispanic Center. Retrieved December 18, 2008, from http://pewhispanic.org/factsheets/factsheet.php?FactsheetID = 35.

U. S. Census Bureau. (2003). *Factfinder: Latino characteristics.* Retrieved on July 24, 2008, from http://factfinder.census.gov/servlet/QTTable?_bm = y&-geo_id = 01000US&-qr_name = DEC_2000_SF4_U_DP2&-ds_name = DEC_2000_SF4_U&-_lang = en&-_sse = on

U. S. Census Bureau. (2005). *Spanish usage in the United States.* Retrieved on September 14, from 2008. http://www.census.gov/Press-Release/www.releases/archives/population/001342.html

CHAPTER FOUR

¡Si, Se Puede! Revisited: Latina/o Workers in the United States

Paul Ortiz

Introduction

Latino/a workers are an integral part of the New Economy, and they have always played a pivotal role in the economic development of the United States. Latina/o peoples have faced structural barriers that have often limited their occupational choices and upward mobility. Conquest and colonization had disastrous effects on Mexican workers as well as their immigrant counterparts from the Latin American and Caribbean diasporas. Today, Latina/o workers confront racism, national-origin discrimination, and sexism in their workplaces. Since new immigrants often have tenuous or nonexistent citizenship rights, they are especially vulnerable to various forms of exploitation, including nonpayment of wages, workplace injuries, and debt peonage.

Latina/o workers have been active in struggles for economic justice and the expansion of democracy in the United States since the nineteenth century. These economic empowerment initiatives, ranging from industrial union organizing to the recent May Day demonstrations, offer insights into how Latina/o laborers philosophically connect work, democracy, and human rights. Latina/o workers have used mass protests and other public forums to expose the often dangerous conditions they work under as well as to offer their ideas on citizen-ship, public policy, and unions.

Latina/o Workers Speak Out

On May 1, 2006—International Workers' Day—Latina/o workers initi-ated one of the largest work stoppages in the history of the Americas. Migrant laborers, *Nuyoricans*, Chicana/os, *Afrocubanos*, *Guatemaltecos*, and immigrants from every continent united in protest of immigration-restriction measures that threatened their families, their livelihoods, and their dignity. Hundreds of thousands of Latina/o workers and their allies sought to end the cycle of isolation and alienation from the broader society that has left them vulnerable to exploitation. The pro-tests were marked by a profound sense of urgency. Politicians, radio talk-show hosts, and some journalists have accused Latina/o immigrant workers of importing disease, terrorism, and crime to the United States. Facing a rising tide of inequality, some white Americans have mistak-enly blamed newer Latina/o immigrants for problems rooted in the larger economic system (Chomsky, 2007; Krugman, 2006; Trumbull, 2006). Even "positive" racial stereotypes of Latina/o immigrants as "hard workers" are sometimes used by employers to pay Latina/o laborers chronically low wages (Kimbriell, 2007). Immigrant workers make a convenient target for political pundits because normally they do not have the power or resources to talk back. On May 1, however, Latina/o workers spoke with a mighty voice. They marched down main streets shouting "*¡Si, Se Puede!*" (Yes We Can!), and they carried signs proclaiming, "You Might Hate Us/But You Need Us," "*Primo de Mayo*," "A Day Without a Mexican," and "This Land Is Your Land, This Land Is Our Land." In New York City, Latina/o workers were joined by thou-sands of Jamaican, Irish, and Chinese immigrants who added their voices to the protests (Siemaszko, 2006).

These mass demonstrations provide a crucial glimpse of the values and aspirations of major segments of the Latina/o working class as well as their centrality to the economic life of the nation. These workers shut down major sectors of the U.S. economy, including meat packing, garment manufacturing, port transportation, and food service in many parts of the country (Bernstein, 2006; Gonzalez, J., 2006a; Gonzalez, V., 2006; Morash, 2006). The May Day protests followed an earlier wave of walkouts that occurred in March and April. These incipient strikes were led in many cases by agricultural and construction workers seeking to boost their wages and to escape poverty conditions (Gonzalez, J., 2006b; Morris, 2006). "In South Florida and Immokalee, things (harvesting) pretty much ground to a halt," said G. Ellis Hunt Jr., the president of

Hunt Bros. Inc., a Lake Wales grower and packinghouse owner with more than five thousand grove acres split equally between Polk and Immokalee (Mojarro, 2006).

In the weeks leading up to International Workers' Day, union organizer Jorge Rodriguez vowed, "There will be 2 to 3 million people hitting the streets in Los Angeles [on May 1] alone. We're going to close down Los Angeles, Chicago, New York, Tucson, Phoenix, Fresno. . . . We want full amnesty, full legalization for anybody who is here. That is the message that is going to be played out across the country on May 1." (Kutalik, 2006; La Botz, 2006; Moffett, 2006). Several days in advance of the gigantic protest dubbed by some organizers as "A Day Without Immigrants," corporations such as Cargill Inc., Tyson Foods, and the Seaboard Corporation announced that they would be closing their operations owing to a lack of personnel (Archibold, 2006; Whitcomb, 2006).

Latina/o marchers vowed to show the American public that they were an essential part of the nation's economic future in the workplace as well as in the marketplace. Nursing home worker Corina Payan, who participated in the Denver march, explained, "I know that without us, they're not going to be able to do anything. They're not going to go out in the field and clean the bathrooms or anything. . . . Everywhere you go, Wal-Mart, anything, all you see are Hispanic people filling their carts to the top. . . . We're the ones making them money." (Nguyen, 2006).

Lucas Benitez of the Coalition of Immokalee Workers in South Florida had earlier explained that Latina/o farm laborers were engaged in a protracted struggle for wages and dignity. "It's a fundamental problem in Immokalee that the workers get no respect from the growers," the farmworker leader noted. "The growers think they have peons, not employees. To find solutions to other problems, we must break down that barrier." (Riley, 2002, p. 55). One agricultural worker in South Florida said that he would forego a day's wages in the tomato fields because "We have to unite and support each other so they see the way we work." (Cardenas, 2006). The demonstrators vigorously expressed their opposition to U.S. House Resolution, H.R. 4437, which threatened to turn undocumented workers and their supporters into felons (Sanchez, 2006; Wiener, 2006).

Latina/o workers organized the demonstrations through the social institutions that have helped sustain their communities, including workers' centers, labor unions, Catholic Church social justice committees, soccer clubs, and civil rights organizations. Many of the regions that witnessed high turnouts of Latina/o workers for the May Day protests had long histories of Latina/o economic and social justice organizing (Milkman, 2007; Fine, 2006; Louie 2001). These areas included South Florida (Coalition of Immokalee Workers, Miami Workers' Center), Los

Angeles (Garment Workers Center, HERE-UNITE and SEIU labor unions), and Chicago (Chicago Interfaith Worker Rights Center, Latino Union of Chicago). These working-class and immigrant-based institutions provide crucial spaces for Latina/o laborers to develop organizing, educational, and leadership skills that allow them to become more effective advocates for their interests and economic well-being.

Struggling for Economic Betterment

Latina/o laborers have taken their case to the larger public in order to challenge public perceptions that immigrant workers "steal jobs" and abuse social welfare benefits. In fact, the jobs that Latina/o workers—especially first-generation immigrants who do not have citizenship—hold in the United States have exposed many of them to terrible forms of abuse. Farmworkers in the Southeast have experiences of being held in debt peonage, and numerous instances of de facto slavery have been uncovered by human rights and labor organizations in recent years (Asbed, 2003; CNN.Com, 2004; Moffett, 2003). Immigrants must often pay labor contractors thousands of dollars in order work in seasonal and unstable occupations in agriculture, construction, and service industries. When these workers arrive in the United States, they find themselves in debt and victimized by firms that sometimes force them to work for little or no wages (Watanabe, 2007). In New Orleans, many immigrants were recruited by labor contractors under the federally mandated H-2 guest worker program to help in rebuilding efforts after Hurricane Katrina only to discover that their employers had no intention of regularly paying them or offering medical care for work-related injuries (Bauer, 2007).

One Latina immigrant hotel worker in New Orleans testified that "Every one of us took out a loan to come here. We had planned to pay back our debt with our job here. They told us we would have overtime, that we could get paid for holidays, that we would have a place to live at low cost, and it was all a lie." Because this worker and her Latina coworkers had signed contracts that bound them to one employer, they risked forfeiting thousands of dollars if they quit their jobs. "I felt like an animal without claws—defenseless. It is the same as slavery." (Bauer 2007, p. 23). Bill Quigley, a lawyer with the New Orleans–based Loyola Law School Legal Clinic noted, "Since the hurricane we've really seen a meltdown of wage and hour laws, OSHA laws, and practically every other standard that exists for work in this country." Luz Molina, another participant in the Loyola legal advocacy program, observed that "The money is going to the big corporations and not to the workers. There is no quality control and no oversight of who they are contracting with" (Brenner, 2006). In most cases, workers do not report these violations because of their fears of being arrested or deported, as well as their sense of isolation from a broader society that they feel looks on them with suspicion and even contempt.

The Answer Is to Raise Wages and Improve Working Conditions

In 2007, Latina/o workers once again marched by the tens of thousands on May Day. They placed workplace abuses, immigration restrictions, and poverty conditions at the center of their reasons for continued protests. In Watsonville, California, a town distinguished by a long history of Mexican American labor organizing, construction worker Carlos Solarzano stated, "We have 11 million people here, cleaning motels, picking the fruits and vegetables, taking care of the homes of rich people." The Jalisco, Mexico, native continued, "We do a lot of things, but people are not thinking about us." (Jones, 2007). Fourteen-year-old Alejandra Onofre, whose parents were born in Mexico observed, "Mexicans do most of the work in this country, and the government should stop picking on them." Alejandra's fellow marchers in Watsonville, Phoenix, Fort Meyers, and hundreds of other towns carried picket signs reading, "We're workers, not criminals," "*Union Si, Migra No,*" and "No One Is Illegal."

Activists used the 2007 May Day protests to express their opposition to congressional proposals to expand existing "guest worker" or H-2 programs, which bind immigrants to specific employers under a government-sponsored work-visa program. Many compared the H-2 program to the U.S. Mexican Farm Labor *Bracero* program that recruited Mexican agricultural workers in the United States between 1942 and 1964 (Marshall, 2007; Krugman, 2007; Galarza, 1964; Ngai, 2004). (Workers in this notorious program were often not paid in full for their labor, and the *Bracero* program was described by the Department of Labor official in charge of it as "legalized slavery.") A new expansion of the guest worker provisions in 2007, many workers feared, would relegate them to permanent dependency on their employers, while imposing insurmountable barriers to earning U.S. citizenship. Under the existing program, ". . . guest workers cannot legally leave their jobs even when their employers are abusive" (Mello, 2007; Democracy Now!, 2007). "The growers are lobbying for a new guest worker law on the grounds that there is not enough labor available," Lucas Benitez observed. "But it's a lie. Every day in the papers you read about the high numbers of unemployed workers. The problem is that most workers in this country do not want to do the work we do for wages we're paid. We average

$7,500 a year and the conditions of exploitation are such that any rea-
sonable person would prefer receiving unemployment benefits. The
answer to the guest worker lobbying effort is to raise wages and
improve working conditions" (Bacon, 2003).

Santiago Rafael Cruz sought to bring this message of economic
empowerment to Latina/o workers on both sides of the border. Cruz,
an organizer with the Farm Labor Organizing Committee (FLOC) was
sent by his union to Monterrey, Mexico, in the spring of 2007 to instruct
H-2A guest workers in Mexico about their rights in the United States.
Cruz was especially interested in promoting an "education campaign
in nearby villages aimed at stopping rogue recruiters from extorting illegal fees from farmworkers headed north." (Ovalle, 2007). On April 9,
Santiago Cruz was tortured and murdered in his union office. FLOC's
president Baldemar Velásquez mourned, "There's a whole ring of opposition to us, from recruiters to growers to all the interests that take
advantage of a low-wage workforce. . . . We're cutting into their corrupt
business and they don't like it" (Mello, 2007, p. 24).

Long pigeonholed by many as docile laborers willing to live in the
shadows of the American economy, Latina/o workers have shattered
cultural stereotypes by marching, demonstrating, and organizing for
social justice in recent years. Through these activities, Latina/o workers
have sought to break through the multiple veils of isolation that render
much of their working lives invisible to the majority of Americans. Lat-
ina/o working-class activism should not come as a surprise, however.
Latina/o workers have been at the forefront of U.S. economic justice
movements for well over a century (Campbell, 2000; Ruíz, 1987; Zavella,
1987; Sánchez, 1993; Vargas, 2005). Indeed, the history of the progressive
labor movements in the United States would be incomplete without the
names of labor leaders such as César Chávez, Luisa Moreno, Dolores
Huerta, and Ernesto Galarza, among many others.

Race, Gender, and Work

Latina/o workers continue to face barriers in their efforts to achieve
economic security. These obstacles include racism, national origin discrimination, limited occupational options, tenuous access to human
rights in the United States, and global economic conditions that determine economic mobility from one generation to the next. Like their
Anglo counterparts, Latina/o workers have felt the impact of global economic integration over the past several decades. According to the Pew
Hispanic Center (Kochhar, 2005, p. ii) "Changes in the structure of
industries, such as the rise of the technology sectors and the decline

of manufacturing, diminished the prospects for upward occupational mobility for Hispanics in the 1990s."

A survey of recent Equal Employment Opportunity Commission (EEOC) cases confirms that sexual and national origin discrimination against Latina/o workers is a pervasive problem in U.S. society (U.S. EEOC, 2001; U.S.EEOC, 2003; U.S. EEOC, 2006). The EEOC recently filed suit against Sizzler Restaurants "for the explicitly targeted harassment of Mexican women by non-Mexican men. Latinas were targeted as 'Mexican bitches only good for sex,' physically and verbally harassed and told 'go back where you come from if you don't like it'" (U.S. EEOC, 2007). Latina workers at another firm, who were subjected to intrusive body searches and paid less than male coworkers were fired and reported to the Immigration and Naturalization Service in retaliation after they reported sexual harassment and national origin discrimination.

The U.S. EEOC cases reveal that Latina/o workers are often paid lower wages than their white peers for doing the same work, regardless of educational attainment. This confirms recent findings of wage discrimination in the scholarly literature on race and wage inequality (Melendez, 1991; Camoy, Daley, & Hinojosa Ojeda, 1990). A survey of labor market studies (Yzaguirre & Kamasaki, 1997) demonstrates that Latina/o workers "earn lower wages and/or experience higher unemployment than similarly qualified White workers, and [they] attribute some portion of the differential (10%–50% of the White-Latino wage gap, cqual to about 4%–16% of Hispanic wages) to employment discrimination." While educational attainment is crucial for improving their prospects in the workplace, educational levels alone cannot explain the economic inequalities that most Latina/o workers face. Racism continues to be a major barrier to Latina/o progress at work and in the larger society.

Contemporary Barriers to Unionization

Latina/o laborers who attempt to unionize in order to improve their economic conditions face severe obstacles. Polls have demonstrated that Latina/o workers are more likely than their white counterparts to support union membership. However, a 2000 Human Rights Watch report shows that U.S. workers are barely able to exercise the freedom to join the union of their choice because of corporate and state hostility. One of the case studies in the report focused on Latina/o and African American workers' experiences in a major union-organizing campaign at a North Carolina meat processing firm. Workers testified that pro-union employees were harassed and fired, while management tried to

convince Latina/o workers that African Americans were organizing to
steal their jobs (Human Rights Watch, 2000, pp. 141–142). One former
manager of the firm admitted that "We were told to fire anyone who
advocated for the union." According to the manager, a company lawyer
instructed her to deal proactively with a union-inclined employee
under her supervision and stated: "Fire the bitch. I'll beat anything she
or they throw at me in court" (Brent Zook, 2003).

Local government officials assisted the firm by distributing anti-
union propaganda at the workplace. Subsequently, state investigators
responded to workers' safety complaints by haranguing them about
their union sympathies. The federal government later targeted this
same factory complex for a raid on suspected illegal immigrants. Union
activist Julio Vargas affirmed that Latina/o and African American workers believed that the government raided their plant "because people
were getting organized" (Bacon, 2007). Latina/o workers seeking to
avoid dependency and to improve their economic conditions faced
opposition from company management as well as local, state, and federal officials. Human Rights Watch concludes "that freedom of association is a right under severe, often buckling pressure when workers in
the United States try to exercise it" (Human Rights Watch, 2000, p. 10).

Comparing Latina/o Workers to Other Immigrants

It has been common to compare the experiences of Latina/o workers
of the twenty-first century with the odysseys of their early-twentieth-
century immigrant peers from Europe. Pundits across the political
spectrum assume that Latina/o immigrants will eventually "assimilate"
to U.S. culture and enjoy upward mobility similar to their Ellis Island
forebears. A wide range of scholars have shown that these comparisons
do not hold up under historical scrutiny (Thurow, 1969; Bloch, 1969;
Grebler, Moore, & Guzman, 1970; Melendez, 1991; Suárez-Orozco &
Páez, 2002). First, while European immigrants faced ethnic discrimination through the Great Depression, they did not have to face generations of racism. In addition, European immigrants arrived during an
overall boom cycle of the U.S. economy, and they did not have to con-
tend with de-industrialization, privatization, the "offshoring" of jobs,
and other global economic factors that have exerted a downward pressure on real wages in the United States over the past several decades
(Ellis, 2007; Galbraith, 1998; Gans, 1992). For example, large numbers of
Puerto Rican immigrants were encouraged by the government's Operation Bootstrap program to migrate to New York in the 1960s, at a time
when the city had already lost approximately 40 percent of its manufacturing base. As a result, the new immigrants faced grim employment
prospects (Lui, Robles, Leondar-Wright, Brewer, & Adamson, 2006).

In the earlier period of immigration, industrial workers were able to organize massive unions in order to improve their economic conditions. Unionization accelerated, especially in the era of the New Deal. Between the 1930s and 1950s millions of U.S. factory workers, many of whom were first-generation immigrants, joined unions and used their newfound economic and political clout to raise families, build communities, and create civic institutions (Cohen, 1990; García, 1995; Metzgar, 2000; Vargas, 2005). However, Latina/o and African American workers in agriculture and domestic service were unable to take advantage of unionization because they were pointedly excluded from the National Labor Relations Act (Galarza, 1977; Daniel, 1981; Hahamovitch, 1997; Katznelson, 2005; Ortiz, 2002). Latina/o workers in factories, canneries, and on the docks did organize and led significant union drives. By the 1970s, however, unions began to crumble, and racial animosities within the working class grew. During the epic Phelps Dodge copper strike in 1983, a white strikebreaker responded to Mexican American unionists by asserting: "I'd rather be rich than an ignorant fucking Mexican union-loving son of a bitch." (Kingsolver, 1983, p. 113). While European immigrants benefited from the explosive growth of industrial unionism in the 1930s, Latina/o migrants of the late twentieth century arrived in a country undergoing rapid union decline and the overall disintegration of working-class power in the workplace and in politics. In general, the experiences of Latina/o workers over the last century appears to be less similar to that of say Irish immigrants of the early 1900s, and more akin to the long-term experiences of African Americans, who also have faced generations of institutional discrimination in labor markets and in the larger political arena.

Wealth and Occupational Mobility

Rakesh Kochhar (2005, p. 2) notes, "A distinctive feature of the occupation profile of Hispanic workers is their lack of representation in professional occupations. Instead, Hispanics are more likely than average to be found in construction and production occupations. This trait is particularly true of Latinos of Mexican or Puerto Rican origin. The ongoing immigration of workers from Mexico has served to reinforce these occupational characteristics during the 1990s." While there are important generational and national origin differences between and within Latina/o communities, it is true that Latinos in the United States have remained a predominantly working-class population. Lui and colleagues (2006) note that a partial exception to this are the Cuban immigrants of the 1960s, who were able to take advantage of generous government social programs that allowed many of them to move into the middle class. Therefore, the slow upward mobility among Latina/o populations is not due to lack of initiative or to cultural flaws. Latina/o parents have been unable to pass down the same levels of wealth to their children that their white counterparts have because of the structural impediments they have faced in the United States. Immigrants who fled from Central America and the Caribbean—sometimes because of U.S.-sponsored trade policies, wars, or coups—often had to leave belongings and financial assets behind in their home countries (La Feber, 1983; Martínez, 1993; Lipsitz, 1998; Grandin, 2006).

Economic historians have estimated that approximately 80 percent of household wealth comes from inheritance rather than labor force participation (Shammas, 1975). "Since the major sources of wealth for most persons today are inheritance and *vivo* transfers," economists William Darity, Jr., and Melba Nicholson (2005, p. 78) write, "a past history of wealth deprivation has dramatic inter-generational effects." State policies have played a major role in this wealth deprivation. For example, Social Security was a program that allowed workers to retire without having to depend on the economic contributions of their children to sustain them, as in earlier times. However, the Social Security Act of 1933 excluded all farm and domestic workers from coverage, thereby depriving many Latina/o laborers of the benefits of this important national program.

Economic Costs of Conquest and Annexation

An equally cogent example of state policy and Latina/o wealth deprivation involves land ownership. While numerous white settlers benefited from the federal government's 1862 Homestead Act, Latino landowners in the Southwest were *losing* their lands in the wake of the U.S. conquest of northern Mexico (Acuña, 1972; Blaner, 1972; Galarza, 1977). Those who refused to give up their land were sometimes driven off of it by avaricious ranchers and cattlemen, or lynched. Judges and law enforcement looked the other way, or sometimes openly participated in the land grabs. In California, the state legislature passed the Foreign Miner's Tax in order to prevent Mexican as well as Chinese miners from competing with white miners for gold claims. Each of these state policies—and there were many others that could be mentioned—effectively limited the economic mobility of the bulk of Latina/o workers in the United States.

Generations of Mexican, Guatemalan, Puerto Rican, and other Latina/o workers have struggled with the after-effects of colonization and conquest in their home countries that have placed them in disadvantageous situations as workers in the United States. The de facto loss of citizenship rights that Mexican Americans suffered in their former homeland after the end of the Mexican-American War (1846–1848) had a negative impact on their working lives and prospects (Luna, 2001). Mexican workers had once traveled freely throughout much of present-day Arizona, New Mexico, California, and other states; after the U.S. takeover, however, they faced increasingly dangerous border crossings and corrupt officials who demanded bribes from them. Mexican laborers who crossed the new border between Mexico and the United States to work in Texas were regularly sprayed with DDT, Zyklon B, and other carcinogenic chemicals by zealous U.S. health inspectors (Romo, 2005). Jose Burciaga, who worked as a janitor in El Paso during the 1920s, recalled that "At the customs bath by the bridge . . . they would spray some stuff on you. It was white and would run down your body. How horrible! And then I remember something else about it: They would shave everyone's head . . . men, women, everybody. . . . The substance was very strong" (Burnett, 2006).

The U.S. conquest of northern Mexico resulted in a dual racial and economic system with similarities to Jim Crow in the southeastern United States. In the copper mining camps of Arizona, there were two wage scales in the early twentieth century: a white one and a Mexican one. In Arizona mines, the top wage for Mexicans was $2.50 per day; $4.00 for "Anglos." (Benton-Cohen, 2003). Ninety-seven percent of the mine foremen in the copper mine camps were Anglos. Pervasive wage differentials in the Southwest gave white workers an incentive to maintain a separate-and-unequal economic system and served as one of the most visible wedges between white and nonwhite labor.

When Mexican workers went on strike in the Arizona mines as well as at the Pacific Electric Railway Company in Los Angeles in 1903, class conflict assumed racial dimensions. Mexican workers argued for an equalization of wages and solidarity between Anglos and Mexicans (Trumpbour & Bernard, 2002, p. 128). In addition, *Mexicanos* called for the assistance of the Mexican Consul in solving the labor disputes and used Spanish-language leaflets to spread word of the struggles. Desirous of preserving the racial wage disparity, white coworkers and Anglo communities responded by siding with employers and repudiated a broader class alliance. Unions often barred Latina/o workers from their crafts, while most skilled jobs were informally reserved for white people. These so-called color bars froze Mexican, Puerto Rican, and other Latina/o workers out of skilled employment across the country. Color bars, wage differentials, and other discriminatory hiring practices were common in U.S. workplaces until the 1964 Civil Rights Act prohibited such practices, at least in theory. In the meantime, Latina/o workers shared little of the tremendous prosperity generated by their labor.

The United Farm Workers

The rise of the United Farm Workers (UFW) in the 1960s was a historic breakthrough in improving the conditions of Latina/o workers. The UFW was founded by César Chávez and Dolores Huerta and was originally called the National Farm Workers Association (NFWA) (Ortiz, 2002). Chávez and Huerta used their organizing experiences learned from the Community Service Organization (CSO) to create the new union. Eschewing a top-down approach, Chávez encouraged workers to identify what they thought were the major crises in their communities and to brainstorm solutions to these problems. NFWA organizers and farmworkers tackled job discrimination, police harassment, voter disenfranchisement, and credit issues. "We'd take the big problems that they [farmworkers] had," Chávez recalled, "some of the police problems, labor problems like nonpayment of wages, and [workers'] compensation cases. We'd service problems at County hospitals, anything that affected them. This was a community union" (Levy, 1975, p.171). Fred Ross, the founder of the CSO and Chávez's mentor, recalled that the younger organizer was adept at encouraging people to develop their own leadership abilities:

> [T]he Service Center, with César in command, was much more than your routine problem clinic; it was a sovereign restorative of human dignity and a means of drawing the people, whose lifestyle had been one of being pushed around by the authorities without a peep, soon learned to stand their ground, speak out, and get what they came after. In the agony of forcing themselves to do this, they suffered a sea change: they got organized. (Ross, 1992, p. 24)

Restoring human dignity and self-respect is the essence of community organizing and positive social change in the workplace. Activists in the fledgling union popularized the slogan "¡Sí, Se Puede!" as an affirmation that ordinary people can do extraordinary things. Workers took turns at leading meetings, and new members were asked to contribute whatever they could—dues, food, time, and so forth—in order to keep the fledgling organization alive. In essence, the NFWA institutionalized reciprocity between working people. Chávez, Huerta, and other NFWA leaders learned by experience that successful organizing begins by building relationships of trust with other people (Greider, 1992). Efforts to build trust and mutual assistance paid off. The United Farm Workers became a successful labor union that lifted thousands of hitherto voiceless working people out of poverty simultaneously.

The UFW's work in building social networks of solidarity extended to their public outreach campaigns. These included consumer boycotts of produce and wines, which broke down barriers of isolation between workers with tenuous claims to citizenship and customers willing to examine their roles in the global economy. Dolores Huerta asserted, "We've got to appeal to the public. We can't go through the legal system because the legal system is stacked." (Ortiz, 1992, p. 269). The UFW as well as FLOC and newer farm labor unions continue to focus on the necessity of winning collective bargaining rights for farmworkers. For César Chávez, the right to negotiate collectively with employers was the linchpin of his philosophy that farmworkers needed power and not public charity. This institutional approach to social change attracted the Rev. Martin Luther King, Jr., to the UFW's struggles and encouraged Dr. King to plow forward with the Poor People's Campaign to end poverty in the United States.

We Must Defend Our Rights

Latina/o immigrant workers have built upon the rich legacies of struggle established by their forebears. For example, Latina/o workers in the meat and poultry processing industries have been especially active in fighting to improve their economic conditions. High line speeds in these factories translate into very high levels of laceration, repetitive-motion, and cumulative trauma injuries (Cook, 1999; Human Rights Watch, 2004; Striffler, 2005). After animals are slaughtered, "the carcasses hurl along evisceration and disassembly lines as workers hurriedly saw and cut them at unprecedented volume and pace" (Human Rights Watch, 2004, p. 1). Employees who are injured on the job are often pressured by supervisors to hide their injuries in order to save their firms money. Historically, poultry and meat processing jobs were unionized and paid well. According to a 2004 human rights exposé of these industries, however, "Many workers who try to form trade unions [in poultry and meat processing] and bargain collectively are spied on, harassed, pressured, threatened, suspended, fired, deported or otherwise victimized for their exercise of the right to freedom of association" (Human Rights Watch, 2004, p. 3).

Guatemalan immigrant workers at Case Farms, Inc. in Morganton, North Carolina, have for more than a decade waged a struggle against what they consider to be dangerously high line speeds and poor working conditions by engaging in a broad range of protests including petitions, strikes, and union organizing. In the summer of 2005, workers at Case Farms went on strike and began to organize a new union after management refused to consider the workers' request to slow production lines and issue appropriate safety equipment (*The News Herald*, 2005; Huffman, 2006). This struggle followed years of in-plant organizing by Latina/o workers, which has led to union-recognition votes, raises, and safer working conditions in the plant. This organizing work has not been easy. Most of the original cohort of employees at Case Farms were Highland Mayans, who brought diverse ethnic, political, and social experiences with them. Like many of their Latin American peers, these workers had skills in running cooperative cultural and economic associations in their home regions. They were able to draw upon previous experiences as active members of *comités cívicos* (community committees) and *directivas* (leadership committees) in Guatemala (Fink, 2003). These first-generation immigrants came to the United States with the knowledge that collective organization paid dividends. Union organizer Luz Rodriguez observed, "We have to stand up for ourselves. We must defend our rights" (OrdoNez, 2006).

The experiences of Latina/o workers in North Carolina and other parts of the country provide us with important ideas on how workplace conditions and economic security for working people in general may be enhanced. Latina/o workers have been at the forefront of new economic justice campaigns but have often been stymied by a variety of factors including fear of harassment, firing, and deportation. As human rights organizations have emphasized in recent years, the internationally recognized freedom of association—the right to join unions and economic organizations for self-improvement—needs to be restored in the United States. Furthermore, because many Latina/o workers enjoy very tenuous claims on citizenship, workplace "rights" need to be recast as human rights. The United Nation's Universal Declaration of Human Rights bars discrimination in the workplace and establishes rights to fair pay and unionization. The United States should honor and protect the human rights of workers at home as vigorously as it promotes the idea of human rights abroad. Finally, Article 23 of the Universal Declaration of Human Rights directly touches on the right of all working people to a "just and favourable" wage. The real federal minimum wage in the United States has been declining for more than a generation. The Coalition of Immokalee Workers as well as labor and interfaith organizations advocate increasing wages to promote better living standards for the lowest-paid workers. There are numerous studies that confirm the economic benefits of raising the minimum wage (Card & Krueger, 1997; Card & Krueger, 2000; Wolfson, 2006).

María Elena Durazo asserts that collective problems require collective solutions. Durazo was the daughter of migrant farmworkers, and she herself picked fruits and vegetables as a young girl in the 1960s. Like so many young people of her generation, she was inspired by the UFW to become a labor activist, and she eventually rose to become one of the top labor leaders in the United States. As the first Latina executive secretary-treasurer of the Los Angeles County Federation of Labor, AFL-CIO, Durazo has fought for the right of all workers, regardless of immigration status, to earn higher wages and to become active in the political arena. In calling for a new living wage movement, Durazo (2006) argues, "We must build a movement with thousands of leaders and millions of supporters that can pressure elected officals and corporations to do the right thing. When we build a movement of the working poor, we will have the power to end poverty."

The isolation and lack of political rights that Latina/o workers toil under often leads to abuses and poor working conditions. It is vital to improve communication between Latina/o workers and consumers as well as investors who benefit from their labor. Workers' centers and educational initiatives that provide organizing experience, leadership training, legal counseling, language proficiency, and health advocacy for Latina/o workers and others should be promoted. For example, the interfaith Western North Carolina Workers' Center has done important work with Latino workers in the region and has helped low-wage workers "file complaints regarding work injury, unpaid wages, discrimination, and other issues" (NC Justice Center, 2006). The educational work that FLOC's Santiago Rafael Cruz was engaged in—advising workers in Mexico about their human rights in the United States—must be encouraged, protected, and deepened. Finally, antiracist education and curricula about the vital roles that Latina/o peoples as well as immigrant workers have played in the U.S. economy should be promoted in primary and secondary schools as well as in colleges and universities. Such educational programs would help dispel numerous popular myths that have negative impacts on the livelihoods of all working people in the United States.

In this chapter, we have explored the proud history of Latino advocacy around the important institution of the marketplace. You have hopefully gained an appreciation of the powerful forces that shape how Latinos engage that marketplace. We have explored how many Latina/o workers are willing to work long hours in some of the most difficult situations in order to provide for their families. The next chapter, the first in the section "Strengths and Vulnerabilities," explores two other key institutions that provide Latinos with strength and resiliency, the family and the community.

For Writing and Reflection

1. What impact will the recent May Day protests have on public policy debates concerning Latina/o workers?

2. What explains historical as well as contemporary income and wealth differences between Latino and non-Latino workers in the U.S. economy?

3. What barriers do Latina/o workers face in achieving upward economic mobility?

4. Why have Latina/o workers persistently attempted to organize and join unions?

5. How do the experiences of Latina/o immigrant workers compare with those of their counterparts in other eras?

References

Acuña, R. (1972). *Occupied America: The Chicano's struggle toward liberation*. San Francisco: Canfield Press.

Aguirre, A., Jr., & Turner, J. H. (1998). *American ethnicity: The dynamics and consequences of discrimination* (2nd ed.). NY: McGraw-Hill.

Archibold, R. (2006, May 2). Immigrants take to U.S. streets in show of strength. *New York Times*, p. 1.

Asbed, G. (2003, March 30). For pickers, slavery tastes like tomatoes. *Palm Beach Post*. Retrieved June 30, 2007, from http://www.ciw-online.org/gapbpoped .html

Bacon, D. (2003, October). Is a new *Bracero* program in our future? *Z Magazine Online*, Vol. 16, No. 10. Retrieved June 13, 2007, from http://zmagsite.zmag .org/Oct2003/baconpr1003.html

Bacon, D. (2007, May 11). Feds crack down on immigrant labor organizers. *The American Prospect Online*. Retrieved June 5, 2007, from http://www .prospect.org

Bauer, M. (2007). Close to slavery: Guest worker programs in the United States. *The Southern Poverty Law Center Special Report* (p. 23–24). Retrieved June 15, 2007, from http://www.splcenter.org/legal/guestreport/index.jsp

Benton-Cohen, K. (2003, June–September). Docile children and dangerous revolutionaries: The racial hierarchy of manliness and the Bisbee deportation of 1917. *Frontiers: A Journal of Women's Studies*, 24, 2–3, 30–50.

Bernstein, R. (2006, May 2). Immigrants' boycott move strikes home. *The Herald-Sun* (Durham, NC), p. A1.

Blaner, R. (1972). *Racial oppression in America*. New York: Harper & Row.

Bloch, H. (1969). *The circle of discrimination*. New York: New York University Press.

Brenner, M. (2006, March). Katrina's aftermath transforms work in the Gulf region. *Labor Notes*. Retrieved September 28, 2008 from http://labornotes.org/ node/201

Brent Zook, K. (2003, Winter). Hog-tied: Battling it out (again) at Smithfield Foods. *Amnesty International Magazine*. Retrieved June 4, 2007, from http:// www.amnestyusa.org/Winter_2003/

Burnett, J. (2006, January 28). The bath riots: Indignity along the Mexican border. National Public Radio. Retrieved June 17, 2007, from http://www.npr.org/ templates/story/story.php?storyId = 5176177

Camoy, M., Daley, H., & Hinojosa Ojeda, R. (1990). *Latinos in a changing U.S. economy: Comparative perspectives in the labor market since 1939.* Inter-University Program for Latino Research. New York: Research Foundation of the City University of New York.

Campbell, D. (2000, April 3). Latinos flexing political muscle in California. *The Guardian* (London), p. 15.

Card, D., & Krueger, A. (1994, September). Minimum wages and employment: A case study of the fast-food industry in New Jersey and Pennsylvania: Reply. *American Economic Review*, Vol. 90, No. 5, pp. 1397–1420.

Card, D., & Krueger, A. (1997). *Myth and measurement: The new economics of the minimum wage.* Princeton, NJ: Princeton University Press.

Card, D., & Krueger A. (2000, December). Minimum wages and employment: A case study of the fast-food industry in New Jersey and Pennsylvania. *American Economic Review*, 84, No. 4, pp. 772–793.

Cardenas, J. (2006, April 28). Workers step from the shadows. *St. Petersburg Times*, p. 1A.

Case Farms workers walked off the job. (2005, June 10). *The News Herald* (Morganton, NC).

Chomsky, A. (2007). *"They take our jobs!" and 20 other myths about immigration.* Boston: Beacon Press.

CNN.Com (2004, February 25). Report: Modern-day slavery alive and well in Florida. Retrieved May 1, 2007, from http://us.cnn.com/2004/US/South/02/25/human.trafficking.ap/

Cohen, L. (1990). *Making a new deal: Industrial workers in Chicago, 1919–1939.* New York: Cambridge University Press.

Cook, Christopher D. (1999, August). Fowl trouble. *Harper's Magazine*, 78–79.

Daniel, C. (1981). *Bitter harvest: A history of California farmworkers, 1870–1941.* Ithaca, NY: Cornell University Press.

Darity, W., & Nicholson, M. (2005). Racial wealth inequality and the black family. In V. McLoyd, N. Hill, & K. Dodge (Eds.), *African American family life: Ecological and cultural diversity.* New York: Guilford Press.

Davey, M. (2006, May 1). With calls for boycott by immigrants, employers gird for unknown. *New York Times.* Retrieved August 14, 2008, from http://query.nytimes.com/gst/fullpage.html?res = 9500E3DD113FF932A35756C0A9609C8B63

Democracy Now! (2007, March 15). Indian guestworker slits wrists after being fired for complaining about squalid work conditions. Retrieved June 12, 2007, from http://www.pacifica.org/program-guide/op,segment-page/segment_id,396/

Durazo, María Elena. (2006). Living wage for all: A plan for a new living wage movement. Center for the Working Poor. Retrieved June 7, 2007, from http://www.centerfortheworkingpoor.org/living%20wage%20for%20all.htm

Eitzen, S. D., & Baca Zinn, M. (2007). *In conflict and order: Understanding society.* Boston, MA: Allyn & Bacon.

Ellis, D. (2007, May 25). Making less than Dad did. CNN.Money.com. Retrieved May 27, 2007, from http://money.cnn.com/2007/05/25/pf/mobility_study/index.htm

An emerging Latino-led radicalism in the US. (2000, April 3). *Manchester Guardian* (UK).

Espín, O. M. (1997). *Latina realities: Essays on healing, migration and sexuality.* Boulder, CO: Westview Press.

Fine, J. (2006). Worker centers: Organizing communities at the edge of the dream. Ithaca, NY: ILR Press/Cornell University Press.

Fink, L. (2003). *The Maya of Morganton: Work and community in the nuevo New South.* Chapel Hill, NC: University of North Carolina Press.

Galarza, E. (1964). *Merchants of labor: The Mexican Bracero story.* Charlotte, NC: McNally& Loftin.

Galarza, E. (1977). *Farm workers and agri-business in California, 1947–1960.* Notre Dame,IN: University of Notre Dame Press.

Galbraith, J. (1998). *Created unequal: The crisis in American pay.* Chicago: The University of Chicago Press.

Gans, H. (1992). Second generation decline: Scenarios for the economic and ethnic futures of the post-1965 American immigrants. *Ethnic and Racial Studies, 15,* 173–92.

García, M. (1995). *Memories of Chicano history: The life and narrative of Bert Corona* (pp. 87–107). Berkeley, CA: University of California Press.

García, M. C. (1996). *Havana USA.* Berkeley, CA: University of California Press.

Gonzales, M. G. (1999). *Mexicanos: A history of Mexicans in the United States.* Bloomington, IN: University of Indiana Press.

Gonzalez, J. (2006a, May 2). On streets of New York, solidarity reigns. *New York Daily News,* p. 6.

Gonzalez, J. (2006b, March 28). "Latino giant" awakens: Demonstrations gaining strength. *New York Daily News,* p. 10.

Gonzalez, V. (2006, May 2). Day without immigrants draws millions to streets; Many local residents take day off to show support. *Star News* (Wilmington, NC), p. A1.

Grandin, G. (2006). *Empire's workshop: Latin America, the United States, and the rise of the new imperialism.* New York: Metropolitan Books.

Grebler, L., Moore, J., & Guzman, R. (1970). *The Mexican-American people.* New York: The Free Press.

Greider, W. (1992). *Who will tell the people? The betrayal of American democracy* (pp. 223–224). New York: Simon and Schuster.

Hahamovitch, C. (1997). *The fruits of their labor: Atlantic Coast farmworkers and the making of migrant poverty, 1870–1945.* Chapel Hill, NC: University of North Carolina Press.

Healey, J. F. (2007). *Diversity and society: Race, ethnicity, and gender* (2nd ed.). Thousand Oaks, CA: Pine Forge Press.

Huffman, T. (2006, October 28). Glove charge sparks strike at Case Farms. *The News Herald* (Morganton, NC).

Human Rights Watch. (2000). Unfair advantage: Workers' freedom of association in the United States under international human rights standards. New York: Human Rights Watch.

Human Rights Watch. (2004). Blood, sweat and fear: Workers' rights in U.S. meat and poultry plants. New York: Human Rights Watch.

Jones, D. (2007, May 2). Nearly 2,000 rally for immigration reform. *Santa Cruz Sentinel.* Retrieved July 21, 2008, from http://www.santacruzsentinel.com/story.php?sid = 48392&storySection = Local&fromSearch = true&searchTerms = alejandra + onofre

Katznelson, I. (2005). *When affirmative action was white: An untold history of racial inequality in twentieth century America.* New York: W. W. Norton & Company.

Kimbriell, K. (2007, May/June). Shifting gears: Frustration over not finding jobs has caused workers from different groups to blame each other. *The Chicago Reporter.* Retrieved June 13, 2007, from http://www.chicagoreporter.com/2007/5–2007/jobs/jobs.htm

Kingsolver, B. (1983). *Holding the line: Women in the great Arizona mine strike of 1983* (Ithaca, NY: Cornell University Press.

Kochhar, R. (2005). The occupational status and mobility of Hispanics. *Pew Hispanic Center Reports and Factsheets.* December 15, 2005. Retrieved June 12, 2007, from http://pewhispanic.org/reports/report.php?ReportID = 59

Krugman, P. (2006, February 27). Graduates versus oligarchs. *New York Times,* p. 19.

Krugman, P. (2007, May 26). Huddled masses: Immigration reform should empower the poorest. *Pittsburgh Post-Gazette,* p. 14.

Kutalik, C. (2006, June). As immigrants strike, truckers shut down nation's largest port. *Labor Notes.* Retrieved July 23, 2008, from http://labornotes.org/node/235

La Botz, D. (2006, May). Millions march for immigrant rights; Virtual strike in some cities. *Labor Notes.* Retrieved August 19, 2008, from http://labornotes.org/node/221

La Feber, W. (1983). *Inevitable revolutions: The United States in Central America.* New York: Norton.

Levy, J. (1975). *Cesar Chavez: Autobiography of La Causa.* New York: Norton.

Lipsitz, G. (1998). *The possessive investment in whiteness: How white people profit fromidentity politics.* Philadelphia, PA: Temple University Press.

Louie, M. (2001). *Sweatshop warriors: Immigrant women workers take on the globalfactory.* Cambridge, MA: South End Press.

Lui, M., Robles, B., Leondar-Wright, B., Brewer, R., & Adamson, R. (2006). *The color of wealth: The story behind the U.S. racial wealth divide.* New York: New Press.

Luna, G. (2001). The treaty of Guadalupe Hidalgo and Dred Scott v. Sandford: "Aren't they all illegal anyway?" In C. Stokes, T. Meléndez, & G. Rhodes-Reed, *Race in 21st century America* (pp. 297–312). East Lansing, MI: Michigan State University Press.

Marshall, R. (2007). Getting immigration reform right. Economic Policy Institute. (Economic Policy Institute Briefing Paper #186.) Retrieved March 30, 2007, from http://www.sharedprosperity.org/bp186.html

Martinez, R. (1993). The other side: Notes from the new L.A., Mexico City, and beyond. New York: Vintage Books.

Melendez, E. (1991). Labor market structure and wage differences in New York City: A comparative analysis. In E. Melendez, C. Rodriguez, & J. Figueroa (Eds.),

Hispanics in the labor force: Issues and policies (pp. 34–45). New York: Plenum Press.

Mello, F. (2007, June 25). Coming to America. *The Nation.* Retrieved June 30, 2007, from http://www.thenation.com/doc/20070625/mello

Metzgar, G. (2000). *Striking steel: Solidarity remembered.* Philadelphia: Temple University Press.

Milkman, R. (2007). Critical mass: Latino labor and politics in California. *NACLA report onthe Americas, 40*(3), 30–38.

Mojarro, Y. (2006, April 11). Local workers protest for rights. *The Ledger* (Lakeland, FL), p. B3.

Moffett, D. (2003, November 23). Slavery? In Florida? In 2003? Yes. *Palm Beach Post,* p. 2E.

Moffett, D. (2006, April 30). We say we don't want illegals here. *Palm Beach Post,* p. 2E.

Morash, C. (2006, May 2). Thousands demonstrate at Springdale Park rally. *Arkansas Democrat-Gazette,* p. A1.

Morris, R. (2006, May 3). Immigrants go back to work in South Florida after one-dayWalkouts. *South Florida Sun-Sentinel.*

Morrow, H. B. (2005). New destinations and immigrant incorporation. *Perspectives in Politics, 3*(4), 781–799.

NC Justice Center. (2006). Profile: The Western North Carolina Workers Center. Retrieved June 15, 2007, from http://www.ncjustice.org/cms/index.php?pid=193

Ngai, Mae. (2004). *Impossible subjects: Illegal aliens and the making of modern America.* Princeton, NJ: Princeton University Press.

Nguyen, K. (2006, May 2). Prompted by anger, a Colorado immigrant marches for principle. The Associated Press.

Oboler, S. (1995). *Ethnic labels, Latino lives: Identity and the politics of (re) presentation in the United States.* Minneapolis, MN: University of Minnesota Press.

Ontiveros, Maria L. (1998). Three perspectives on workplace harassment of women of color. In R. Delgado & J. Stefancic (Eds.), *The Latino condition: A critical reader* (pp. 531–535). New York: New York University Press.

OrdoNez, F. (2006, November 12). Worker unrest at Case Farms: Employees at poultry plant meet to discuss forming union. *The Charlotte Observer,* p. B3.

Ortiz, P. (2002). From slavery to César Chávez and beyond: Farmworker organizing in the United States. In C. Thompson & W. Wiggins (Eds.), *The human cost of food: Farmworkers' lives, labor and advocacy* (pp. 249–275). Austin, TX: University of Texas Press.

Ovalle, D. (2007, May 3). Murder of Mexican union organizer alarms workers, activists. *McClatchy Newspapers.* Retrieved June 15, 2007, from http://www.mcclatchydc.com/world/story/16229.html

Padilla, F. (1985). *Latino ethnic consciousness: The case of Mexican Americans and Puerto Ricans in Chicago.* South Bend, IN: University of Notre Dame Press.

Portes, A., & Rumbaut, R. G. (2006). *Immigrant America: A portrait.* Berkeley, CA: University of California Press.

Riley, N. (2002). *Florida's farmworkers in the twenty-first century.* Gainesville, FL: University Press of Florida.

Romo, D. (2005). *Ringside seat to a revolution: An underground cultural history of El Pasoand Juárez, 1893–1923.* El Paso, TX: Cinco Puntos Press.

Ross, F. (1992). *Conquering Goliath: Cesar Chavez at the beginning* (p. 24). Detroit, MI: Wayne State University Press.

Ruíz, V. (1987). *Cannery women, cannery lives: Mexican women, unionization, and the California food processing industry, 1930–1950.* Albuquerque, NM: University of New Mexico Press.

Ruiz, V. (2000). (Ed.). *Las obreras: Chicana politics of work and family.* Los Angeles: UCLA Chicano Studies Research Center.

Sanchez, C. (2006, May 3). Protesters hope to create a political movement. *Sarasota Herald-Tribune,* p. A3.

Sánchez, G. (1993). *Becoming Mexican American: Ethnicity, culture and identity in ChicanoLos Angeles, 1900–1945.* New York: Oxford University Press.

Shammas, C., Salmon, M., & Dahlin, M. (1987). *Inheritance in America: From colonial times to the present* (p. 3). New Brunswick, NJ: Rutgers University Press.

Siemaszko, C. (2006, May 2). N.Y. immigrants rally for rights. *New York Daily News.* Retrieved September 1, 2008, from http://www.nydailynews.com/

Striffler, S. (2005). *Chicken: The dangerous transformation of America's favorite food.* New Haven, CT: Yale University Press.

Suárez-Orozco, M., & Páez, M. (2002). The research agenda. In M. Suárez-Orozco & M. Páez (Eds.), *Latinos remaking America.* Berkeley, CA: University of California Press.

Thurow, L. (1969). *Poverty and Discrimination.* Washington, DC: Brookings.

Trumbull, M. (2006, August 3). New treasury head eyes rising inequality. *Christian Science Monitor.* Retrieved June 12, 2007, from http://www.csmonitor.com/2006/0803/p03s03-usec.html

Trumpbour, J., & Bernard, E. (2002). Unions and Latinos: Mutual transformation. In M. Súarez- Orozco & M. Páez (Eds.), *Latinos Remaking America* (pp. 126–145). Berkeley, CA: University of California Press.

U.S. Equal Employment Opportunity Commission. (2001, August 8). EEOC settles suit against Arizona company for $3.5 million on behalf of low-wage workers. Retrieved April 20, 2007, from http://www.eeoc.gov/press/8-8-01.html

U.S. Equal Employment Opportunity Commission. (2003, July 18). Central casino to pay $1.5 million in EEOC settlement for national origin bias. Retrieved April 20, 2007, from http://www.eeoc.gov/press/7-18-03a.html

U.S. Equal Employment Opportunity Commission. (2006, April 12). EEOC settles lawsuit on behalf of Hispanic employees. Retrieved April 20, 2007, from http://www.eeoc.gov/press/4-13-06.html

U.S. Equal Employment Opportunity Commission. (2007, February 28). Statement of William R. Tamayo. Retrieved May 3, 2007, from http://www.eeoc.gov/abouteeoc/meetings/2-28-07/tamayo.html

Vargas, Z. (2005). *Labor rights are civil rights: Mexican American workers in twentieth-century America.* Princeton, NJ: Princeton University Press.

Watanabe, T. (2007, May 16). Civil activists join Latino wage suit. *Los Angeles Times.* Retrieved June 18, 2007, from http://www.ijjblog.org/2007/05/

Whitcomb, D. (2006, April 28). U.S. Latinos expect a momentous May Day. *The Star-Ledger* (Newark, New Jersey), p. 3.

Wiener, J. (2006, May 2). L.A.'s two May Day marches. *The Nation*. Retrieved July 1, 2008, from http://www.thenation.com/blogs/notion?bid=15&pid=81085

Wolfson, P. (2006, November 27). *State minimum wages: A policy that works*. Economic Policy Institute Briefing Paper, No. 176.

Yzaguirre, R., & Kamasaki, C. (1997). Comment on the Latino civil rights crisis: A research conference. The Civil Rights Project/Proyecto Derechos Civiles, University of California, Los Angeles. Retrieved October 9, 2007, from http://www.civilrightsproject.ucla.edu/research/latino97/latino97.php

Zavella, P. (1987). *Women's work and Chicano families: Cannery workers of the Santa Clara Valley*. Ithaca, NY: Cornell University Press.

PART II

Strengths and Vulnerabilities

CHAPTER FIVE

Family and Community as Strengths in the Latino Community

Sandra Magaña
Marci Ybarra

Introduction

The focus of this chapter is Latino families and communities. We will discuss the macro picture of Latino communities as a review of the literature and examine the micro issues of families through the lens of our research on Latino families who have children with disabilities.

There are tremendous strengths in Latino families and communities, which are often overlooked in social work practice. Strengths and values like familism and deep-rooted kin- and community-based networks work to support Latino families and communities in important ways. Like other U.S. ethnic groups, Latinos are a heterogeneous people with historical, social, political, geographic, and cultural differences. At the same time, certain aspects of Latino history help to create a shared background of colonization, regional proximity, language, and religious affiliation that shapes culture and values across the Latino population in general (Tienda & Ortiz, 1986; Cauce & Domenech-Rodríguez, 2000).

While there are also challenges and vulnerabilities in Latino families and communities, other chapters in this book will shed light on these social problem areas and also tie in the use of strengths discussed in this chapter to resolve these problems. Our hope is to provide important examples and background information about the strengths of

Latino families and communities so they can be better understood in light of the challenges and social work practice implications.

Importance of Community

Given the increasing number of Latinos in the United States, understanding and serving this community is now at the forefront. The Latino community has a long and rich history in the United States. For example, as early as the late nineteenth century, Latinos began to organize, largely to meet the needs of members who were underserved by traditional organizations (Camarillo, 1991). More recently, scholars have found that Latinos are more likely to look within their own community to access community resources and/or social services, rather than access formal services that typically serve mainstream populations (Delgado & Tennstedt, 1997). Oftentimes, Latinos choose both formal and informal services provided within and by their own community because of fears of discrimination, disrespect, and difficulty in accessing culturally sensitive services (Boerstler & de Figueiredo, 2003).

Current population trends indicate that the Latino population will continue to increase in the coming years, requiring social workers to develop better strategies to serve them. For example, some midwestern and southern rural communities are experiencing significant increases in Latino immigrants. Many of these communities, with their limited interaction with and knowledge of the Latino community, may be ill-equipped to handle both linguistic and culturally competent practice vital for assisting new immigrants. Social workers could play an important role in such communities by assisting community members and local organizations alike in developing and implementing services that address the needs of Latinos.

Historical Context

Early community-based Latino organizations were known as *mutualistas*, or mutual aid societies, and were designed to support an array of services related to both economic stability and Latino rights (Gregory, Steinberg, & Sousa, 2003; Hernández, 1983). Early *mutualistas* illustrate the historical (and current) trend in which Latino community organizations were often initiated and maintained by the Latino community members themselves (Tirado, 1974; Center on Philanthropy & Civil Society, 2003). *Mutualistas* provided valuable services and were largely developed to:

... [protect] against economic, political, and cultural imperialism. These early *mutualistas* provided services from "the cradle to the grave," such as caring for the physically and mentally ill, placement of homeless children, funeral arrangements, financial benefits for surviving family members, and friendly visiting services. On an economic and political development level, credit unions were established, agricultural assistance was provided for the entire community, and voting rights were upheld. Thus, *las mutualistas* exemplified indigenous self-help movements based on the values of self-determination, inclusion, and altruism.(Aranda, 2001 p. 255)

The more recent attributes associated with community-based Latino organizations are related to the development of *mutualistas* that focused on providing for and protecting the rights of Latinos (Gregory, Steinberg, & Sousa, 2003). Latino community-based support as a response to community needs continues today and serves as one of the most valuable strengths of the community overall.

As a Network

The strength of the Latino community as a network is largely rooted in the overlap of two traditions. First, the need to increase and protect the rights of Latinos helped to shape the Latino community, which functioned as both an active and collective network (Cárdenas, 2004; Gregory et al., 2003). In other words, Latinos were *active* participants in their own advocacy, who worked *collectively* as a community to better address issues related to Latinos. Second, the traditional values of familism and collectivism help to create community-based networks that focused on providing culturally relevant resources and support that members can access within their own communities (Delgado & Humm-Delgado, 1982). It is their ties to both community and kinship networks that help Latinos access vital information concerning family-related, social, and economic issues (Delgado, Jones, & Rohani, 2005). Latino community-based networking fosters a sense of trust and confidence between members (Levitt, 1995) that, in turn, leads to community members being regarded as extended family. Through these community and kin-based networks involving organizations, businesses, and families, or "natural systems of support" (Delgado & Humm-Delgado, 1982; Delgado, 1996; Delgado & Tennstedt, 1997), Latinos are able to access services they might not otherwise utilize. The strength of Latino networking both in the community and kin-based associations leads to better information and access in areas such as employment, services, social affiliations and membership, and educational needs (Barnes, 2007).

Community and Collectivism

Underpinning the Latino community is the cultural value of collectivism. Collectivism is centered on the family or community rather than the individual. The Latino value of collectivism is often contrasted with the mainstream U.S. cultural value of individualism. U.S. values place the achievement of the individual (often tying success to economic achievement) as primary, while Latino culture emphasizes the importance of family over the individual. The value of collectivism plays out in the community, with many efforts focused on the success and survival of the family rather than on individuals. The Latino family is rooted in an intricate extended network of families and friends, based on a collectivistic belief system (Falicov, 2001) that in turn works as a network. An example of the significance of family-and-friend networks for Latinos can be found in the vignette section later in this chapter. The vignette highlights how such networks interact to offer support of individual decision making while simultaneously upholding cultural values of the larger Latino community.

Organizations and businesses located and serving predominantly Latino communities operate within the community-network frame (Delgado, 1996; 1997). For example, businesses that serve Latino community members often perform multiple roles such as providing a forum for the exchange of information concerning social and economic issues as well as providing services (Delgado, 1997). Moreover, businesses located in the Latino community broker valuable information such as access to services, community-related news, and assistance in interacting with other formal support systems, such as public programs (Delgado, 1996), which ultimately empower members. For example, Latina salon owners were found to have a significant belief in community responsibility, particularly in areas of family and violence, and were willing to collaborate with social service agencies to better meet the needs of their clients (Delgado, 1997). Similarly, Latino-owned restaurants and groceries have been found to be a vital meeting space for connecting community members to important social networks; they provide informal services such as assistance with language barriers, and owners are often considered important community leaders (Delgado, 1996). These examples illustrate important networking opportunities that social workers should keep in mind when attempting to foster relationships with the Latino community. Extending our outreach to non-traditional social service providers, such as Latino-owned businesses, may be an important part of reaching the Latino community.

Current Issues: Community and Culturally Competent Treatment

How do cultural values of collectivism in the Latino community work to improve conditions for families and communities overall? Some evidence suggests that collectivist practices translate into a shared-responsibility framework in which individual members feel a familial (Triandis, Bontempo, Villareal, Asai, & Lucca, 1998) or community responsibility (Levitt, 1995) that improves conditions for all members. For example, scholars have found that Latino social support leads to improved conditions in areas of health (Padilla & Villalobos, 2007), access to systems of support (Delgado & Humm-Delgado, 1982), and improved trust in services received (Antshel, 2002). Overall, collectivism and familism are linked by a broader expectation of responsibility toward one's family and community (Delgado, 1996).

Valuing culture and community has shaped Latinos' growing demand for culturally competent services, and the social work profession has been an important voice in the call to provide such services. The broader Latino community is an important player in our ability to secure and implement culturally competent services to Latino clients. For example, the importance of recruiting and collaborating with local Latino leaders has been suggested as a point of entry for social workers who desire to work with the Latino community (Delgado 1996; 1997). Latino leaders are often seen as people in the community regarded with *respeto* and thought to have great knowledge of the community's needs. *Respeto* is also an important cultural value among Latinos, for whom deference to authority figures is important (Zea, Garcia, Belgrave, & Quezada, 1997); however, it is often a reciprocal relationship. Recent scholarship supports the notion that Latino community leaders recognize their responsibility to the larger community, feel a sense of duty, and are willing to collaborate with public-sector programs to assist other community members (Levitt, 1995). Community-based programs that have incorporated culturally responsive services have often utilized community members, businesses, churches, leaders, and language-appropriate materials when working with the Latino community.

In the preceding section on the Latino community, we saw how the roles of community, family, and cultural values intersect and contribute to its overall well-being. We will now move from macro to more micro issues with Latinos and discuss cultural values within the family.

Latino Families and Familism

We use our research on Latino families and developmental disabilities to give the reader an understanding of familism and work with families from an empirical perspective. We then present a case vignette that demonstrates how familism plays out for a family who has a child with special needs. The case can also give us an example of how to take into account familism in working on the micro and macro levels.

When starting our research, we wanted to understand how caring for a family member with a disability was unique for Latino families compared to non-Latino white families. As Latinas who have worked and lived in Latino communities, we know there are differences in the way Latino families relate to one another compared to non-Latino white families, but this is considered anecdotal information. We wanted to be able to document unique cultural values among Latinos and understand how they approached caring for a child with a developmental disability. Accounts in the scholarly literature described various Latino cultural values and norms including familism, *respeto*, attitudes about gender roles, *personalismo*, and *sympatia*, among others. While most of the accounts were consistent with one another, very few of them were based on empirical studies. It is important to empirically study these values and norms in order to understand to what extent they reflect the reality of Latinos we work with in social work contexts. Here we will discuss familism, which is the focus of our research.

Familism has sometimes been presented as a dysfunctional characteristic of Latino families because it may appear to resemble enmeshment, which in family-systems therapy implies an unhealthy over-involvement and closeness of family members who lack boundaries between them (McGoldrick, Giordano, & Pearce, 1996). Other scholars were interested in countering these "deficit model" views of Latino culture with a better understanding of how culture may in fact be a strength or protective factor (García Coll et al., 1996). Thus, an important focus of our research was to understand how familism might be a cultural strength for mothers caring for a child with a developmental disability across the life course.

Familism is a cultural value that includes strong feelings of loyalty, reciprocity, and solidarity among family members (Marín & Marín, 1991). Sabogal, Marín, Otero-Sabogal, and Marín (1987) emphasized the importance of distinguishing between attitudinal familism and behavioral familism. *Attitudinal familism* has to do with the beliefs that people have about their family, the support it provides, and its importance with respect to obligations and identification. *Behavioral familism* is what the family actually does with respect to closeness, interaction, and providing support to one another. The two constructs may complement each other, but not necessarily. In other words, individuals' beliefs and attitudes may be based on some level of what is actually taking place in the family; but new immigrants with strong familistic beliefs may be unable to demonstrate familistic behaviors because they live far from their family. Sabogal and colleagues (1987) defined three dimensions of familism: support provided by the family, one's obligations to the family, and use of relatives as referents. The latter dimension refers to the extent to which a person consults with relatives about important matters, and to what extent family members' behavior reflects on the individual. This dimension taps into the collectivist nature of familism, that individuals in familistic cultures make decisions and behave with respect to what is important to the family as a group as opposed to what is important to the individual. These authors also examined whether there were differences between different Latino groups, between Latinos and non-Latino whites, and differences according to levels of acculturation (Sabogal et al., 1987). They found that the Latino groups were similar to one another, but rated significantly higher than non-Latino whites on the familism scale. With respect to acculturation, two dimensions changed: higher levels of acculturation were associated with lower levels of both *obligation to the family* and *families as referents*. However, the dimension *support from the family* did not change with acculturation. Furthermore, acculturated Latinos still rated higher on the familism scale than non-Latino whites. This study was one of the first to confirm differences between Latinos and non-Latino whites in terms of family orientation, similarities between Latino groups, and the durability of some aspects of familism across acculturation levels. More recent research has confirmed the stability of family support across acculturation levels (Steidel & Contreras, 2003), higher rates of familism among Latinos when compared to non-Latino whites (Ramírez et al., 2004), and similarities across Latino subgroups on attitudinal familism measures (Ramírez et al., 2004; Villarreal, Blozis, & Widaman, 2005).

Recent research has also shown how familism may be protective for family members. Romero and Ruiz (2007) found that for Mexican American youth, familism was associated with less risky coping behavior and more parental monitoring. Perceived family support has been linked to greater psychological well-being or better mental health outcomes among Latinos (Castillo, Conoley, & Brossart, 2004; Rodriguez, Mira, Paez, & Myers, 2007).

In order to study whether familism provided protection to Puerto Rican mothers who lived with and cared for an adult child with intellectual disabilities (ID), we used the attitudinal familism scale, which measured the three dimensions described previously (Sabogal et al., 1987). However, we did not find any relationships between the attitudinal scale and the psychological distress of the mothers, primarily because most of the mothers rated very high on the familism scale, and there was little variation. For this reason, we decided to examine measures in the study that could be proxies for behavioral manifestations of familism.

Initially, we focused primarily on the dimension *support from the family* by examining instrumental support (day-to-day caregiving tasks) and emotional support (the mothers' social support network). Key findings were that many immediate and extended family members were involved in day-to-day caregiving tasks (instrumental support), but what contributed most to lower levels of depression and burden were the size of the social support network and maternal satisfaction with the network (emotional support). These findings suggest that while instrumental support may be expected from family members, emotional support from family members may hold the most meaning for mothers (Magaña, 1999).

Next we focused on the *family members as referents* dimension of familism. As stated earlier, this dimension is based on the collectivist nature of familism, which emphasizes the needs of the group versus the needs of the individual. Consequently, individuals who are from a familistic culture may be more likely to consider the well-being of the family before considering their own. In collaboration with colleagues from the University of Miami, we conducted a comparison between Puerto Rican and Cuban American mothers of adults with mental retardation, in which we examined family problems and their relationship to maternal depression and burden (Magaña, Seltzer, Krauss, Rubert, & Szapocznik, 2002). We hypothesized that problems that emerged in the family as a result of caregiving would be the most important predictor of maternal depression and burden, because the mother's perception of how well the family was doing would be expected to affect her own emotional well-being. We found that having more family problems was a significant predictor of higher depression and burden for both groups. However, the Cuban American mothers reported having more family problems than the Puerto Rican caregivers and as a result were significantly more burdened. These findings suggest that while familism may be equally meaningful to both Latino groups, different ethnic and environmental contexts may account for the differences in the mother's perception of family problems and burden (Magaña et al., 2002). We then compared Latina and non-Latina white mothers:

> Subsequently, we examined whether family problems had a stronger affect on a Latino sample compared to a non-Latino white sample, and found that the relationship between family problems and maternal depressive symptoms was significantly stronger for the Puerto Rican mothers than it was for the non-Latina white mothers. (Magaña, Seltzer, & Krauss, 2002)

With Miami colleagues, we developed a stress-process model that incorporates family functioning more comprehensively for Latino caregivers. The primary aim was to better understand the mechanisms by which family problems mediated the relationship of maladaptive behaviors and caregiver distress as we found in previous studies. Our findings validated a model that emphasized family burden rather than subjective caregiver burden. Traditionally, in caregiving research, subjective caregiver burden is conceptualized as how caregiving impacts the individual lives of the caregivers. We argued that it would be more relevant in research on Latina mothers to examine the impact of caregiving on the lives of all family members, including their own. We found that more maladaptive behaviors are related to worse family relationships, which in turn are related to greater family burden. Greater family burden was then related to poorer caregiver outcomes (Magaña, Schwartz, Rubert, & Szapocznik, 2006). These findings reinforce previous findings about the importance of family functioning to the Latina caregiver's personal well-being.

A study in which we compared Latina and non-Latina white mothers of adolescents and adults with an autism spectrum disorder (ASD) focused on the familism dimension *obligation to family members*. The obligation to care for a family member with an illness or disability in the home may be considered a cultural preference among Latinos. It was hypothesized that Latina mothers would be more satisfied with co-residence than non-Latina white mothers, and that satisfaction with co-residence would lead to more positive outcomes for the Latina mothers. When controlling for demographic characteristics, non-Latina white mothers were more distressed and had lower levels of psychological well-being than Latina mothers, and, as hypothesized, satisfaction with co-residence mediated this difference (Magaña & Smith, 2006).

CASE STUDY

The experience of a Puerto Rican family that had a son with autism who was placed in a residential program gives us insights into how familism plays out. The mother in this family, Mrs. Lopez, was separated from her husband and living with her son, Jorge, a young adult of twenty-two years with autism, and an adolescent daughter, Araceli. Jorge had many service needs that could only be met in a residential school facility as these services were not made available to families at home. Mrs. Lopez indicated that it was an important cultural value to maintain her son at home, and she did not want to consider placement. This demonstrates the *obligation to the family* aspect of familism. Mrs. Lopez consulted with other family members including those in Puerto Rico, and the majority of the family was not in favor of placement. This is an example of *family members as referents*. It was only upon meeting with a Puerto Rican mental health professional, who was able to take into account Mrs. Lopez's cultural values and frame the situation in terms of the needs of the entire family, that the mother agreed to placement. He discussed the needs of Mrs. Lopez's adolescent daughter, suggesting that her decision should also take into account what was best for Araceli. Thus, he appealed to Mrs. Lopez's strong sense of identification with her family. Even though Mrs. Lopez decided to place her son in the residential school, she insisted upon home visits every weekend. This was against the policy of the residential program because the administrators believed that problematic behaviors would be exacerbated by the home visits. The administrators finally agreed, however, and the mother reported that the weekly home visits worked out well for all involved. This is an example of an appropriate cultural adaptation that the facility made. While the administrators were initially reluctant, the negative outcomes they predicted did not occur, and the family was able to maintain a level of closeness with Jorge that was important to them culturally. Eventually, Jorge moved back to live with Mrs. Lopez because she viewed the placement as temporary in order for Jorge to receive needed services.

In Massachusetts where this family lived, a placement in a residential school setting was seen as a stepping-stone to a permanent out-of-home placement for young adults with disabilities. However, this expectation of independent living is not satisfactory to many Latino families, as many young adults live with their parents whether they have a disability or not. For Latino families, placement of a son or daughter with a disability outside the home may involve deliberation of many different family members, and require more frequent parental contact.

This case demonstrates both micro and macro issues. On the micro level, social workers who are doing case management with families such as this should understand the difference between the cultural values of the dominant society and those of the family. In the field of developmental disabilities, independence is valued by the dominant society, whereas in many Latino families, interdependence is valued. Because most services for adults with disabilities are geared toward independence from their families, social workers need to find ways to make exceptions to the norm and serve as an advocate when there is resistance to this by larger systems. Also, when families are making important life decisions, as demonstrated in the case study, the social worker needs to recognize and respect that the client may need to defer to family members in the decision-making process, even when they seem to the social worker to be distant family. Furthermore, effective counseling by a bilingual and bicultural counselor is needed. If the social worker does not meet these criteria, a referral to someone who does would be appropriate.

On a macro level, social workers need to advocate for more services that are congruent with the needs of families from different backgrounds. For example, this case demonstrates a need to develop more services that are family- and home-based rather than based out of residential placements. The social worker can appeal to statewide policy makers and agencies toward this end. Additionally, social workers in macro practice may actually become administrators of agencies. In this case, it is important to recognize the need to be flexible and change the rules for some cases, as the administrators ultimately did in the case study.

To link this case study to the issues of Latino community networking discussed in the first part of the chapter, we can think about how to involve the Latino community in making policy changes. In Massachusetts, where our research was conducted and the case study came from, there were a number of Latino service coordinators (mostly social workers) who worked with Latino families all over the state. They did many things to organize the community and involve families in change: They organized a family and provider conference specifically for Latino families. One of the Latina social workers was an administrator and conducted a study within her agency documenting disparities in services to Latinos, which she shared at this conference. The service coordinators decided to get together and form a statewide group that could advocate for the needs of Latino families in the developmental disability policy world.

We involved these service coordinators in our research so that they could have data to use in their advocacy efforts. They were invited to a meeting to review the findings of the research and help with the interpretation of it. A report was put together from the study for the providers to use in policy advocacy as well. The social workers also organized support groups of Latino families, some of which became empowerment groups that began to work on community-level issues. Additionally, the service coordinators created links to broader Latino community-based organizations in the state. They were able to partner with these agencies to develop programs that served Latino families that had children with developmental disabilities. These service coordinators recognized that there is strength in numbers and that the tradition for community action in the Latino community is important to tap. These actions are all good examples of practices that social workers can engage in and/or assist with. Social workers can also be important allies to Latino community workers on these kinds of initiatives.

In this chapter, we explored two institutions, family and community, which have helped Latinos survive and thrive. Families and communities are two strengths that Latinos have used to survive numerous challenges, and in the process, have created rich and textured cultural experiences. In the next chapter, the authors explore another important strength in the Latino community, spirituality. As you shall see, the manner in which spiritually is expressed within the Latino community reflects the theme of commonality and diversity. While social workers must develop the skills to help all their clients utilize their spiritual beliefs and religious institutions as sources of strength and resiliency, this may be particularly true for the Latino community.

For Writing and Reflection

1. Describe cultural values of the dominant U.S. society. How do these values manifest themselves in different social work settings?

2. How might these values differ from Latino values of collectivism and familism in these social work settings?

3. How do the values of collectivism and familism shape Latino community-based networking and social service utilization? What impact might Latino community networking have on service delivery and/or planning for social service agencies?

4. How and where might social workers seek out Latino community leaders? How would you identify leaders? Is this different from how you might identify community leaders from other groups? If yes, how?

References

Antshel, K. M. (2002). Integrating culture as a means of improving treatment adherence in the Latino population. *Psychology, Health, & Medicine, 7*, 435–451.

Aranda, M. P. (2001). The development of Latino social work profession in Los Angeles. *Research on Social Work Practice, 11*, 254–267.

Barnes, S. (2007). An intra-ethnic analysis of social affiliations among Latinos in the United States. *Journal of Poverty, 11*, 107–134.

Boerstler, H., & de Figueiredo, J. M. (2003). Pathways of low-income minority patients to outpatient psychiatric treatment. *American Journal of Psychiatry, 160*, 1004–1007.

Camarillo, A. (1991). Mexican Americans and nonprofit organizations: An historical overview. In H. E.Gallegos & M. O'Neill (Eds.), *Hispanics and the nonprofit-sector* (pp. 15–32). New York: The Foundation Center.

Cárdenas, G. (2004). *La causa: Civil rights, social justice, and the struggle for equality in the Midwest.* Houston, TX: Arte P?blico Press.

Castillo, L., Conoley, C., & Brossart, D. (2004). Acculturation, white marginalization, and family support as predictors of perceived distress in Mexican American female college students. *Journal of Counseling Psychology, 51*, 151–157.

Cauce, A.M., & Domenech-Rodríguez, M. (2000). Latino Families: Myths and realities. In *Latino children and families in the United States: Current research and future directions.* Contreras, J.M., Kerns, K.A., & Neal-Barnett, A.M. (Eds.) Westport, Connecticut: Praegar.

Center on Philanthropy & Civil Society. (2003). *Latino philanthropy literature review.* The Graduate Center, City University of New York. Available at: http://www.philanthropy.org/programs/literature_reviews/latino_lit_review .pdf

Delgado, M. (1996). Puerto Rican food establishments as social service organizations: Results of an asset assessment. *Journal of Community Practice, 3*, 37–57.

Delgado, M. (1997). Role of Latino-owned beauty salons in the Latino community. *Social Work, 42*, 42–51.

Delgado, M. (1998). Linking schools, human services, and community: A Puerto Rican perspective. *Social Work in Education, 20*, 121–130.

Delgado, M. (2006). *Social work with Latinos: A cultural assets paradigm.* New York: Oxford University Press.

Delgado, M., & Barton, K. (1998). Murals in Latino communities: Social indicators of community strengths. *Social Work, 43*, 346–356.

Delgado, M., & Humm-Delgado, D. (1982). Natural support systems: Source of strength in Hispanic communities. *Social Work, 27*, 83–89.

Delgado, M., Jones, K., & Rohani, M. (2005). *Social work practice with refugee and immigrant youth in the United States.* Boston, MA: Pearson.

Delgado, M., & Tennstedt, S. (1997). Making the case for culturally appropriate community services: Puerto Rican elders and their caregivers. *Health & Social Work, 22*, 246–255.

Falicov, C. J. (2001). The cultural meanings of money: The case of Latinos and Anglo-Americans. *American Behavioral Scientist, 45,* 313–330.

Fix, M. E., & Zimmerman, W. (1999). All under one roof: Mixed family status in an era of reform. *Urban Insitute.* Available at: http://www.urban.org/Upload edPDF/409100.pdf

García Coll, C., Lamberty, G., Jenkins, R., McAdoo, H., Crnic, K., Wasik, B., & Vázquez García, H. (1996). An integrative model for the study of developmental competencies in minority children. *Child Development, 67,* 1891–1914.

Gonzalez H. M., Haan, M. N., Hinton, L. (2001). Acculturation and the prevalence of depression in older Mexican Americans: Baseline results of the Sacramento Area Latino Study on Aging. *Journal of the American Geriatrics Society, 49,* 948–953.

Gonzalez, N. A., Deardorff, J., Formoso, D., Barr, A., & Barrera, M. (2006). Family mediators of the relation between acculturation and adolescent mental health. *Family Relations, 55,* 318–330.

Gregory, P. G., Steinberg, Y. J., & Sousa, C. M. (2003). *Voluntary community involvement of Latinos: A literature review.* Unpublished manuscript. Available at: http://www.ucce.ucdavis.edu/files/filelibrary/5433/8114.pdf

Hernández, J. A. (1983). *Mutual aid for survival: The case of the Mexican Americans.* Malabar, FL: Robert E. Krieger Publishing Co.

Holleran, L. K., & Waller, M. A. (2003). Sources of resilience among Chicano/a youth: Forging identities in the borderlands. *Child and Adolescent Social Work Journal, 20,* 335–350.

John, R., Resendiz, R., & De Vargas, L. W. (1997). Beyond familism? Familism as explicit motive for eldercare among Mexican American caregivers. *Journal of Cross-Cultural Gerontology, 12,* 145–162.

Latapí, A. E., Martin, P., Castro, G. L., & Donato, K. (1997). Factors that influence migration. In *Migration between Mexico and the United States. Mexico-United States Bi-national study.* U.S. Commission on Immigration Reform. Available at: http://www.utexas.edu/lbj/uscir/binational/full-report.pdf

Levitt, P. (1995). A todos les llamo primo (I call everyone cousin): The social basis for Latino businesses. In M. Halter (Ed.), *New migrants in the marketplace: Boston's ethnic entrepreneurs* (120–140). Boston, MA: University of Massachusetts Press.

Magaña, S. (1999). Puerto Rican families caring for an adult with mental retardation: The role of familism. *American Journal on Mental Retardation, 104,* 466–482.

Magaña, S., Schwartz, S., Rubert, M., & Szapocznik, J. (2006). Hispanic caregivers of adults with mental retardation: The importance of family functioning. *American Journal on Mental Retardation, 111,* 250–262.

Magaña, S., Seltzer, M., & Krauss, W. (2002). Service utilization patterns of adults with intellectual disabilities: A comparison of Puerto Rican and non-Latino white families. *Journal of Gerontological Social Work, 37,* 65–86.

Magaña, S., Seltzer, M., Krauss, M., Rubert, M., & Szapocznik, J. (2002). Well-being and family role strain among Cuban American and Puerto Rican mothers of adults with mental retardation. *Journal of Human Behavior in the Social Environment, 5,* 31–55.

Magaña, S., & Smith, M. J. (2006). Psychological distress and well-being of Latina and non-Latina white mothers of youth and adults with an autism spectrum disorder: Cultural attitudes towards co-residence status. *American Journal of Orthopsychiatry,76,* 346–357.

Marín, G., & Marín, B. (1991). *Research with Hispanic populations.* Newbury Park, CA: Sage Publications.

McGoldrick, M., Giordano, J., & Pearce, J. (1996). *Ethnicity & family therapy.* New York, NY: Guilford Press.

McQueen, A., Getz, J. G., & Bray, J. H. (2003). Acculturation, substance use, and deviant behavior: Examining separation and family conflict mediators. *Child Development, 74,* 1737–1750.

Morín, J. L. (2005). *Latino/a rights and justice in the United States.* Durham, NC: Carolina Academic Press.

Padilla, Y. C., & Villalobos, G. (2007). Cultural responses to health among Mexican American women and their families. *Family Community Health, 30,* 24–33.

Pardo, M. (1998). *Mexican American women activists.* Philadelphia, PA: Temple University Press:

Parra, R. (2004). Latinos in the Midwest: Civil rights and community organization. In G. Ca'rdenas (Ed.), *LA CAUSA: Civil rights, social justice, and the struggle for equality in the Midwest* (pp. 1–18). Houston, TX: Arte Público Press.

Raffaelli, M., & Ontai, L. L. (2004). Gender socialization in Latino/a families: Results from two retrospective studies. *Sex Roles, 50,* 287–299.

Ramírezs, J. R., Crano, W. D., Quist, R., Burgoon, M., Alvaro, E. M., & Grandpre, J. (2004). Acculturation, familism, parental monitoring, and knowledge as predictors of marijuana and inhalant use in adolescents. *Psychology of Addictive Behaviors, 18,* 3–11.

Rivera, J. (1998). Domestic violence against Latinas by Latino males. In R. Delgado & J. Stefancic (Eds.), *The Latino/a condition: A critical reader* (pp. 501–507). New York: New York University Press.

Rodriguez, N., Mira, C., Paez, N., & Myers, H. (2007). Exploring the complexities offamilism and acculturation: Central constructs for people of Mexican origin. *American Journal of Community Psychology, 39,* 61–77.

Romero, A., & Ruiz, M. (2007). Does familism lead to increase parental monitoring?: Protective factors for coping with risky behaviors. *Journal of Child and Family Studies, 16,* 143–154.

Sabogal, F., Marín, G., Otero-Sabogal, R., & Marín, B. (1987). Latino familism and acculturation: What changes and what doesn't? *Hispanic Journal of Behavioral Sciences, 9,* 397–412.

Steidel, A., Contreras, J. (2003). A new familism scale for use with Latino populations. *Hispanic Journal of Behavioral Sciences, 25,* 312–330.

Tirado, M. D.(1974). Mexican American community political organization "The key to Chicano political power." In F. G. Garcia (Ed.), *La causa politica: A Chicano politics reader* (pp. 105–127). Notre Dame, IN: University of Notre Dame Press.

Tienda, M., & Ortiz,V. (1986). Hispanicity and the 1980 census. *Social Science Quarterly, 67* (2), 3–20.

Triandis, H. C., Bontempo, R., Villareal, M. J., Asai, M., & Lucca, N. (1998). Individualism and collectivism: Cross-cultural perspectives on self-ingroup relationships. *Journal of Personality and Social Psychology, 54,* 323–338.

Valenzuela, A., & Dornbusch, S. M. (1994). Familism and social capital in the academic achievement of Mexican origin and Anglo adolescents. *Social Science Quarterly, 75,* 18–36.

Villarreal, R., Blozis, S., Widaman, K. (2005). Factorial invariance of a pan-Hispanic familism scale. *Hispanic Journal of Behavioral Sciences, 27,* 409–425.

Williams, B. (2003). The worldview of dimensions of individualism and collectivism: Implications for counseling. *Journal of Counseling and Development, 81,* 370–374.

Xavier, R. E. (1999). Politics and Chicano culture: Luis Valdez and el treato campensson, 1964–1990. In D. Montejano (Ed.), *Chicano politics and society* (175–200). Austin, TX: University of Texas Press.

Zea, M. C., Belgrave, F. Z., Garcia, J. G., & Quezada, T. (1997). Socioeconomic and cultural factors in rehabilitation of Latinos with disabilities. In J. G. Garcia, M. C. Zea (Eds.), *Psychological interventions and research within Latino populations.* Needham Heights, MA: Allyn & Bacon, Inc.

CHAPTER SIX

Spirituality as a Strength in the Latino Community

Clay Shorkey
Eunice Garcia
Liliane Windsor

Introduction

RELIGION AND SPIRITUALITY IN SOCIAL WORK

Christian, Jewish, and humanistic values constitute the historical foundation of social work, and it is only more recently that religion and spirituality in social work practice and theory have been increasingly emphasized. The history of American social work has been conceptualized in three broad phases revealing the connection of professional practice with religion and spirituality. Prior to the 1920s, social work was largely based on Christian and Jewish values, with sectarian services and ideologies characterizing social service provision. From the 1920s to the 1970s, the increasing professionalization and secularization of social work contributed to the detachment of social work education from religion and spirituality. Starting in the 1970s, and rapidly expanding in the 1990s to the present, the trend toward integrating religion and spirituality with social work is marked by significant increases of related research and publication, an expansion of diverse perspectives concerning religion and spirituality, and an intensification of attention to religious and spiritual themes in social work education (Canda & Furman, 1999).

The journal *Social Work and Christianity*, which began publication in 1974, is devoted to integrating Christian faith with social work practice, and *The (Jewish) Social Work Forum* was first published in 1964. The journal *Social Thought*, which was founded in 1978, changed its name to the *Journal of Religion and Spirituality in Social Work* in 2004 to reflect a broader contemporary focus. Also noteworthy is the foundation of the Society for Spirituality and Social Work in 1990, and the publication of the Society's newsletter, *The Spirituality and Social Work Forum*, beginning in 1994. According to Canda and colleagues (Canda, Nakashima, Burgess, Russel, & Barfield, 2003), there are more than seventy courses in social work schools related to spirituality and more than seven hundred publications on spirituality and social work. The argument to vigorously include spirituality as an integral part of social work practice was made by Cornett (1992), who presented the view that social work should broaden current focus of practice to a biopsychosocialspiritual model, thereby making "spiritual issues a legitimate clinical focus and provide for a more complete understanding of clients' strengths, weaknesses, and problems" (p. 102).

While there has been an increased focus on spirituality in social work, little emphasis has been placed on spirituality in practice with Latinos. The available literature, which reflects limited understanding and integration of religion and spirituality in practice with Latino individuals and their families, points to the pressing need for culturally sensitive social services. For example, *Spiritual Diversity and Social Work: A Comprehensive Bibliography* (Canda et al., 2003) includes only ten articles reflecting the social work literature on the spiritual beliefs and religions of Latinos. Canda and Furman (1999) emphasize spirituality as "the heart of helping." This is especially true in work with Latino individuals, families, and communities, where a mixture of traditional and contemporary religious values frequently permeate their way of life. Spirituality has always been an important aspect of Latino culture, whether practiced in the form of Catholicism, other varieties of Christianity, indigenous religions, indigenous folk healing, or a deep connection with spirits or naturalistic gods. This chapter addresses the broader Latino community; however, much of the research base is drawn from information related to Mexican Americans in the United States.

Religion, Spirituality, and Latino Health

An ever-expanding amount of research literature is available that supports the relationship between religious involvement and personal spirituality, and positive aspects of physical and mental health (e.g., Koenig & Larson, 2001; George, Ellison, & Larson, 2002; Hill & Pargament, 2003). For example, religious attendance and subjective assessment of health was studied with a sample of 1,125 Mexican Americans in San Antonio, Texas. A significant relationship between religious attendance and positive subjective ratings of health was found for all ages of women, who made up two-thirds of the sample (Levin & Markides, 1986). A study by Marsiglia and colleagues (Marsiglia, Kulis, Nieri, & Parsai, 2005) of more than seven thousand white and Mexican American middle-school youth examined the relationship between religious involvement and use of alcohol, cigarettes, and marijuana. Results supported religious involvement as a protective factor in chemical use. Skinner and colleagues (Skinner, Correa, Skinner, & Bailey, 2001) carried out a study investigating the importance of religion in the lives of families with children with mental retardation or developmental delays. More than 250 parents of Mexican American or Puerto Rican children viewed themselves as religious, were members of a church, and participated in religious activities. The parents considered their affiliation with organized religion supportive, but rated personal religious beliefs as providing the most psychological and social support. In an interesting study, Moadel and colleagues (1999) asked ethnically diverse cancer patients to indicate the prevalence of their spiritual and existential needs related to their illness. Greater need for spiritual support was found in Hispanic patients compared to white or black patients. Sixty-one percent of Hispanics identified five or more spiritual or existential needs compared to 25 percent of whites and 41 percent of blacks.

In a longitudinal study conducted more than two decades ago, Markides (1983) studied three measures of religiosity and life satisfaction for a sample of Mexican Americans and Anglos. Of the three areas of religiosity, only church attendance showed a significant effect on life satisfaction as opposed to reported private prayer or self-related religiosity. More recently, a study by Hill, Angel, Ellison, and Angel (2005) reported that the risk of mortality among older Mexican Americans appears to be reduced by weekly church attendance. Based on a sample of 3,050 Mexican Americans age sixty-five and older in Texas, California, New Mexico, Arizona, and Colorado, the researchers found a 32 percent reduction in risk of mortality for individuals who attend church weekly compared with others who never attend religious services. Weekly religious attendance had a stronger effect on mortality risk than factors such as cardiovascular health, mobility, and activity limitations.

Historical Trajectories, Globalization, and Acculturation Influencing Latino Spirituality

Latinos share a historical trajectory that includes conquest and a broad range of indigenous and imposed cultural traditions (McLemore &

Romo, 1985). These factors, as well as acculturation and increasing globalization, cause Latino individuals, families, and communities to draw
upon a diverse range of religious and spiritual belief systems as sources
of strength, healing, and empowerment to address life's challenges.
Globalization has resulted in families being spread across not only several cities and states but often two or more countries. These different
localities may possess distinct differences in social and cultural environments and the challenges faced by families. Acculturation is influenced by the person's or family's ability to adapt and adjust to new
aspects of reality (Urrabazo, 2000). The degree of acculturation is a
major survival factor for many individuals, influencing their conception
of spirituality and church selection in a new environment. Variations of
acculturation of individuals and among family members create a spectrum of belief systems from indigenous spirituality through beliefs associated with European and American variations of Christian religions.
The importance of spirituality in Latino culture parallels the significance of spirituality to African American survival, which gave "Black
people the strength to go on when . . . oppressive forces were seeking
to strip them of their humanity . . . [and] gave them a will to live and
the determination to make life worth living" (Martin & Martin, 2002, p.
1). For Latinos, religion also serves as "a mechanism for survival. It is
the way to understand and put order in the universe," amounting to "a
way of looking at the world that has been passed down from one generation to the next in order to give meaning and purpose to living" (Urrabazo, 2000, pp. 212–213). For Latinos and African Americans alike,
spirituality provides a source of inspiration and hope to both celebrate
important life milestones and mitigate sufferings and losses. Sensitivity
to the history, language, and variations in the acculturation level of Latinos in the United States provides the basis for effective therapeutic
services.

Blending Indigenous and Catholic Spiritual Beliefs

Since Latinos include people of diverse origins, their spirituality, too, is
diverse in terms of its original form and the changes that have evolved
through religious influences promoted by conquering European
nations and cultures. In Peru, for instance, the Incas left Machu Picchu,
the ancient city propped on a mountaintop where modern visitors still
go to experience a mystic "magical" setting that promotes the healing
of spirit and soul. In Mexico, the Mayas left concrete proof of their belief
system that included deities linked to natural entities, such as the moon
and the sun, as sources of power and nurturance. Similarly, in the
northeastern area of the southern state of Oaxaca, as well as in the

northwestern outskirts of Mexico City, numerous archeological sites bear witness to the indigenous daily inclusion of spirituality (León-Portilla, 1963).

Western thought, in particular, Catholicism, was introduced in Latin American colonies by social influence and through forced methods beginning in the fifteenth century. Prescott's (1855) early history of the Spanish conquest of Mexico notes that the conversion of the Mexican natives to Catholicism was the heart of the colonial project. Having "somewhat of the air of a crusade," the task of conversion through instruction and persuasion often gave way to violent means: "The sword," Prescott (1855) writes, "was a good argument when the tongue failed" (p. 269). Many of the traditional spiritual places of worship, sacred texts, beliefs, and practices were destroyed, forced into hiding, or melded with Catholic forms of symbolism and ritual (Canda & Furman, 1999).

An important technique of evangelization, which is particularly relevant to the Christianization of the southwest and southern regions, was the parallel effort used by the conquistadors via the religious staff they included in all of their military planning. Monks and priests were ministering to the military staff while working diligently to convert the indigenous population to Christianity, more specifically, to Catholicism, as the history of the Spanish missions attests. Eventually new converts were included in the Spanish settlements and charged with the indoctrination of new converts in territory that is now U.S. soil. The rituals in the Church were conducted in Latin until the Second Vatican allowed for use of other languages. Thus, Catholicism was initially forced, with "infidels" slain during the years of the Inquisition, but later adopted by families and carried on in traditions from generation to generation as "folk Catholicism"—meaning a faith-based religion practiced within the teachings of the Catholic Church.

Contemporary Latino conceptions of spirituality have evolved from a mixture of earth-oriented beliefs and the beliefs and traditions of the Catholic Church. For example, Tonantzin, the Aztec goddess who evolved into the Virgen de Guadalupe, helped facilitate the initial conversion of indigenous people to Catholicism in Mexico. In the ecclesiastical account of the apparition of the Virgen de Guadalupe, it is noteworthy that the Catholic Madonna appeared to Juan Diego, an indigenous believer, in 1531 at the site of Tonantzin's temple. Furthermore, the new Madonna was given the name *Guadalupe*, the same as the Madonna in West Central Spain. She was further depicted as the dark Madonna (*virgen morena*), also similar to the Madonna in Spain. This affirmation of cultural blending and adaptation by the Catholic Church led to adoption of La Virgen de Guadalupe as the patron saint of the Americas.

An example of the blending African, indigenous, and Western religious traditions, a process known as religious syncretism, took place in colonial Brazil, where slaves were prohibited from practicing their African spiritual rituals while being encouraged to practice Catholicism. As a result, slaves incorporated Catholicism into their indigenous spiritual practices and beliefs, developing new religions, including "Candomblé," "Umbanda," and "Macumba." A way in which these religions incorporate Catholicism is that they have parallel sacred entities, where each Catholic saint has a corresponding *orixá* (highly evolved spiritual being). For instance, the Catholic Lady of the Conception is the corresponding saint of Iemanjá. Both figures essentially represent the same entity, who is responsible for governing bodies of water and protecting fishermen (Johnson, 2002).

The blending of indigenous and Christian beliefs also influenced how traditional Mexican culture accepts death as part of life. The most notable expression of this is *El Dia de los Muertos*, the Day of the Dead, at which time it is believed that the spirits of loved ones visit their descendants. To welcome these spirits, the family builds an altar in honor of deceased loved ones, cooks family dishes in their honor, and places photos and mementos on the altar. In the most traditional communities in Mexico, the 1st of November is *Dia de los Angelitos*, in honor of the children who have died, and November 2nd is *El Dia de los Muertos*, in honor of the older deceased. The night between these days is believed to be the time when the spirits of the dead pay a special visit. Traditional families spend all day at the cemetery bringing floral offerings and food to join in celebration of the living and dead (Aguilar-Moreno, 1998). The same spiritual fervor and communal experience takes place when a family faces a crisis or experiences death. Religious rituals are often included, but it is the faith expression of the people that makes it an experience. For instance, the *novena*, or daily rosaries for nine days with a grieving family, provides support and guidance to the bereaved in a religious manner, but usually in the family's home (Williams, 1990).

Curanderismo *and Other Folk-Healing Practices*

Religion and spirituality are at the core of the traditional health care system. The most well-known indigenous healing system, *curanderismo*, includes a broad range of folk-healing practices such as herbal remedies, oils, poultices, prayers, candles, massage, and a range of healing rituals that include soul retrieval and intercession with saints or spirits (Krassner, 1986). Many *curanderas* are older women, often referred to as *señoras*. *Curanderismo* stresses the interrelatedness of the physical, mental, emotional, and spiritual components of the soul (Avila, 1999). Some healers practice *curanderismo* in a manner compatible with Catholic beliefs and traditions, while others emphasize the individual's relationship with Mother Earth. Some people are considered special by the community because they interact with spirits and are seen as "mediators" between the human and the divine (Abalos, 1986). These healers draw upon any force viewed as lending support to the person who is hurting, be it physically, mentally, socially, or spiritually (Avila, 1999).

Curanderos rely as much on the *fé* (faith) of the person with whom they are working as on knowledge of health issues and methods for re-creating balance in an individual's life. As in a social work assessment, the *curandero* builds trust and mutuality in the helping relationship and uses them to facilitate expression of concerns and preferences in the person's physical, psychosocial, and spiritual life. Referral to conventional medical resources may occur if the person shows symptoms of physical distress beyond the realm of *curanderismo*. If the person shows symptoms of mental and spiritual distress, indigenous and/or religious resources, such as cleansings (*barridas* or *limpias*) and blessings by clergy, are recommended. If the person shows symptoms of spiritual and mental concerns, a comprehensive assessment of the source of the problem and possible interventions may also be recommended. The *curandero* relies on the faith and collaboration of the person seeking help (through *platicas*, or conversations), social support from the family, and the spiritual/religious/cultural tradition in order to reconnect the person to the desired state of equilibrium (Avila, 1999).

Several studies relating to the use of *curanderos* by women and/or elderly Mexican Americans found that those individuals comprise the majority of people who have used or would consider using traditional health practices as a supplement to professional health care (Applewhite, 1995; Mayers, 1989). Lopez (2005) found that even highly assimilated Mexican American women maintain traditional, indigenous beliefs and practices related to health care. A recent study by Zacharias (2006) has provided initial evidence for the effectiveness of healing methods of *curanderos* in the treatment of mental illness. The research was conducted in Oaxaca, Mexico, following clients of three native healers. The clients were diagnosed with mild or moderate psychiatric symptoms. Treatment was evaluated pre, post, and at six months follow-up using semi-structured interviews and instruments to measure psychiatric symptoms, level of functioning, and degree of distress. Results based on study data concluded that the treatment by the *curanderos* resulted in complete recovery in six of the eight cases and partial recovery in the other two. These improvements continued to be observed at the six-month follow-up. The two cases that did not completely recover included a schizophrenic client and a second client described as having high levels of symptom severity. The author suggests that there is greater likelihood of complete improvement for clients with less severe illnesses, whereas clients with severe psychiatric disorder show limited improvement.

Latinos also access other health care traditions. *Espiritismo* and *Santeria* are spiritual approaches that also provide healing practices in Cuba, Puerto Rico, throughout the Caribbean, Brazil, and in the United States. *Espiritismo* (spiritualism) was originally introduced to Cuba by Yorubas from Nigeria. This belief system focuses on the important role of souls or spirits of one's ancestors. This approach emphasizes the interaction with spirits and their active role in daily life. These spirits are invoked for healing through rituals by mediums (Delgado, 1977). *Santeria*, or *La Regla Lucumi* (The Way of the Saints), is another spiritual tradition that began in Cuba and likewise spread through the Caribbean and the United States, and it also blends Yoruba beliefs with aspects of Catholicism. This tradition centers on the *Orishas*, spirits that are often associated with Catholic saints and that are invoked to assist in a variety of areas of life. Worship and rituals are carried out to maintain positive relationships with the *Orishas* and to ensure their help and support (Paulino, 1995).

Modern medical systems' lack of acknowledgment and at times outright rejection of traditional healing systems, as well as the protective stance of Latino communities, has inhibited further study and understanding of these approaches as alternative resources for Latinos. Many Latinos nevertheless continue to consider *curanderismo, espiritismo,* and *Santeria* as healing resources, depending on the geographic location and acculturation level of the person who is experiencing difficulty.

Contemporary Religious Influences in the United States

Seventy percent of Latinos in the United States are Catholic, approximately 29 million persons in 2005 (Murray, 2006). However, a growing number, 9.5 million or about twenty-three percent, identify themselves as mainline Protestants or other Christian affiliations such as Pentecostals, Jehovah's Witnesses, and Mormons. One percent identifies itself as following another major religion other than Christianity, 6 percent report no religious preference, and less than half of 1 percent report that they are atheists or agnostic (Espinosa, Elizondo, & Miranda, 2003). Eighty-five percent of the Latino Protestants identify themselves as Pentecostals or Evangelists (Murray, 2006). The Pentecostal church has been most aggressive in efforts to convert Latinos, and Pentecostals account for the largest subset of Protestants. Their beliefs are often attractive to Latinos possessing strong indigenous beliefs, given, for example, the Pentecostal belief that bodies can be inhabited by the Holy Spirit and the belief in miraculous physical, mental, or spiritual healing. Fundamentalist groups make literal interpretation of the New Testament passage (James 5:14–15) that promises that through anointing with oil and calling on the name of Jesus, the sick can be cured (Ness & Wintrob, 1981).

A study by Hunt (2000) analyzed data for persons of Spanish origin in the General Social Surveys conducted between 1972 and 1996 to determine differences between Hispanics related to religious and church involvement and indicators of socioeconomic status. Religious groups represented in the study included Catholics, mainline Protestants (e.g., Lutherans, Methodists, and Unitarians), and conservative Protestants (e.g., Pentecostal, Holiness, Assembly of God, and Jehovah's Witnesses). Conservative Protestants had higher church attendance, viewed their religion as of greater subjective importance, and were more involved in a church-related group than Catholics or mainline Protestants. Mainline Protestants differed from Catholics only on greater participation in church-related groups. Mainline Protestants, including Methodists, Presbyterians, and Baptists, had clearly higher socioeconomic status than Catholics or conservative Protestants on indicators such as education, family income, and occupational prestige, indicating participation in mainline churches may be associated with lifestyles and beliefs that are more in line with those of mainstream society.

Churches, both Catholic and Protestant, are centers for religious worship, education, socialization, and community organization (Selee, 2006, p. 23). Research suggests that Latino Catholics, Protestants, and other Christians report that religion provides a "great deal of guidance" in their day-to-day life (Espinosa et al., 2003, p. 17). From birth to death, religious rituals such as baptism, confirmation, marriage rituals, anniversary celebrations, prayers and blessings in times of sickness or injury, as well as death and dying, mark important points in the lives of individuals, families, and communities. Urrabazo (2000) describes the strong identification of poor Latinos with Jesus, who was poor, and with his mother Mary, who is viewed as the nurturing and protective mother. Latino Catholics also often seek assistance from saints, and may have selected special saints for themselves and their families. These may be displayed in the form of statues or candles, appearing with a crucifix and images of the Virgin of Guadalupe throughout the home. In addition to providing structure, rituals, and values to guide the lives of individuals, families, and communities, some churches also provide the leadership, legitimacy, and influence to promote the rights of Latinos through social activism, involving, for example, migrant workers (Espinosa, Elizondo, & Miranda, 2005).

Latino-Oriented Faith-Based Programs

Social work has paid very limited attention to the use and integration of faith-based social service programs with public and secular nonprofit organizations. Although there are thousands of faith-based organizations that have served millions of individuals and families, no current data exist to highlight the magnitude of this contribution (Cnaan, 1999). A national study group organized to research common ground among faith-based organizations concluded that the social welfare programs play a unique role as their emphasis on the spiritual dimension provides a powerful ingredient for personal change in individuals who have not been reached by other methods (Working Group, 2002). Many faith-based programs are focused on the Latino population or offer a broad range of services specifically geared to this population. Data examining the national impact of faith-based programs with Latinos is, however, very limited.

Faith-based programs often share many core components with public programs but clearly emphasize Christian spiritual beliefs, activities, and rituals, and focus on developing a long-term relationship with God (McCoy, Hermos, Bokhour, & Frayne, 2004; Neff, Shorkey, & Windsor, 2006). The types and range of services by faith-based programs for Latinos are diverse, and serve a broad range of needs of Latino individuals and families. Refugee resettlement programs, located mainly in border states, serve individuals from Mexico, Central and South America, as well as the Caribbean. In central Texas, for example, Catholic charities provide shelters, classes, and access to basic social and legal services. Similarly, the Episcopal dioceses provide health care, language classes, legal assistance, counseling, and leadership development for Latino individuals and families. At the national level, Episcopal Migration Ministries provides resettlement, advocacy, and outreach services to immigrants through a network of thirty-three affiliate offices in twenty-seven church dioceses (www.episcopalchurch.org/emm). Catholic Charities USA operates thousands of programs nationwide, with special services for Latinos in states with large Latino populations (Catholic Charities USA, 2006). Citing a biblical obligation to "speak on behalf of the stranger," Texas Baptist leaders recently announced the creation of a national initiative for churches to provide legal assistance to immigrants seeking legal residency or citizenship (Flynn, 2007).

Several national and regional faith-based programs provide rehabilitation services for Latinos with alcohol and drug abuse problems. Victory Ministries, with headquarters in San Antonio, Texas, has more than twenty-five programs throughout the Southwest as well as programs in Mexico, Honduras, Nicaragua, and Peru (Stertzer, 2001). Victory Ministries International, with headquarters in Southern California, has more than 350 programs nationwide, with 43 programs throughout the United States specifically serving Spanish-speaking alcoholics and addicts. Available data from twenty-four programs from 2006 indicates that over 2,500 clients were served (J. Parra, personal communication, May 15, 2007). Finally, Esperanza USA, funded by a grant from the U.S. Department of Health and Human Services, provides communication coordination and capacity building to a network of more than fifty faith-based agencies throughout the United States to serve Latino individuals, families, and communities. The programs are viewed as providing "Faith in Action" and reflect the verse in Matthew 22 of the New Testament, "Love thy neighbor as yourself." These programs vary in their service orientation by locality but generally include basic social services, counseling, GED, language, literacy, cooking, and computer classes, sports and activities for youth, chemical dependence education and treatment, training programs for community and business leadership, arts, music, after-school care, day care, food banks, housing, home-buyer preparation programs, parenting skills, and others (www .esperanza.us).

Political and social upheaval in Central America in the 1980s created a pressing need for assisting refugees crossing into the United States. Protestant and Jewish churches and congregations joined a movement led by the Catholic Church to protect refugees from abuse. This network, referred to as the Sanctuary Movement, has been compared "to the role the black church and its white allies played in the civil rights movement" (Williams, 2006). Sanctuary Movement churches across the United States provided housing and help to refugees. This movement has not been without its critics, who believed the churches were acting in defiance of U.S. law. Today, congregations across the country have begun to revitalize the Sanctuary Movement for current immigrants to the United States. This "new" Sanctuary Movement aims to protect immigrant families whose civil rights may be violated in the form of hatred, discrimination, and unjust deportation.

Implications for Social Work: Incorporating Spiritual Strengths into Work with Latinos

Social workers serve an increasing Latino population in the United States, and therefore, an understanding of the specific existential, as well as spiritual and religious, dimensions of Latino culture is crucial for culturally relevant practice. Diversity within the Latino community produces individuals who have different beliefs regardless of their specific cultural background. Thus, social workers must employ culturally sensitive communication skills to earn trust and to learn about the religious and spiritual history, beliefs, and practices of individual clients and their families (Garcia, 2001). Knowledge of the degree of acculturation from traditional cultures to mainstream American culture provides general information useful in understanding Latino spiritual and religious beliefs. New immigrants who maintain strong traditional culture may turn from traditional Catholicism to Spanish-speaking churches that espouse evangelical beliefs and practices that are more consistent with their indigenous culture. Understanding what church—Catholic, mainstream Protestant, or fundamentalist—an individual or family belongs to, the extent of their participation in it, and the importance of church support in their daily lives is important information for professional social workers.

Established principles of effective counseling, including *personalismo* (person-to-person interaction, based on equality rather than status) reflected in a *platica* (heart-to-heart talk) with clients, allow the worker and client to interact more comfortably in the context of a helpful and trustful relationship. Urrabazo (2000) suggests that information concerning religion and spirituality should flow naturally from the interaction and explores when it is relevant to the content presented by the client. For many Latino clients, an important component to address and remediate problems and/or help with attainment of important life-goals may be interaction with a priest, minister, or lay counselor. (Tan, 1999).

Existing problematic, stressful, or painful situations experienced by the client and/or his or her family may be reduced through prayer, meditation, attendance at religious services, religious readings, and visitation to shrines or sacred sites. Design of individualized rituals for the client and/or family may provide an important mechanism to deal with grief, loss, separation, divorce, or illness. Canda and Furman (1999) in *Spiritual Diversity in Social Work Practice: The Heart of Helping*, provide guidelines to assist clients to develop meaningful and effective rituals to deal with difficult life events.

Latino spirituality also has important implications for social policy. It is known that when the state fails to provide services, the church is often the organization that becomes responsible for filling these gaps. As previously discussed, there are many faith-based agencies providing a variety of services ranging from shelter to substance abuse treatment. It is important that the diverse religions within Latino communities be acknowledged and understood. Policies affecting faith-based service provision must be developed based on a thorough understanding of Latino spirituality to protect the community while also allowing these organizations to provide valuable service to their communities. More importantly, service providers must be willing to provide Latino individuals, families, and communities with comprehensive programs that acknowledge spirituality as a cultural strength.

CASE STUDY

Laura Sanchez, a twenty-year-old student attending college at a major midwestern university, became withdrawn and suffered severe headaches soon after her neighbor was sexually attacked in their apartment complex. The neighbor took refuge in Laura's apartment, and it was Laura who first heard the account of a horrific experience, called the police, and accompanied her friend/neighbor for medical exams. Laura remembered how, against her parents' advice, she had moved from her parents' home to attend college over a thousand miles away. She now felt particularly vulnerable. She prayed, she called her parents just to hear their voices, and she did everything possible to regain a sense of balance, but she could not concentrate on school assignments or tasks involved in her part-time job, and lost her appetite and much sleep. Final exams were approaching, and in spite of a good academic record, Laura lacked confidence in her ability to successfully complete the semester. She decided she had no choice but to go to the campus health clinic to see if she could get medical assistance for her symptoms. Her parents pleaded for her return home. She decided, owing to the distance and expense of travel, to try the university health clinic first.

Laura's family lives in a Mexican American neighborhood in south Texas and is very involved in the local Catholic parish and community. Traditional responses to her situation, had she been at home, would have been different. She would have had access to a *señora* (*curandera*) who could treat her for *susto* (fright sickness) by cleansing her with a *barrida* and prescribing prayers and herbal teas to serve as a mild sedative. One or two *barridas* or *platicas* (cleansings or conversations with the *señora*) might have been sufficient for her to get cultural support by which to emerge from the secondary trauma suffered via her neighbor/friend's attack and its aftermath. She might have also been able to go to church, or to a shrine, to thank a patron saint for intercession on her behalf as she survived this traumatic experience.

Social work continues to improve its exploration of heretofore unappreciated domains of human functioning, in particular coming to understand spirituality as a personal and cultural strength. However, it has only infrequently explored the importance of the arts to psychosocial well-being. The following chapter presents the value and importance of the arts in the Latino community. The author traces the history of the arts to the pre-Columbian world and connects this work to Latino art today. He explores the role of the artist in creating personal and community change. This unique chapter shows, through narrative, art, and the analysis of art, the manner in which Latinos have utilized the arts for their own personal and group well-being and empowerment.

For Writing and Reflection

1. What are the roles that religiosity and spirituality play with individual Latinos, families, and the broader community?

2. How should social workers incorporate spirituality and religiosity in providing services to Latinos and their families?

3. What are some ways that your own values and spiritual or religious beliefs may interact with the values and beliefs of Latino clients?

4. Discuss the previous questions for reflection in relation to the case example of Laura Sanchez.

References

Abalos, D. T. (1986). *Latinos in the United States: The sacred and the political.* Notre Dame, IN: University of Notre Dame Press.

Aguilar-Moreno, M. (1998). *The cult of the dead in Mexico: Continuity in a millennial tradition.* Austin, TX: Mexic-Arte.

Applewhite, S. L. (1995). Curanderismo: Demystifying the health beliefs and practices of elderly Mexican Americans. *Health and Social Work, 20*(4), 247–253.

Avila, E. (1999). *Woman who glows in the dark: A curandera reveals traditional Aztec secrets of physical and spiritual health.* New York: Jeremy P. Tarcher/Putnam.

Calderón, J. (1992). "Hispanic" and "Latino": The viability of categories for panethnic unity. *Latin American Perspectives, 19*(4), 37–44.

Camarillo, A. (Ed.). (1986). *Latinos in the United States: A historical bibliography.* Santa Barbara, CA: ABC-Clio.

Canda, E. R., & Furman, L. D. (1999). *Spiritual diversity in social work practice: The heart of helping.* New York: The Free Press.

Canda, E. R., Nakashima, M., Burgess, V. L., Russel, R., & Barfield, S. T. (2003). *Spiritual diversity and social work: A comprehensive bibliography with annotations.* Alexandria, VA: Council on Social Work Education.

Catholic Charities USA. (2006). *Annual survey, 2005.* Washington, DC: Center for Applied Research in the Apostolate.

Cnaan, R. A. (1999). *The newer deal: Social work and religion in partnership.* New York: Columbia University Press.

Cornett, C. (1992). Toward a more comprehensive personology: Integrating a spiritual perspective into social work practice. *Social Work, 37*(2), 101–102.

Delgado, M. (1977). Puerto Rican spiritualism and the social work profession. *Social Casework, 58*(8), 451–458.

Espinosa, G., Elizondo, V., & Miranda, J. (Eds.). (2003). *Hispanic churches in American public life: Summary of findings.* Notre Dame, IN: Institute for Latino Studies.

Espinosa, G., Elizondo, V., & Miranda, J. (Eds.). (2005). *Latino religions and civic activism in the United States.* Oxford: Oxford University Press.

Flynn, E. E. (2007, June 26). Baptists plan to offer aid to immigrants. *Austin American- Statesman,* A01.

Garcia, E. C. (2001). Parenting in Mexican American families. In N. B. Webb (Ed.), *Culturally diverse parent-child and family relationships: A guide for social workers and other practitioners* (pp. 157–179). New York: Columbia University Press.

George, L. K., Ellison, C. G., & Larson, D. B. (2002). Explaining the relationship between religious involvement and health. *Psychological Inquiry, 13*(3), 190–200.

Giménez, M. E. (1992). U. S. ethnic politics: Implications for Latin Americans. *Latin American Perspectives, 19*(4), 7–17.

Hill, P. C., & Pargament, K. I. (2003). Advances in conceptualization and measurement of religion and spirituality: Implications for physical and mental health research. *American Psychologist, 58*(1), 64–74.

Hill, T. D., Angel, J. L., Ellison, C. G., & Angel, R. J. (2005). Religious attendance and mortality: An 8-year follow-up of older Mexican Americans. *Journal of Gerontology, 60B*(2), S102–S109.

Hirschman, C., Alba, R., & Farley, R. (2000). The meaning and measurement of race in the U.S. census: Glimpses into the future. *Demography, 37*(3), 381–393.

Hunt, L. L. (2000). Religion and secular status among Hispanics in the United States: Catholicism and the varieties of Hispanic Protestantism. *Social Science Quarterly, 81*(1), 344–362.

Johnson, P. (2002). *Secrets, gossip, and gods: The transformation of Brazilian Candomblé.* New York: Oxford University Press.

Koenig, H. G., & Larson, D. B. (2001). Religion and mental health: Evidence for an association. International *Review of Psychiatry, 13,* 67–78.

Krassner, M. (1986). Effective features of therapy from the healer's perspective: A study of curanderismo. *Smith College Studies in Social Work, 56,* 157–183.

León-Portilla, M. (1963). *Aztec thought and culture: A study of the ancient Nahuatl mind.* Jack E. Davis (Trans.). Norman, OK: University of Oklahoma Press.

Levin, J. S., & Markides, K. S. (1986). Religious attendance and subjective health. *Journal for the Scientific Study of Religion, 25*(1), 31–40.

Lopez, R. A. (2005). Use of alternative folk medicine by Mexican American women. *Journal of Immigrant Health, 7*(1), 23–31.

Markides, K. S. (1983). Aging, religiosity, and adjustment: A longitudinal analysis. *Journal of Gerontology, 38*(5), 621–625.

Marsiglia, F. F., Kulis, S., Nieri, T., & Parsai, M. (2005). God fordid! Substance use among religious and nonreligious youth. *American Journal of Orthopsychiatry, 75*(4), 585–598.

Martin, E. P., & Martin, J. M. (2002). *Spirituality and the black helping tradition in social work.* Washington, DC: NASW Press.

Mayers, R. S. (1989). Use of folk medicine by elderly Mexican-American women. *Journal of Drug Issues, 19*(2), 283v295.

McCoy, L. K., Hermos, J. A., Bokhour, B. G., & Frayne, S. M. (2004). Conceptual bases of Christian, faith-based substance abuse rehabilitation programs: Qualitative analysis of staff interviews. *Substance Abuse, 25*(3), 1–11.

McLemore, S. D., & Romo, R. (1985). The origins and development of the Mexican American people. In R. O. de la Garza, F. D. Bean, C. M. Bonjean, R. Romo, & R. Alvarez, (Eds.), *The Mexican American experience: An interdisciplinary anthology* (pp. 3–32). Austin, TX: University of Texas Press.

Moadel, A., Morgan, C., Fatone, A., Grennan,.J., Carter, J., Laruffa, G., Skummy, A., & Dutcher, J. (1999). Seeking meaning and hope: Self-reported spiritual and existential needs among an ethnically-diverse cancer patient population. *Psycho-Oncology, 8*, 378–385.

Murray, B. (2006). *Latino religion in the U. S.: Demographic shifts and trends.* Retrieved April 17, 2007, from http://www.facsnet.org/issues/faith/espinosa.php

National Institute on Drug Abuse. (2003). *Drug use among racial/ethnic minorities revised.* NIH Publication No. 03–3888. Bethesda, MD: U.S. Department of Health and Human Services.

Neff, J. A., Shorkey, C. T., & Windsor, L. C. (2006). Contrasting faith-based and traditional substance abuse treatment programs. *Journal of Substance Abuse Treatment, 30*, 49–61.

Ness, R. C., & Wintrob, R. M. (1981). Folk healing: A description and synthesis. *American Journal of Psychiatry, 138*(11), 1477–1481.

Obeler, S. (1992). The politics of labeling: Latino/a cultural identities of self and others. *Latin American Perspectives, 19*(4), 18–36.

Obeler, S. (1995). *Ethnic labels, Latino lives: Identity and the politics of (re)presentation in the United States.* Minneapolis, MN: University of Minnesota Press.

Paulino, A. (1995). Spiritism, Santería, Brujería, and Voodooism: A comparative view of indigenous healing systems. *Journal of Teaching in Social Work, 12*(1), 105–124.

Prescott, W. H. (1855). *History of the Conquest of Mexico, with a Preliminary View of Ancient Mexican Civilization, and the Life of the Conqueror, Hernando Cortés.* (3 vols.). 3rd ed. Boston, MA: Phillips, Sampson, & Co.

Selee, A. (2006). Mexican immigrants and religious communities. In X. Bada, J. Fox, & A. Selee (Eds.), *Invisible no more: Mexican migrant civic participation in the United States* (pp. 23–26). Washington, DC: Mexico Institute.

Sierra, C. M. (1989). Mexicans in the United States: History, evolution, and transformation. *Latin American Research Review, 24*(2), 218–230.

Skinner, D. G., Correa, V., Skinner, M., & Bailey D. B. (2001). Role of religion in the lives of Latino families of young children with developmental delays. *American Journal of Mental Retardation, 106*(4), 297–313.

Stertzer, C. C. (August, 2001). When God came to the barrio. *Charisma and Christian Life, 27*(1), 47–56.

Tan, S-Y. (1999). Cultural issues in spirit-filled psychotherapy. *Journal of Psychology and Christianity, 18*(2), 164–176.

Urrabazo, R. (2000). Therapeutic sensitivity to the Latino spiritual soul. In M. T. Flore & G. Carey (Eds.), *Family therapy with Hispanics: Toward appreciating diversity* (pp. 208–227). Boston: Allyn & Bacon.

U.S. Census Bureau. (2006). *Facts for features: Hispanic Heritage Month, Sept. 15 –Oct. 15, 2006.* Public Information Office Document CB06-FF.14. Retrieved April 17, 2007, from http://www.census.gov/Press-Release/www/releases/archives/facts_for_features_special_editions/007173.html

Williams, J. (2006, April 10). A Hispanic civil rights movement. *The Washington Post,* A17.

Williams, N. (1990). *The Mexican American family: Tradition and change.* Dix Hills, NY: General Hall, Inc.

Working Group on Human Needs and Faith-based and Community Initiatives. (January, 2002). *Finding common ground: 29 recommendations of the Working Group on Human Needs and Faith-based and Community Initiatives.* Washington, DC: Consensus Council, Inc.

Zacharias, S. (2006). Mexican *curanderismo* as ethnopsychotherapy: A qualitative study on treatment practices, effectiveness, and mechanisms of change. *International Journal of Disability, Development, and Education,* 53(4), 381–400.

CHAPTER SEVEN

Art as a Source of Strength in the Latino Community

George Rivera

Introduction

When one thinks about art and social change, one usually thinks about art therapy as an individual mode of treatment (Kaplan, 2006). Art therapy has been used when working with the homeless (Braun, 1997), and it has been very effective with homeless women (Lighthall, 2006) and children (Baumann, 1995). Art has been used in work with children in therapy (Dillenburger, 1992), with inner-city children (Adams et al., 1996), and with refugee children (Perry, Drumm, & Pittman, 2000). Recently, art has proved effective for those dealing with grief (Finn, 2003) and post-traumatic stress disorder (Chapman, Morabito, Ladakakos, Schreler, & Knudson, 2001). Thus, art therapy brings about change at the individual level.

When an individual needs help for a mental health issue, their illness is often embedded in social relations, which may lead therapists to choose therapy for a couple or for the family as a whole. In other words, therapists look for issues in the collective that have precipitated a mental health problem. I would like to present a model for art that is collective, as a strength in the community.

I propose that to heal an individual, one must first heal a community. One must reach out to the whole community to make members aware that their individual problems are related to social issues. C. Wright Mills called this "the sociological imagination" (Mills, 1959). Art has the capacity to do this.

The artists of the Chicano Movement in the 1970s used murals to make the barrio community aware of its identity, heritage, and culture. It was an effort to communicate directly to the Mexican/Latino community in order to instill a positive image of self. The same was done by Mujeres Muralistas to bring feminist issues into the forefront of Chicano consciousness. In California, a mural for homeless people was created to inform them of where to find services such as health care, food, and so on.

Art has been used in border communities to make others aware of the exploitation of immigrants. David Avalos and others did this in San Diego by putting signage on city buses that addressed this problem (Felshin, 1995). They also used billboards to make the city aware of discrimination against immigrants.

Though art in public places continues to be made, a lot of art by Chicanos/Latinos is now being shown in galleries and museums. This art communicates to a different audience; one must deliberately step into these venues to see the art. Its audience includes decision makers, middle- and upper-class Chicanos and Anglos. Thus, Chicano/Latino art continues to seek social change, if at another social level.

To paraphrase Marcuse, art does not change the world, but it can change people who can change the world (Marcuse, 1978). Art, when it can be understood, serves as a strength in a community; if it can be understood, it can serve as a mechanism for social change. Art created by professional artists has yet to make its mark as a therapeutic device to be used by psychiatrists, psychologists, social workers, and other mental health care providers. This chapter examines how art can be used as a strength in the Chicano (a term herein used interchangeably with Latino or Hispanic) community. It includes a survey of art exhibitions that address HIV/AIDS, death, and the effects of war.

Prelude

When one thinks about art as a strength in the Latino community, one usually conjures up murals. During the civil rights movement of the 1960s and 1970s, Chicanos (Mexican Americans) produced murals throughout the Southwest (Arizona, California, Colorado, New Mexico, and Texas). The Chicano mural movement even extended beyond the Southwest to the Midwest. Much of this artwork was highly influenced by "*Los Tres Grandes*" of Mexico: Diego Rivera, David Alfaro Siqueiros, and Jose Clemente Orozco.

Like the Mexican muralists, Chicanos produced work in public places where barrio (community) members could view it. These artists wanted to convey the strength of Mexican culture by celebrating history and contemporary Chicano life in the United States. This movement was about expressing civil rights, cultural revitalization, and mobilizing the community.

This was a time when the mainstream art world did not include Chicanos in museums and galleries. Chicano artists took to the streets, bypassing the institutional art world. Artists of all stripes, mostly self-trained in art, began to paint exterior murals on building walls and cement beams under bridges. This was not graffiti. It was art that could be understood by people of Mexican descent. It included depictions of Mexican revolutionary heroes like Emiliano Zapata and Pancho Villa, and Aztec and Mayan pyramids. It proudly included images of the indigenous peoples of Mexico. It also included local heroes, like César Chávez and others, in order to connect the present situation with past struggles.

Though the mural movement still exists in the present era, it has waned and lost much of its original influence. Much of this has to do with the difficulties in obtaining funding for public art that addresses contemporary Chicano issues. This is exacerbated by the attitudes of public-funding committee boards, who make decisions about what is and is not appropriate for public consumption.

A new group of Chicano artists is emerging, and it consists of artists who have received master of fine arts degrees from universities. For the most part, these artists are not muralists; they are primarily painters, and though some do not address issues facing Chicanos in the present day, most still have a Chicano consciousness that is revealed in their visual images. Thus, another model of visual art is emerging in the Chicano community.

In this chapter, I will present the nonmural approach to reaching the Latino community. One perspective uses the artwork of children and another solicits Chicano/Latino artists to address social issues. Both of these utilize museum or gallery space, for the most part in Chicano/Latino venues. After the Chicano mural movement took hold during the 1960s and 1970s, Chicano art centers emerged throughout the Southwest. Among the first Chicano art venues to surface was one started by Carlos Santistevan at the Crusade for Justice in Denver, Colorado.

Chicano art centers that arose throughout the Southwest, and in the Midwest, were located in Chicano/Latino neighborhoods so that local Latinos could view exhibitions about Chicano/Mexican/Latino culture and attend workshops for youth and adults. They continue their work as cultural centers of art in the Chicano community to the present day.

Art Journey: A Personal Account of an Art Activist

I am a Chicano artist, curator, and art critic. Since 1994 I have been a professor of art and art history at the University of Colorado and am head of our Integrated Arts area. I have a doctorate in sociology and have taught in the Department of Sociology at my university for twenty-four years. In other words, I am an artist with a sociological perspective. My life-goal in art is to visually present the history, culture, and life of Chicanos (people of Mexican descent born and living in the United States) and more generally to address social problems and social change. I will speak in the first person because what I present is a personal history of my efforts to use art for the purposes of educating and empowering the Chicano/Latino community. I also must admit that I wish to communicate with non-Latinos so that they may understand our experience, and perhaps influence them to help resolve the social issues that confront our communities. I made the transition from sociology to art because my publications and presentations were only communicating with professionals in sociology. I was presenting papers at social science and sociological conferences, and sociologists were reading my publications. Though I was committed to bringing Chicano/Latino perspectives into this discipline, I did not feel that my work was reaching the community. Thus, I began to think about alternate strategies.

While I was in the Department of Sociology, I started writing about the HIV/AIDS epidemic in Mexico and in the United States, as it related to the Chicano/Latino community. I conducted ethnographic studies and intensive interviews to gather information. After publishing my first findings on AIDS awareness of prostitutes in Mexico, I was left with an empty feeling that my work was again not reaching the "right" audience. Prostitutes should have been reading my work, not academics. After all, it was their lives that were at stake. In addition to conducting research, I began to be involved with efforts to address issues of HIV/AIDS in our community. That put me in touch with many agencies and organizations that were trying to reach the Latino community with AIDS education.

During this time, I started working with members of the Mile High Chapter of the American Red Cross. They had received grant monies to educate the Chicano/Latino community and solicited my help. They asked me to apply for a grant utilizing whatever ideas I had about what would be the best way to communicate an AIDS awareness message to our community.

As a sociologist, I studied and wrote exclusively about Chicanos/Latinos, and I used my intuitive and scholarly knowledge about my culture to design the proposal. I concluded that the best way to communicate information about HIV/AIDS to our community was through our children. I knew how important the family was in our culture and the high value that we placed on children. However, I did not want to interview just any children. I wanted to interview only Chicano/Latino children who knew something about HIV/AIDS.

I put together a proposal to interview children in the Denver, Colorado, area who had a family member with HIV or one who had died from AIDS. In addition, I would collect artwork by these children, who I instructed to "show me what is inside your head when you think about AIDS." Furthermore, these interviews and accompanying artwork would be published as a book by the Red Cross and would be made available to schools, organizations, and community members. Needless to say, the grant was funded.

Art Exhibitions

HIV/AIDS: IMAGES OF HISPANIC YOUTH

The American Red Cross published the book *HIV/AIDS: Images of Hispanic Youth* in 1990 (Rivera, 1990). The book contained transcripts of forty-four interviews with children ages six to seventeen. It included sixteen drawings.

Among the artwork was a piece by a girl, age ten, whose father had died from AIDS and whose mother was HIV-positive (Rivera, 1990, p. 42). In this artwork (see Figure 1) we are reminded of the importance of the family, an institution that is highly valued in Chicano/Latino culture. It shows a heart (a symbol of love) broken in half with the word "AIDS" written in throughout the break. The heart is divided into two parts separating the child from her mother and father. The message on the right of the heart is her advice to others to prevent AIDS from literally breaking up their families. Notice that the word "family" is underlined.

A boy, age thirteen, whose uncle died from AIDS, made an image of his uncle before and after AIDS (Rivera, 1990, p. 123). It showed his uncle in a wheelchair after AIDS destroyed his health (see Figure 2). At the top of this drawing, we encounter a message about what AIDS does to one's health. The image is divided into two parts: one-half contains the essence of the drawing and the other half, again, advice for others. On the left side we see a health image of his uncle lifting weights (notice his size). An abrupt break is depicted by a lightning bolt and a man in a wheelchair with the word "AIDS" above him. Note that the man in the wheelchair is crying and that his body is very small and withered, the "wasting" that accompanies the last stages of AIDS. On the right side of the work one finds written text. The top text emphasizes the progression of AIDS and the child's perception that it cannot be stopped once (with "once" underlined) one is infected. This drawing

FIGURE 1 *Mom + Dad, AIDS, Me*

was done before drug "cocktails" and inhibitor drugs were found to be effective against the effects of AIDS. The bottom text stresses that a small word (AIDS) can fool us into complacency.

In Figure 3, a boy, age ten, whose uncle died from AIDS created a drawing that addressed the use of syringes in transmitting AIDS through sharing needles (Rivera, 1990, p. 87). This image was created by a child who lived in an impoverished area known as a haven for injecting heroin. It is a simple image with a strong visual statement. The vial contains the word "AIDS" with lines going through it to indicate "NO." The needle is dripping blood, the medium by which AIDS is transmitted when sharing needles.

Art created by Hispanic children who had directly seen the effects of HIV/AIDS could help both children and adults learn about this disease. For example, people could learn that they should protect themselves. These children did not mince words in their interviews concerning how AIDS is transmitted. A sixteen-year-old girl, whose mother was HIV-positive, stated that one can get AIDS "through sharing needles or having sexual [sic]" (Rivera, 1990, p. 139). Another girl, age eight, whose cousin was living with AIDS, said that you can get AIDS by "drugs with a needle or had a blood transfusions with blood that had AIDS in it, or having sex with someone who had AIDS" (Rivera, 1990, p. 27).

FIGURE 2   *AIDS Is a Health Destruction*

FIGURE 3   *AIDS*

Other children made direct reference to the transmission of HIV through homosexual contact. For example, a girl, age sixteen, whose distant cousin had died from AIDS, said, "I guess mostly gay people get it. It's not all of them though" (Rivera, 1990, p. 142). Another young adult, a girl, age seventeen, said: ". . . there are people that go every six months just to make sure, and they do needles, even bi[sexuals], how can I say, gay, gay, gay people" (Rivera, 1990, p. 159). Views of children are difficult to ignore. One finds it difficult to distance oneself from their message that calls for empathy, not judgment.

This book, with accompanying artwork, gained much attention during a time that HIV/AIDS information to the Hispanic community was difficult to convey. Our first venue for the exhibition was the Chicano Humanities and Arts Council Gallery, a Chicano (Mexican American) art gallery in Denver, Colorado. It then traveled to other venues, including non-Hispanics ones.

CHICANO/LATINO ART: IMAGES IN THE AGE OF AIDS

After using art to convey the thoughts of children, I started another art project that resulted in the publication of a catalog entitled *Chicano/ Latino Art: Images in the Age of AIDS* (Rivera & Lucero, 1992). Sixteen Chicano/Latino artists residing in Colorado participated in this exhibition.

Since most of the artists knew very little about AIDS and had never had contact with any Latino who had been infected, I asked them to attend a workshop presented by the Colorado Latino AIDS Community Network. At this meeting, the artists heard presentations by Latino men who were infected through sex with men, a Latina woman infected through intravenous drug use, and a Chicana woman who had lost two brothers to AIDS. The purpose of this encounter was to provide Chicano/Latino artists with a realistic basis for their artwork.

The Reverend Marshall Gourley, pastor of Our Lady of Guadalupe Church in Denver, Colorado, wrote the introduction to the catalog. He wrote, in part, "AIDS has, for so many, filled life's journey with much agony and sorrow. Religion, being such an integrated part of life in our community, is called upon to offer her heart, hope and images in response. That is the reason that these artists have chosen to create these offerings" (Rivera, 1992, p. 3).

Tony Ortega created a piece entitled *Una Oracion a Guadalupe* (see Figure 4). He made the following comments on his artwork for this exhibition: "My work explores the interactions of Chicano/Mexican environments. As I have looked at my own cultural life, I have become more aware of contemporary surroundings and of current events such as the impact of AIDS in my community.

FIGURE 4   *Una Oracion a Guadalupe*

"The use of prayer, or *oracion*, to the Virgin for protection is the theme represented in *Una Oracion a Guadalupe*; condoms appear in the aura around her. 'My Virgin—give me the sweet miracle, always with protection in nights of Mexican passion plays,' reads the poem by George Rivera, Jr., that I have quoted. I feel it is important to present an image of empowering the woman in these decisions about love, and life and death" (Rivera, 1992, p. 13).

Ortega's art depicts two lovers embracing, with the center of the piece occupied by an image of *La Virgen de Guadalupe* (Our Lady of Guadalupe), a religious icon highly regarded among Chicanos and Latinos. *La Virgen* is known as the patron saint of the Americas and is known worldwide as an apparition of the Virgin Mary that appeared to Juan Diego, an Aztec, on a hill in Tepeyac in Mexico City in 1531. The rays of the sun that always surround her have been replaced by condoms. At the bottom of the work is a payer (*oracion*) written by George Rivera petitioning the Virgin Mary to protect us from AIDS.

Sylvia Montero, another artist, created a piece entitled *Viva el Condon* (see Figure 5). She wrote the following to accompany her artwork:

> "Viva el Condon"—"Long live the condom," proclaims my
> work in this exhibit. The myth of the poor and uneducated

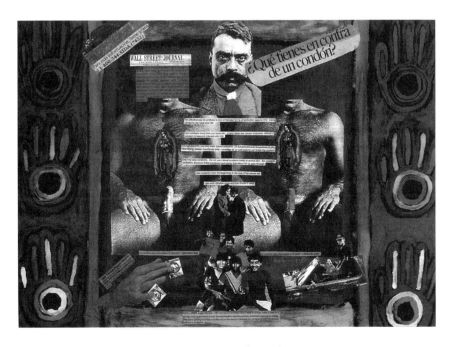

FIGURE 5   *Viva el Condon*

as the only ones who don't use condoms is completely inaccurate, as discussions among my friends and colleagues have
revealed. But the condom has to become a part of our way
of life—it has to become part of common sense that if you
don't use a condom, you might die. "What do you have
against a condom?" my work asks. There needs to be a "condom revolution" among Chicana and Latina women—they
have to make a choice of wanting to live, and not being afraid
to say "No!" instead of wanting to please the male. At the
same time, men have to feel more sensitive—not just to their
mates, but to themselves, for their own lives. Take a moment
to think use a condom to live. (Rivera, 1992, 12)

Montero's artwork addresses a topic that was once highly taboo
among Catholics. However, she speaks to a reality that must be confronted in the quest to prevent AIDS—the use of condoms. In the top
middle of her work is an image of Emiliano Zapata, a Mexican revolutionary hero very popular among Mexicanos and Chicanos in the
United States. Zapata has a stern, serious look on his face and a caption
in Spanish coming from him that states: "What do you have against
the use of a condom?" Montero has appropriated a style often used in
advertising that uses icons to "sell" merchandize.

In the middle of the piece, on the chests of the two naked men, is an
image of Our Lady of Guadalupe. Montero is associating this religious
icon, Mexico's most famous cultural image, with the message of condom use. Thus, religion, another institution important to Chicano/Lat-
ino culture, is evident here. Both of the men have an erect penis
protected by a condom. Note that *La Virgen* is located directly above
each erect penis, as if appearing once again. The bottom part of the
work contains images of youth posing in a group and a couple in a
convertible car. To the left of these images is a hand offering condoms.
On the left and right sides of her artwork are images of hands that represent symbols of control and allude to the hand *milagro* use in offerings
in the Catholic Church. The remainder of the work contains text from
newspaper articles about AIDS, including the AIDS hotline phone number to call for more information.

Patty Ortiz made a piece entitled *If You See Me in the Street . . .* (See
Figure 6). She said about it:

One of the things I love about my culture is our sense of
"familia." When one person in my family hurts, we all hurt.
Yet, many people are sick and dying and we are closing our
eyes. In doing the pieces for this show, I looked at how we
are all still in a state of tremendous avoidance and denial

FIGURE 6   *If You See Me in the Street . . .*

about AIDS and, through this avoidance, we are forcing the people who have this disease to hide and be alienated. (Rivera, 1992, p. 14)

Ortiz's artwork addresses the feeling of isolation and shame created in the minds of those infected with HIV/AIDS. This is a direct response to the discrimination that they experience once it is known that they have the disease. At the bottom of the piece are three faces covered by blindfolds, protecting their identities. Moreover, this work addresses the public's denial of AIDS in our society by making the disease and those who have it invisible.

LATINOS: YOUTH LIVING WITH HIV/AIDS IN THE FAMILY

After publishing *HIV/AIDS: Images in the Age of AIDS* and having toured the *Chicano/Latino Art: Images in the Age of AIDS* exhibition, another Latino health organization contacted me. The Illinois Prevention Resource Center in Chicago, Illinois, asked me to write a book similar to my *HIV/AIDS: Images in the Age of AIDS*, but with Latino children in Chicago who were either living with HIV/AIDS themselves because they had been infected through blood transfusions, or who had a relative who was HIV-positive or a relative who had died from AIDS as a result of intravenous drug use.

Thus, another book of interviews and art was published, entitled *Latinos: Youth Living with HIV/AIDS in the Family* (Rivera, 1993). It included thirty-one interviews and thirty-two pieces of artwork. Most of the children in this book were Puerto Ricans, and others were Guatemalans, Mexicans from Mexico, and children of mixed ethnicity (Mexican American, Italian, Mexican Polish).

The art included in this project was exhibited at the Mexican Fine Arts Center Museum, Chicago, Illinois (1992). Other exhibitions in Illinois followed, all sponsored by the Illinois Prevention Resource Center.

In Figure 7, a child (a Puerto Rican boy, age five) whose mother was HIV-positive drew a picture that was figurative yet highly abstract of a person lying down (and/or rising) that he entitled *Die in the Winter and Come Back to Life in the Spring* (Rivera, 1993, p. 2). The bottom part of this drawing contains a dark mass of lines, perhaps evidencing the chaos that AIDS brings to a family. Behind the image of the mother are images of a disintegrating body that is also rising until it becomes a faint mass at the top left. The title implies change and transformation.

In Figure 8, another child (a Guatemalan girl, age nine) drew a picture of a hospital visit to her adopted little sister who was HIV-positive. The image depicts an effort to cheer up her sister by blowing up balloons (Rivera, 1993, p. 16). All too often, we forget that there are

FIGURE 7   *Die in the Winter and Come Back to Life in the Spring*

children who are born HIV-positive, having contracted AIDS in the womb of an infected mother. In this case, the child has been abandoned by her mother and adopted by a compassionate family.

The significance of religion is evident in the artwork of a Hispanic boy, age fourteen, whose father had died from AIDS, and whose mother and little brother were HIV-positive (see Figure 9). The piece is entitled

FIGURE 8   *My Sister and I*

You're in the Lord's Hands (Rivera, 1993, p. 64). Again we see the importance of religion.

In Figure 10, a Puerto Rican boy, age seventeen, whose uncle died
from AIDS, drew a picture of various weeping faces with the title *AIDS
Does Not Care if You Are Black, White, 17 or 40. AIDS Does Not Discriminate* (Rivera, 1993, p. 102). All of the faces are different shades of black
to indicate that people of all races can contract AIDS. The message is
clearly stated: AIDS does not discriminate. On the right side of the piece
is a plea: "Help Find the Cure Please!"

In Figure 11, the importance of the family in Latino culture is depicted
by a Puerto Rican/Mexican boy, age sixteen, who was HIV-positive, as
were his two brothers. Here we see a faint image of a family all holding
hands and facing their predicament together (Rivera, 1993, p. 88).

The children in this project were either born HIV-positive, having
been infected before birth from an HIV-positive mother, or they were
hemophiliacs who had been infected through blood transfusions.
Examples of comments made by these children or their siblings follows.

A Mexican girl, age six, whose mother died from AIDS and whose
little sister was HIV-positive, found out about her sister's illness when
". . . she was sick, and then my mother had her as a little baby. And

FIGURE 9   *You're in the Lord's Hands*

then when she was a little baby, she grew up. And my mother, she died" (Rivera, 1993, p. 4).

One Puerto Rican/Mexican boy (age sixteen), a hemophiliac who was HIV-positive, recounted the following upon learning about his illness:

"In the hospital, they told me, me and my brothers, that we were infected with HIV. Well, they haven't told me anything.

FIGURE 10   *AIDS Does Not Care if You Are Black,*
White, 17 or 40. AIDS Does Not Discriminate

They wanted to talk to my parents to talk to them about everything. And then they decided to tell me. They called me in later on to the room where they were talking. And then they told me that I caught it because of the factor I get in the blood product." (Rivera, 1993, p. 89)

Another boy, age thirteen, whose mother and little sister were HIV-positive, said that his mom told him the following about his sister: ". . . she's going to live until a certain age, and she's gonna be all right. But she ain't gonna be healthy. My mom said it was a disease—HIV. Bad" (Rivera, 1993, p. 54).

There also were children, part of families with an infected family member, who made the following observations:

(Mexican boy, age sixteen, whose uncle was living with AIDS)

"I guess most of the time that he stayed here, he just comes around and stays for a while, does his stuff here—drugs. Then after a while, he just leaves. Instead of helping the family, he gets in a lot of trouble" (Rivera, 1993, p. 85).

FIGURE 11   *The Cure for AIDS Is Love and Support from Your Family!*

(Mexican girl, age fourteen, whose uncle died from AIDS, and whose aunt and cousin were HIV–positive)

"I felt like he was in the fault too for using needles with my other aunt, but my other aunt doesn't have AIDS. And I was pretty shocked because I felt that even though he had AIDS, that it was his fault too, you know. And it was cause he should know better not to be doing drugs and all that" (Rivera, 1993, p. 69).

NOCHE DE MUERTOS: CHICANO JOURNEY INTO A MICHOACAN NIGHT

Not only can art be used as a strength in the Latino community to address health issues, but it also can help generate dialogue on other societal issues that deserve attention. For example, art can help us deal with death. In 1993, I decided that I needed to organize an exhibition for the Days of the Dead (November 1 and 2). However, I wanted the Chicano artists to create artwork based on experiential knowledge of death rather than on their ideas about the Days of the Dead. Thus, I took a group of artists to Tzintzuntzan, Michoacan, to observe all-night vigils in the local cemetery, where the indigenous population decorates graves and stays throughout the night to await the return of their dead. Afterward, we returned to Colorado to create artwork based on this experience.

The resulting exhibition was entitled *Noche de Muertos: Chicano Journey into a Michoacan Night* (Rivera, 1993). The exhibition traveled to three venues: CU Art Galleries, Boulder, Colorado (1993); Museo de las Americas, Denver, Colorado (1993); and Valle del Sol Community Center, Capulin, Colorado (1995). It consisted of twenty-one works by seven artists and included photographs, paintings, and installations. I will focus here on the altars that were created for the exhibition.

Day of the Dead altars, as evident in our examples, usually include flowers, objects dear to the deceased, food and drink, incense, candles, and photographs. The flowers (usually marigolds) and incense are for the returning souls to smell in order to find their way back. The food and drink are so that they can eat and drink the spirit of these items because it is believed that they will be hungry and thirsty upon their return. Objects dear to the deceased are there for recognition of their earthly selves and include photographs so that they can recognize their human faces.

An altar was created by Aileen Lucero and Sylvia Montero entitled *Altar Para Nuestras Abuelas/Altar For Our Grandmothers: Carlota A. Lucero, Guadalupe Molina, y Eulalia V. Pulido* (see Figure 12). This altar was dedicated to grandmothers who had sacrificed their lives so that generations of Mexicanas would not perish (Rivera, 1993, p. 24).

Tony Ortega and myself created another altar in a collaborative effort. It was entitled *Solis Present/Presente* (see Figure 13). It was dedicated to Raul "Rudy" Solis, my brother, who died on July 13, 1990, of cancer. He worked for the U.S. Post Office in Houston, Texas. All of the photographs surrounding the altar are of his mother, wife, and children. The altar is a gift (present) to him and an affirmation of his spiritual presence in the lives of those who loved him (Rivera, 1993, p. 27).

Altars are constructions of memory. When grief and loss overcome us, we need to remember what our loved ones meant to us. We remember them, and in remembering them they are once again present for us. This is the power of memory. In this way, altars serve as therapy in the grieving process.

NEW MILLENNIAL GUERNICA: ANTIWAR ART BY CHICANOS AND LATINOS

Since art also has the function of educating and informing others, I more recently turned my attention to addressing issues that comment on our involvement in Afghanistan and Iraq. There is growing dissent throughout the United States against a war that is daily taking the lives of our sons and daughters.

In 2004, I curated an exhibition entitled *New Millennial Guernica: Antiwar Art by Chicanos and Latinos*. It included fourteen artists who were primarily Chicanos, but also included artists living in the United

FIGURE 12   *Altar Para Nuestras Abuelas: Carlota A. Lucero,*
Guadalupe Molina, y Eulalia V. Pulido

States who had been born in Argentina, Brazil, and Colombia, as well as
one artist of Cuban descent. This exhibition was shown at the Chicano
Humanities and Arts Council Gallery in Denver, Colorado.

The army that is fighting this war is primarily composed of volun-
teers, and many of these soldiers are returning home with post-traumatic stress disorder. I reasoned that addressing the effects of war in
general, and the Iraq War in particular, would facilitate a dialogue that
would enable us (as Chicanos/Latinos) to talk about what war does to

FIGURE 13   *Solis Present/Presente*

individuals. Moreover, I felt a responsibility to express views against the war to empower young people to think before they enlisted.

Figure 14, Quintin Gonzalez's artwork *The Berserkers Pact* (Rivera, 2004, p. 7), depicts two individuals being shaken violently. This is how head injuries, which many returning soldiers have experienced, occur. In order to understand what is happening to those who return with such injuries, we need to understand the impact of improvised explosive devices, whereby a person is killed or injured and their brain is shaken violently against their skull.

FIGURE 14   *The Berserkers Pact*

Upon returning home, soldiers with brain injuries experience lapses in memory and an inability to concentrate, or focus. Family members find that they are not the same as when they left. An image such as Gonzalez's allows us to talk about how brain injuries occur and their effects on behavior.

Figure 15 shows a work by Eugene Stewart-Huidobro entitled *Moral Chaos #6* (Rivera, 2004, p. 13). It addresses what occurred at the Abu Ghraib Prison where Iraqi soldiers were tortured and abused. Stewart-Huidobro's art informs us of the moral issues inherent in doing this to other human beings. Many of the soldiers returning with post-traumatic stress disorder are deeply troubled by what they did or witnessed during interrogations.

A favorable review of the exhibition in *La Voz Nueva*, one of Denver's main Hispanic newspapers, concluded with the following statement:

> The opening last week was well attended, provoking a great deal of sincere discussion. In what promises to be a devisive election year with widely disparate views on the war and immigration, open forums, open dialogue and open

FIGURE 15   *Moral Chaos #6*

minds are what's sorely needed. This exhibit at CHAC is a small, but perhaps invaluable, beginning. (Bain, 2006, p. 13)

Another review in the *Denver Post* noted:

> The Chicano Humanities and Arts Council is among the first area art institutions of any kind to address head-on the continuing Iraq war. . . . In today's charged sociopolitical climate, where taking an antiwar position is sometimes equated with being unpatriotic or even anti-American, such a presentation is a daring undertaking. (MacMillan, 2006, p. 5FF)

Conclusion

One way to define art could easily be as cultural work. Art can clarify values, allow us to probe meaning in our lives, and metaphorically lift us beyond our present situation. Art has power. The Chicano/Latino artists presented here are all cultural workers. They are artists who have chosen to assert that art is for society's sake, not just art's sake. To them, art is more than decorative.

We have reviewed art by children who have been impacted by HIV/ AIDS either directly (themselves) or indirectly (a family member). We also examined an exhibition wherein professional artists addressed the HIV/AIDS epidemic through their art. Such exhibitions served to educate the Chicano/Latino community, as well as the general public and schoolchildren. In addition, we reviewed exhibitions by professional artists that addressed death and grief, as well as the impact of war.

All of these presentations were shown in Chicano community art centers, where community members living in the area attend exhibitions, and where local schools bring students as well. Hopefully, what follows is an open discussion in the community (and homes) about the issues raised.

Not only do individuals need to heal, but whole communities do as well. We provided a model for using local artists to address social issues in exhibitions located where the people live, not on gallery row. Though we focused our attention on the arts as a strength in the Chicano/Latino community specifically, such strategies can be used in all communities. In our next chapter, we explore other areas that need whole-community health and wellness strategies: mental health and health care.

References

Adams, K., Cole, P., Cole, W., Faltermayer, C., Labi, N., Lofaro, L., Mcwhirter, W., Rubin, J., and Waller, D. (1996, August 26). Local heroes. *TIME Magazine*, 148(10), 11.

Bain, D. (2006, January 11). War—what is it good for? *La Voz Nueva* (Denver, Colorado), 1:13.

Baumann, S. L. (1995). Two views of homeless children's art: Psychoanalysis and Parse's human becoming theory. *Nursing Science Quarterly, 8*(2), 65–70.

Braun, L. N. (1997). In from the cold: Art therapy with homeless men. *Journal of the American Art Therapy Association, 14*(2), 118–122.

Chapman, L., Morabito, D., Ladakakos, C., Schreler, H., & Knudson, M. (2001). The effectiveness of art therapy interventions in reducing post traumatic stress disorder (PTSD) symptoms in pediatric trauma patients. *Art Therapy Journal, 18*(2), 100–108.

Dillenburger, K. (1992). Communicating with children: The use of art in social work. *Practice, 6*(2), 126–134.

Felshin, Nina (Ed.). *But Is It Art?* Seattle, WA: Bay Press, 1995.

Finn, C. (2003). Helping students cope with loss: Incorporating art into group counseling. *The Journal for Specialists in Group Work, 28*, 155–165.

Kaplan, Frances (Ed.). (2006). *Art therapy and social action*. London: Jessica Kingsley Publishers.

Lighthall, W. D. (2006). Social work project combines art and research coming together photos on display through Nov. 29. Web site: http://www.news.utoronto.ca/bin6/06114-2741.asp

MacMillan, K. (2006 January 20). "Antiwar art" and the beauty of books, *The Denver Post*, 5FF; 11FF.

Marcuse, Herbert. *The Aesthetic Dimension.* Boston: Beacon Press, 1978.

Mills, C. Wright. *The Sociological Imagination.* New York: Oxford University Press, 1959.

Perry, S., Drumm, R., & Pittman, S. (2000). Three social workers and an NGO. *Reflections*, 6(2), 53–57.

Rivera, G. (1990). *HIV/AIDS: Images of Hispanic youth.* Washington, DC: American Red Cross.

Rivera, G. (1993). *Latinos: Youth living with HIV/AIDS in the family.* Chicago: Illinois Prevention Resource Center.

Rivera, G. (1993). *Noche de muertos: Chicano journey into a Michoacan night.* Boulder, CO: CU Art Galleries.

Rivera, G. (2006). *New millennial Guernica: Antiwar art by Chicanos and Latinos.* Boulder, CO: ARTNAUTS Publications.

Rivera, G., & Lucero, A. F. (1992). *Chicano/Latino art: Images in the age of AIDS.* Boulder, CO: CU Art Galleries.

CHAPTER EIGHT

Barriers to Health Care Utilization among Latinos in the United States

Recommendations for Social Workers

Marcia Shobe
Maren J. Coffman

Introduction

Health disparities among Latinos have become an important concern in the United States over the past two decades, particularly given the rapid influx of Latino immigrants. In general, Latinos have more markers of disadvantage than non-Hispanic whites in terms of lower incomes, language barriers, undocumented status, health illiteracy, and limited education. These indicators tend to have long-term and costly negative effects on health and well-being (James, Thomas, Lillie-Blanton, & Garfield, 2007).

This chapter will supplement the text by describing health disparities experienced by Latinos in the United States and by suggesting how social workers and other health professionals can respond to health care access and treatment disparities. We begin by describing important barriers to health care access and treatment for Latinos, including issues related to health insurance, language, acculturation, legal status, and what has been termed the "Latino health paradox." We include a discussion of health-related social policies and their impact on health care access and utilization for Latinos. We also incorporate a case study of the Ramirez family to provide an example of health-related barriers experienced by low-income Latino immigrants. Finally, we provide several suggestions as to how social work practitioners can address health disparities among Latinos in the United States. This chapter concludes with several study questions designed to assist the social work practitioner consider the many ways in which social work practice and policy are correlated and to explore ways to address health care barriers that currently exist.

Barriers to Health Care Access and Treatment

This section provides an overview of key barriers to health care access and treatment for low-income Latinos in the United States. A discussion of health disparities cannot take place without including key social policies that impact Latinos and society as a whole. For example, despite the billions of dollars that employed Latino immigrants contribute to the tax rolls, Social Security and Medicare systems, welfare reform, and immigration and tax policies have banned many Latinos from accessing health care resources for prevention and treatment.

LEGAL STATUS

It is estimated that 11 million people, most of them Latinos, currently live in the United States without legal authorization (Passel, 2005). While most Latino immigrants come to the United States for employment purposes (Camarota, 2004), undocumented Latinos living in the United States often fear deportation and may resist any situation, including treating a serious illness, that draws attention to them. In addition, undocumented immigrants who work in the United States often contribute to the tax rolls, health care, and Social Security systems without reaping the benefits. One of the reasons for this is related to social policy legislation that was passed more than twenty years ago. The Immigration Reform and Control Act of 1986 penalizes employers who hire undocumented workers. As a result, an unwritten "don't ask, don't tell" policy was adopted, whereby undocumented immigrants purchase counterfeit Social Security numbers to demonstrate citizenship and employers feign ignorance of this fact (Porter, 2005). This resulted in an estimated 50 percent of all undocumented employed immigrants receiving earnings paid through the traditional payroll system. As a result, in 2002 undocumented workers allocated approximately $4,000 each in federal taxes per year (Camarota, 2004).

In addition, while they do not benefit from Medicare or Social Security, many undocumented immigrants pay into this system. In fact, undocumented workers contribute as much as $7 billion per year in

Social Security and $1.5 billion in Medicare revenue through payroll taxes (Mohanty et al., 2005; Porter, 2005). Despite their contributions, undocumented Latinos who do not seek professional health care services for fear of deportation (Berk & Schur, 2001) often miss out on preventive health care (Doty & Holmgren, 2006), and discount symptoms until emergency care is inevitable.

CULTURAL TRADITIONS

Owing to a combination of cultural preferences and limited access to formal health services in the United States, many Latinos utilize folk medicine as a part of their healing traditions. Faith healers have many titles depending on the Latino subgroup to which they belong and may include *curanderos* for Mexican Americans, *santeros* for Cuban populations, or *espiritista* for Puerto Rican populations. Folk healers are consulted to provide medical advice and to perform healing. Most alternative healing practices are used in conjunction with professional health services and are not disclosed to the medical provider (Foster, Phillips, Hamel & Eisenburg, 2000). Alternative health practices are most prevalent among less-educated, foreign-born Latinos (Loera, Black, Markides, Espino, & Goodwin, 2001). Though some researchers have examined alternative-care practices, there is little agreement on its prevalence. However, one study found that 56 percent of elderly Latinos reported the use of herbal supplements to treat gastrointestinal and other ailments, 25 percent reported the use of home remedies, and 8 percent reported the use of *curanderos* or other faith healers (Najm, Reinsch, Hoehler, & Tobis, 2003). It is important that social workers not blame Latinos themselves for this lack of communication. Mistrust of health care and social service providers runs deep within many minority populations, and often is created by a lack of culturally competent practices.

LANGUAGE BARRIERS

Estimates suggest that in 2005, approximately 74 percent of Latinos in the United States were Spanish-speaking (Roslow Research Group, 2005). The lack of English proficiency among patients and limited Spanish-language proficiency among health care providers negatively affects health care access and treatment. For example, in a two-year retrospective study among Spanish- and Portuguese-speaking patients, researchers found that the primary barrier between health care providers and patients involved communication (Jacobs et al., 2001). Recent studies indicate that health care access and treatment quality decreased for Spanish-speaking patients; many patients indicated that they often had to wait in long lines and felt that medical providers did not listen to them or provide appropriate services (Weech-Maldonado et al., 2003; Woloshin, Bickell, Schwartz, Gany, & Welch, 1995). Researchers also found that professional interpreter services increased the delivery of health care services among limited-proficiency patients (Jacobs et al., 2001).

Even when patients receive medical care, compliance remains an issue. One reason for this resistance is related to *health literacy*. In fact, recent reports indicate that more than 90 million Americans have difficulty reading and understanding health-related information (Nielson-Bohlman, Panzer, & Kindig, 2005). Health-literacy skills include reading, writing, and understanding oral communications with health care providers (Schillinger, Bindman, Wang, Stewart, & Piette, 2004). Low health literacy may contribute to poor health care access and outcomes; in fact, health literacy has been cited as an important indicator of health status, hospitalization rates (Paasche-Orlow, Parker, Gazmararian, Nielson-Bowman, & Rudd, 2005), and comprehension of chronic illnesses including diabetes (Gazmararian, Williams, Peel, & Baker, 2003).

Health literacy is problematic for populations whose native language is not English. For example, 62 percent of Latinos tested in Spanish scored either low or marginal on health-literacy instruments (Paasche-Orlow et al., 2005). Health literacy is also related to education levels; recent findings indicate that only 52 percent of Latino adults have completed high school compared to 85 percent of non-Hispanic whites (Bauman & Graf, 2003).

Acculturation

Acculturation is the "process of culture learning and behavioral adaptation" (Marin & Marin, 1991, p. 36) that occurs as individuals are exposed to a new culture. Though individuals often retain many traditional values and practices, as acculturation occurs, adoption of the values, behaviors, and norms of the predominate group occur. Low acculturation levels in Latinos have been linked to decreased participation in preventive health care activities such as cancer screenings (Hulme et al., 2003). According to research, poorly acculturated women are the least likely to have had a mammogram, clinical breast exam, or Pap exam. In addition, although Latina women have a lower incidence of breast cancer than other women, they are more likely to be diagnosed at a later stage, thereby resulting in a poorer long-term prognosis (O'Malley, Kerner, Johnson, & Mandelblatt, 1999; Peragallo, Fox, & Alba, 2000).

Low acculturation also influences dietary practices and often results in overweight and obese states. Approximately 75 percent of Mexican adults living in the United States are overweight, and 40 percent of Mexican American women are obese (Ogden et al., 2006). Sundquist and Winkleby (2000) found that increased abdominal obesity was found in women with lower levels of acculturation, and women whose primary language is Spanish. As Latino immigrants acculturate to the United States and adopt American dietary food customs, their nutritional risks grow. For example, once in America, Latinos begin to consume fast food, resulting in diets higher in fat and lower in fruits and vegetables (Neuhouser, Thompson, Coronado, & Solomon, 2004). The cost, quality, and availability of familiar fresh fruits and vegetables may be a factor in the decreased nutritional choices (Cason, Nieto-Montenegro, & Chavez-Martinez, 2006). Acculturation to U.S. dietary ways also reverses the positive health status that many Latino immigrants have when they arrive.

Health Care Disparities

Health care disparities in the United States continue to be problematic. While appropriate health care is vital to individual well-being, the level of health care as a right to *all* individuals remains an issue of debate (Raiz, 2006). In terms of outcomes, disadvantaged racial and ethnic groups tend to have higher mortality rates, are less likely to have health insurance, and access fewer formal health care services than non-Hispanic whites (Kaplan et al., 2006). Disparities in health care among Latinos in particular continue to be a problem, particularly as they relate to health care access, risk factors, and morbidity (Martinez & Carter-Pokras, 2006). In fact, in a 2002 National Survey of Latinos, researchers note that 15 percent of those surveyed reported that a family member went without needed medical care because of an inability to pay for services, and 22 percent described difficulty paying medical bills (Kaiser Family Foundation, 2004). A more recent survey found that in 2004 approximately 31 percent of adult Latinos had no usual source of health care, and 27 percent had not had a physical exam in the past year (James et al., 2007).

Health care systems in some parts of Latin America are at times more accessible to their citizens; in fact, many countries have a socialized system that provides access to all citizens. For example, in the Latin American Caribbean, the island of Cuba has impressed and perplexed other developed countries, including the United States, throughout the years owing to its scarce economic resources but high health outcomes

(Spiegel & Yassi, 2004). Cuba boasts inclusive and extraordinary disease-prevention efforts, comprehensive primary care services, and high physician-to-patient ratios (Spiegel & Yassi, 2004). In addition, Cuba has extremely low infant mortality rates and high immunization and life span rates (Nasmith, 2006).

While important concerns regarding prescription costs, doctor-patient relations, long waits, and personal care remain among many patients surveyed, a recent study suggests that community health centers and Social Security health clinics in urban and rural Costa Rica and Panama are viewed positively by citizens for their physical and social accessibility and for their community focus (Leon, 2003). However, in poorer countries such as El Salvador, Guatemala, Honduras, and Nicaragua, problems with health care service access and treatment continue to have negative effects on the health and well-being of adults and children (World Bank, 2007a).

Turning to other areas of Latin America, while several smaller countries including Ecuador and Colombia continue to experience problems with health care access and quality, Brazil and, more recently, Mexico have proved to be frontrunners in making health care improvements. This is particularly true among the traditionally underserved in these countries. Brazil's Unified Health System was initiated in the 1988 Constitution and has made important and consistent strides in terms of free and equitable access to health care treatment among the poor through increased government funding and a focus on primary care (World Bank, 2007b). Some of the positive changes over the past fourteen years include a 46 percent decrease in infant mortality, an increase in adult life expectancy, and a leveling off of new HIV/AIDS cases. Many of these improvements are due to increased monitoring, preventive measures, and education initiatives. Important regulatory challenges remain, however, particularly given the need for increased funding, administrative oversight, and accountability measures (World Bank, 2007b).

While Mexico previously outperformed other countries in terms of child immunizations (95 percent success rate), it has historically functioned poorly in other areas of health care access and quality, particularly for its low-income citizens (Barraza-Lloréns, Bertozzi, González-Pier, & Gutiérrez, 2002; Frenk, 2006). However, recent health care reform in Mexico has proved to be a model for other countries struggling with health disparities. In 2004, Mexico instituted the Seguro Popular (Popular Health Insurance); this health-reform policy was designed to gradually expand its membership over seven years so that as many as 50 million low-income Mexican residents are included in its social insurance program (Fineberg, 2006; Frenk, 2006). Initial outcomes suggest that the legislation is successful not only in terms of health care access and quality for traditionally underserved Mexicans but also for

the government's commitment to health promotion and disease prevention through its Community Health Services Fund (Frenk, 2006).

CURRENT HEALTH CARE PRACTICES

It is important to provide an overview of current health care practices
among Latinos. Upon arrival to the United States, Latino immigrants
often have a limited understanding of how to access health care services, particularly given the complexities of the U.S. health care system.
As a result of this and other barriers, Latinos living in the United States
are more likely than non-Hispanic whites to have low health care utilization rates and higher rates of mortality and morbidity. Because of
persistent barriers, including a lack of affordable health care services,
Latinos tend to underutilize preventive health care and only use formal
services as a last resort (Carillo, Treviño, Betancourt, & Coustasse, 2001).
Patterns of health care use that are prevalent among Latinos include
the lack of primary care services, overuse of emergency departments,
and alternative health care practices.

In fact, research suggests that Latinos tend to use emergency departments (ED) as their primary source of health care. According to a study
of undocumented Latinos, the main reasons for seeking care in hospital
emergency rooms include lack of health insurance, limited information
regarding health care access and treatment, and difficulty obtaining
care at other sites (Chan, Krishel, Bramwell, & Clark, 1996). Approximately three-quarters of those surveyed sought care in the ED because
of perceptions of lower cost, and over half reported lack of information
regarding alternative health care sources. Furthermore, undocumented
Latinos who feared deportation perceived the ED as a place to obtain
health care without being identified.

In an effort to offset the perceived costs associated with emergency
room utilization by undocumented immigrants, Congress passed the
Medicare Modernization Act of 2003 and allocated $250 million in
funds to emergency rooms. However, most of the funding has gone
unspent (Ng'andu, 2006). One reason for this may be that undocumented Latino immigrants are generally young and in good health and
therefore use disproportionately fewer medical services and less public
resources than originally anticipated (Goldman, Smith, & Sood, 2006;
Mohanty et al., 2005). For example, in 2000, 21 percent of total public
medical costs were allocated to the native-born, while 16 percent were
allocated to the foreign-born (Goldman et al., 2006).

Medical practitioners in the United States have been baffled by this
phenomenon and have labeled it the Latino "health paradox." This
contradiction suggests that, despite socioeconomic disadvantages, Latino immigrants in the United States tend to be healthier than their non-
Hispanic white counterparts (Dey & Lucas, 2006). In support of this

theory, adult and infant mortality rates in the United States among Latinos are lower than rates for non-Hispanic whites (Chung, 2006).

Caution is suggested when interpreting these outcomes. While specific health indicators may support the concept of a health paradox, the notion that Latinos, particularly Latino immigrants, do not need health care services is dangerous for several reasons. First, the longer immigrants remain in the United States, the more their health suffers, particularly in terms of obesity, self-reported hypertension, and cardiovascular disease (Dey & Lucas, 2006). Second, the lack of health care access and treatment not only affects Latino immigrants in the long-term, but it also affects the health of their children. In 2002, nearly 10 percent of U.S. births were to undocumented immigrant women, 45 percent of whom were originally from Mexico (Camarota, 2005). Preventive care, such as immunizations, is vital for decreasing future health disparities among Latino children (Niederhauser & Stark, 2005). It is important to note that health care costs for the children of immigrants who are born in the United States are much higher, since child-citizens are entitled to Medicaid, food stamps, education, and other public assistance benefits (Camarota, 2004). Thus, support for the assumption that all Latino immigrants are healthy negatively influences current and future health care policies and practices (Ng'andu, 2006). Third, many Latino immigrants return to their country of origin to access treatment when ill (Chung, 2006), making it impossible for researchers to capture data on their health care status and needs.

HEALTH INSURANCE

The ethnic minority group in the United States with the largest percentage of individuals without health insurance is Latinos. In 2004, approximately 34 percent (or 13.7 million) of non-elderly Latinos were uninsured, and 23 percent were in receipt of public health insurance through Medicaid (DeNavas-Walt, Proctor, & Lee, 2005; James et al., 2007). A significant number of Latinos report that a lack of health insurance and the high cost of care are barriers to health care access (Doty & Holmgren, 2006).

In terms of immigration status, undocumented immigrants are less likely to have health insurance (32 percent) than their documented (77 percent) counterparts (Goldman, Smith, & Sood, 2005). Despite assumptions to the contrary, 63 percent of uninsured Latinos are employed (Kaiser Family Foundation, 2004); however, having less than a high school education is one barrier to securing employment that provides health benefits (Carrillo et al., 2001). Because the costs are considerable, most undocumented immigrants do not purchase health care coverage independent of plans subsidized by an employer. According to one estimate, Latino families living below the federal poverty line would have to spend up to 40 percent of their income to purchase health insurance (Quinn, 2000). Thus, lack of health insurance coverage is considered the most serious health problem among Latino immigrants (Carrillo et al., 2001).

Health care access is also a concern of major significance to Latino immigrants who often live in poverty, are not proficient in English, and have jobs that do not provide health insurance. However, due to the high cost of health care and the complexities of the health care system in the United States, many Latinos avoid traditional health care services altogether, even when the need is extreme. As a result, alternative health care practices are often sought in order to avoid the cost and discomforts associated with using the U.S. health care system.

CASE STUDY

A young Latino mother without employer- or government-sponsored health insurance describes a recent health care emergency experienced by her family. Mrs. Ramirez states, "The other day my son fell and cut himself on the forehead. My husband was very concerned and told me to take him to the hospital. I told him I didn't want to take him because I knew my son would need stitches. I knew that if we took him to the hospital, we were going to get a very expensive bill. The last time I went to the emergency room, I translated the bill the best I could and noticed that they charged me for the doctor, the chair, the time, even for occupying the room. Everything! So I am thinking about the stitches, the anesthesia. . . . No!!! I told my husband, we are not going to take him to the hospital! I ended up spending the whole night holding my son's forehead closed. We went to Latin stores looking for penicillin for him to take. I even opened some capsules and I put the liquid antibiotic and some bandages on his forehead and finally, it got better." (Coffman, Shobe, & O'Connell, 2008)

As highlighted in the previous case vignette, the strongest predictors of health care utilization for Latino immigrants are insurance coverage and economic status (DeNavas-Walt et al., 2005; Hsia et al., 2000).

On average, Latinos are less likely than other ethnic groups to have a usual source of care, and the uninsured are at greatest risk for not receiving professional health care (Agency for Healthcare Research and Quality, 2005). Further, Latinos are the most likely to go without needed care. For example, 21 percent of Latinos in the United States with a chronic health condition or other health problem had not visited a doctor in the previous year, compared to 9 percent of non-Hispanic whites (Doty & Holmgren, 2006). Having a regular source of health care is instrumental in quality care and participation in preventive health care services. In a recent study conducted by the Commonwealth Fund (Beal, Doty, Hernandez, Shea, & Davis, 2007), researchers found that health disparities by race and ethnicity are significantly reduced or eliminated when adults have health insurance and a regular health care provider who offers quality prevention, treatment, and other health care services.

Despite the lack of health care benefits to Latino immigrants, a growing concern associated with the exponential growth of the undocumented Latino population and its potential effect on public health care costs gained political attention in the mid-1990s. As a result, landmark social policy changed the landscape of economic assistance and health care support for low-income Latinos, including Latinos newly arrived to the United States and undocumented Latinos. The Personal Responsibility and Work Opportunities Reconciliation Act of 1996 played an important role in decreasing health care coverage for Latinos. Also known as the Welfare Reform Act, this legislation mandated that most Latino immigrants were not eligible to apply for public assistance benefits, including Medicaid, until they had lived in the United States for five years (Mohanty et al., 2005; Shah & Carrasquillo, 2006).

Individual states had the option of enacting legislation to provide health care services to undocumented immigrants (Berk, Schur, Chavez, & Frankel, 2000). Estimates suggest that in 2002 nearly half of all immigrants in the United States were undocumented (Goldman et al., 2006). Despite the fact that immigrants are less likely to use public programs, one of the driving forces of this legislation was related to the growing political ideology suggesting that undocumented immigrants, Latinos in particular, would bankrupt the health care system. For undocumented immigrants who are eligible to access the health delivery system, a fear of deportation has been found to negatively affect care-seeking behaviors (Berk et al., 2000).

During this time (1993 to 2000), the rates of Latinos with private and public health insurance were also decreasing. While employers of Latinos who experienced Medicaid losses due to the Welfare Reform Act were often unable to make up the difference in employee coverage rates, Latinos did benefit from Medicaid expansion plans between 2000 and 2004. Unfortunately, Latinos who were new to the United States did not fare as well, with undocumented Latinos experiencing the highest uninsured rates (Shah & Carrasquillo, 2006).

Social Work Implications

It is important that social workers in the health care field understand and address the barriers to health care access and treatment for Latinos in order to provide optimal services. While language and cultural obsta-cles often receive the most attention in the literature, they do not com-prise the only barriers to effective health service utilization (Scheppers, van Dongen, Dekker, Geertzen, & Decker, 2006). Based on a review of the literature regarding health care disparities among ethnic minorities, researchers suggest that not only should health care providers focus on improvements in communication and health care policy, but also on preventive and ancillary services, health care screening, and follow-up (Martinez & Carker-Pokras, 2006; Scheppers et al., 2006).

GLOBAL KNOWLEDGE OF HEALTH CARE

As we discussed, the health care systems in Latin American countries are very different from those in the United States; therefore it is impor-tant for social work practitioners to actively learn about the systems in the countries from which their clients came. Social work practitioners can also learn from successful health care practices in countries like Cuba and Mexico and become directly involved in improving access to and the quality of preventive and treatment services in the United States. In addition, social work practitioners are in a key position to educate Latino immigrants about the health care delivery system in the United States.

MEDICAID REFORM

Given that immigrants use less health care resources than politicians originally anticipated, it may be that changes in health care policy for undocumented adult immigrants, particularly Latinos, would be appro-priate to address barriers to access and treatment (Mohanty et al., 2005). Legislation that allows undocumented immigrants to gain legal status could have a significant impact on short-term health care access and treatment and long-term public costs associated with untreated illnesses. For example, insured Latinos could participate in preventive services related to their dental, hearing, vision, and mental health needs, thereby offsetting future costs related to the lack of treatment (Martinez & Carter-Pokras, 2006).

Health care policy changes would also impact the U.S. economy. While amnesty would result in a tax revenue increase, critics suggest that even billions of dollars in increased funds would not offset the increase in public assistance and social insurance benefit usage that was previously unavailable to undocumented immigrants (Camarota, 2004). For example, one of the problems with affording undocumented immigrants amnesty is that the United States would be left with an unprecedented number of low-income, unskilled laborers in a market economy that cannot host them. As a result, this has the potential to bankrupt the welfare state (Camarota, 2004). Social policy development that examines the ways in which Cuba, a country with limited resources, is able to provide universal health coverage to its citizens can help with policy development, implementation, and evaluation.

COMMUNICATION

One way in which social workers and other health care providers can improve services to Spanish-speaking clients is to increase Spanish-proficient provider services either through the providers themselves or via the availability of professional interpreter service delivery. Informal translation services through friends and family members are often problematic since the individuals do not have the skills to parley important medical information to their loved ones (Scheppers et al., 2006). Effective communication between client and health care provider offers Latino clients the opportunity to participate in health care decisions regarding their treatment (Hablamos Juntos, 2005). Patients who receive health care support in their native language report increased use of preventive and treatment services and increased satisfaction with the quality of service provision (Jacobs et al., 2001).

Health care should be provided in a manner that considers the linguistic and cultural needs of the client. Unfortunately, there remains a dearth of social workers who speak Spanish and understand cultural differences in terms of health care access, prevention, and treatment in newly developed Latino communities in the United States. (Vidal de Haymes & Kilty, 2007). In response to the need for appropriate care, the Office of Minority Health of the U.S. Department of Health and Human Services issued its "National Standards for Culturally and Linguistically Appropriate Services in Health Care (CLAS)" (Office of Minority Health, n.d.). There are fourteen CLAS standards, which include recommendations for culturally appropriate care measures and mandates for linguistic accommodations in health care settings. Any agency that receives federal funds as payment for health care services is required to adhere to CLAS standards. Social workers who work with Spanish-speaking populations should be aware of the client's rights to receive interpretation services, linguistically appropriate documents, and culturally competent care.

Treatment services in Spanish can also help increase the health literacy of Latino patients. Health care providers need to increase their awareness of the Latino community in which they serve and their understanding of the barriers to health care access and treatment. Given the complexity of the U.S. health care system, many Latinos do not understand where or how to access health care services (Scheppers et al., 2006). Providers can help clients access supportive networks that can help with their health care needs (Martinez & Carter-Pokras, 2006). In addition, they can help explain the complexities of the U.S. health care system in a way that is beneficial to Latino clients.

COMMUNITY NETWORKING

The development of a network of community resources can play an important role in the long-term prevention of health disparities among Latinos. Internationally renowned health-disparities researcher, H. J. Geiger (2005) found that, controlling for health insurance, income, education, and a host of other factors, in addition to other minority groups, Latinos in the United States are more likely to be treated poorly than non-Hispanic whites by health care providers. While cultural competency training of health care workers has gained interest in the medical field, the focus of training has been on patient behaviors instead of health care provider racial and ethnic biases (Geiger, 2006). For example, researchers collected survey data from 193 physicians to examine the degree to which race (African American versus white) and socioeconomic status affect their perceptions of 618 patients. Findings indicate that physicians perceive low-income and African American patients in a less positive light on a number of dimensions than they do their white, middle- or upper-income patients (van Ryn & Burke, 2000).

Communities also need to assess the ways in which they support the health care needs of their Latino residents. Geiger (2005) suggests that understanding the "organizational culture of the health-care providing institution" is vital for the provision of culturally competent health care. He suggests that community-based advocacy groups and community organizations assemble collectively to ensure that health care organizations are available in low-income and racially and ethnically diverse communities.

The ways in which current social problems are interrelated make it necessary for social workers to collaborate with professionals from other disciplines (Bronstein, 2003). For example, in terms of health care, social work practitioners are in a position to collaborate with physicians, public health nurses, occupational therapists, and Latino groups to develop and maintain interdisciplinary health care resources in Latino communities. As a result, given their educational training and experience with diversity, advocacy, and community development, social workers are in a unique position to provide case management and outreach services to the Latino community (Anderson & Eamon, 2005; Seipel & Way, 2007).

Researchers suggest that social supports in the form of friends and family members have been found to increase health status for Latino immigrants (Chung, 2006) and daily prenatal care for low-income, pregnant Mexican women (Sherraden & Barrera, 1997). Social workers and other health professionals need to recognize the important impact that these supports can have on Latino health and well-being. A more holistic approach to understanding a health care system that recognizes the contributions that family and community make to overall health and well-being may improve overall health care treatment.

Social workers have historically, since the dawn of the profession, collaborated with other professions (Bronstein, 2002). Today, social workers are in a key position to continue with this tradition in order to help address health care disparities among Latinos in the United States. Thus, it is imperative that social workers develop and maintain an effective knowledge base regarding the Spanish language, culturally competent community development approaches, national and state health care policy, immigration and naturalization laws, and eligibility requirements for health care services (Vidal de Haymes & Kilty, 2007). In addition, it is essential that social workers develop interdisciplinary relationships with other health care professionals to provide effective health care services to Latino populations.

Hopefully, you have gained an appreciation for the many variables that influence, and are influenced by, the health of Latinos. None of the issues that are addressed in this book can be viewed in isolation. This is particularly true for the issue of violence, which has strong implications for physical and mental health and other attributes of well-being. The next chapter explores the impact that violence has had upon the Latino community, with a special focus on intimate-partner violence, gangs, and victimization.

For Writing and Reflection

1. Using a micro-practice approach, develop an individualized plan to work with Mrs. Ramirez to solve the problems she listed in the case vignette. In collaboration with your colleagues, discuss and describe the strengths and limitations of your plan.

2. As a community-based social work practitioner, how might you address the health care access and utilization barriers Mrs. Ramirez and other Latinos experience? With whom could you collaborate to support your efforts (e.g., client, key players in the community, etc.)?

3. Using information from this chapter, list several ways in which social policy influences social work practice. How can social workers participate in policy practice? What unique contributions can social workers and their clients bring to social policy development that other professionals cannot?

References

Agency for Health care Research and Quality. (2005). *National health care disparities report.* (AHRQ Publication No. 06–0017). Rockville, MD: Author.

Anderson, S. G., & Eamon, M. K. (2005). Stability of health care coverage among low-income working women. *Health and Social Work, 30*(1), 7–17.

Barraza-Lloréns, M., Bertozzi, S., González-Pier, & Gutiérrez, J. P. (2002). Addressinginequity in health and health care in Mexico. *Health Affairs, 21*(3), 47–56.

Bauman, K. J., & Graf, N. L. (2003). *Educational attainment, 2000: Census 2000 brief. (C2KBR-24).* Washington, DC: U.S. Census Bureau.

Beal, A. C., Doty, M. M., Hernandez, S. E., Shea, K. K., & Davis, K. (2007). *Closing the divide: How medical homes promote equity in health care: Results from the Commonwealth Fund 2006 Health Care Quality Survey.* The Commonwealth Fund. Retrieved on July 15, 2007, from http://www.commonwealth fund.org/usr_doc/1035_Beal_closingedivide_medical_homes.pdf?section= 4039

Berk, M. L., & Schur, C. L. (2001). The effect of fear on access to care among undocumented Latino immigrants. *Journal of Immigrant Health, 3*(3), 151–156.

Berk, M. L., Schur, C. L., Chavez, L. R., & Frankel, M. (2000). Health care use amongundocumented Latino immigrants. *Health Affairs, 19*(4), 51–64.

Bronstein, L. R. (2002). Index of interdisciplinary collaboration. *Social Work Research, 26*(2), 113–126.

Bronstein, L. R. (2003). A model for interdisciplinary collaboration. *Social Work. 48*(3), 297–306.

Camarota, S. A. (2004). *The high cost of cheap labor: Illegal immigration and thefederal budget.* Washington, DC: Center for Immigration Studies.

Camarota, S. A. (2005). *Births to immigrants in America, 1970–2002.* Washington, DC: Center for Immigration Studies.

Carillo, J. E., Treviño, F. M., Betancourt, J. R., & Coustasse, A. (2001). Latino access to health care. In M. Aguirre-Molina, C. W. Molina, & R. E. Zambrana (Eds.), *Health issues in the Latino community* (pp. 55–75). San Francisco: Jossey-Bass.

Cason, K., Nieto-Montenegro, S., & Chavez-Martinez, A. (2006). Food choices, food sufficiency practices and nutrition education needs of Hispanic migrant workers in Pennsylvania. *Topics in Clinical Nutrition, 21*(2), 145–158.

Chan, T. C., Krishel, S. J., Bramwell, K. J., & Clark, R. F. (1996). Survey of illegal immigrants seen in an emergency department. *Western Journal of Medicine, 164*(3), 212–216.

Chung, J. (2006, August 28). Poor patients who are healthy? *Los Angeles Times.* Retrieved May 27, 2007, from http://infoweb.newsbank.com

Coffman, M. J., Shobe, M. A., & O'Connell, E. (2008). Self-prescription practices of recent Latino immigrants. *Public Health Nursing, 25*(3), 203–211.

DeNavas-Walt, C., Proctor, B. D., & Lee, C. H. (2005). *Income, poverty, and health insurance coverage in the United States: 2004 (P60–229).* Washington, DC: U.S. Census Bureau.

Dey, A. N., & Lucas, J. W. (2006). *Physical and mental health characteristics of U.S.- and foreign-born adults: United States, 1998–2003.* Washington, DC: U.S. Centers for Disease Control.

Doty, M. M., & Holmgren, A. L. (2006). Health care disconnect: Gaps in coverage andcare for minority adults. The Commonwealth Fund. Retrieved on August 15, 2006, from http://www.cmwf.org/usr_doc/941_Doty_hlt_care_discon nect_dispariti es_issue_bri.pdf

Fineberg, H. V. (2006). Health reform in Mexico: A work in progress. *Lancet, 368.* 1755–1756.

Foster, D. F., Phillips, R. S., Hamel, M. B., & Eisenburg, D. M. (2000). Alternative medicine use in older Americans. *JAGS, 48,* 1560–1565.

Frenk, J. (2006). Bridging the divide: Global lessons from evidence-based health policy in Mexico. *Lancet, 368,* 954–961.

Gazmararian, J. A., Williams, M. V., Peel, J., & Baker, D. (2003). Health literacy and knowledge of chronic disease. *Patient Education and Counseling, 51,* 267–275.

Geiger, H. J. (2006). *Creating a synthesis of research: Racial and ethnic disparities.* Princeton, NJ: Robert Wood Johnson Foundation.

Geiger, H. J. (Fall/Winter 2005). *What we know and should be doing about disparities in health care.* Decatur, GA: Doctors for Global Health. Retrieved on May 27, 2007, from http://www.dghonline.org/nl15/hcdisparities.html

Goldman, D. P., Smith, J. P., & Sood, N. (2005). Legal status and health insurance among immigrants. *Health Affairs, 24*(6), 1640–1653.

Goldman, D. P., Smith, J. P., & Sood, N. (2006). Immigrants and the cost of medical care. *Health Affairs, 25*(6), 1700–1711.

Hablamos Juntos. (2005). *Affordable language services: Implications for health care organizations.* Retrieved on May 24, 2007, from http://www.hablamosjun tos.org/search/default.search.asp

Hsia, J., Kemper, E., Sofaer, S., Bowen, D., Kiefe, C., Zapka, J., et al. (2000). Is insurance a more important determinant of health care access than perceived health? Evidence from the Women's Health Initiative. *Journal of Women's Health & Gender Based-Medicine, 9*(8), 881–889.

Hulme, P. A., Walker, S. N., Effle, K. J., Jorgensen, L., McGowan, M. G., Nelson, J. D., et al. (2003). Health-promoting lifestyle behavior of Spanish-speaking Hispanic adults. *Journal of Transcultural Nursing, 14*(3), 244–254.

Jacobs, E. A., Lauderdale, D. S., Meltzer, D., Shorey, J. M., Levinson, W., & Thisted, R. A. (2001). Impact of interpreter services on delivery of health care to limited-English-proficient patients. *Journal of General Internal Medicine, 16*(7), 468–474.

James, C., Thomas, M., Lillie-Blanton, M., & Garfield, R. (2007). *Key facts: Race, ethnicity & medical care.* Washington, DC: Kaiser Family Foundation.

Kaiser Family Foundation. (2004). *Health care experiences.* Washington, DC: Author. Kaplan, S. A., Calman, N. S., Golub, M., Davis, J. H., Ruddock, C., & Billings, J. (2006). Racial and ethnic disparities in health: A view from the South Bronx. *Journal of Health Care for the Poor and Underserved, 17*(1), 116–127.

Leon, M. (2003). Perceptions of health care quality in Central America. *International Journal for Quality in Health Care, 15*(1), 67–71.

Loera, J. A., Black, S. A., Markides, K. S., Espino, D. V., & Goodwin, J. S. (2001). The use of herbal medicine by older Mexican Americans. *Journal of Gerontology, 56A*(11), M714-M718.

Marin, G., & Marin, B. V. (1991). *Research with Hispanic Populations.* Newbury Park, CA: Sage.

Martinez, I. L., & Carter-Pokras, O. (2006). Assessing health concerns and barriers in a heterogeneous Latino community. *Journal of Health Care for the Poor and Underserved, 17,* 899–909.

Mohanty, S. A., Woodhandler, S., Himmelstein, D. U., Pati, S., Carrasquillo, O., & Bor, D. H. (2005). Health care expenditures of immigrants in the United States: A nationally representative analysis. *American Journal of Public Health, 95*(8), 1431–1438.

Najm, W., Reinsch, S., Hoehler, F., & Tobis, J. (2003). Use of complementary and alternative medicine among the ethnic elderly. *Alternative Therapies, 9*(3), 50–57.

Nasmith, L. (June 2006). Focus on Cuba's accomplishments. *Canadian Family Physician,* 813–814.

Neuhouser, M. L., Thompson, B., Coronado, G. D., & Solomon, C. C. (2004). Higher fat intake and lower fruit and vegetables intakes are associated with greater acculturation among Mexicans living in Washington State. *Journal of the American Dietetic Association, 104,* 51–57.

Ng'andu, J. (2006). *Immigrants, refugees, asylees, and the undocumented: Understanding laws that impact their health and well-being.* Washington, DC: National Council of La Raza.

Niederhauser, V. P., & Stark, M. (2005). Narrowing the gap in childhood immunization disparities. *Pediatric Nursing, 31*(5), 380–386.

Nielson-Bohlman, L., Panzer, A., & Kindig, D. (2005). *Health literacy: A prescription to end confusion.* Washington DC: National Academies Press.

Office of Minority Health. (n.d.). National Standards on Culturally and Linguistically Appropriate Services (CLAS). Retrieved on May 17, 2007, from http://www.omhrc.gov/templates/browse.aspx?lvl=2&lvlID=15

Ogden, C. L., Carroll, M. D., Curtin, L. R., McDowell, M. A., Tabak, C. J., Flegal, K. M. (2006). Prevalence of overweight and obesity in the United States, 1999–2004. *Jama, 295,* 1549–1555.

O'Malley, A. S., Kerner, J., Johnson, A. E., & Mandelblatt, J. (1999). Acculturation and breast cancer screening among Hispanic women in New York City. *American Journal of Public Health, 89*(2), 219–227.

Paasche-Orlow, M. K., Parker, R. M., Gazmararian, J. A., Nielson-Bohlman, L. T., & Rudd, R. R. (2005). The prevalence of limited health literacy. *Journals of General Internal Medicine, 20,* 100–184.

Passel, J. S. (2005). *Unauthorized migrants: Numbers and characteristics.* Washington, DC: Pew Hispanic Center. Retrieved January 19, 2006, from http://www.pewtrusts.org/pdf/PHC_immigrants_0605.pdf

Peragallo, N. P., Fox, P. G., & Alba, M. L. (2000). Acculturation and breast self-examination among immigrant Latina women in the USA. *International Nursing* Review, 47(1), 38–45.

Porter, E. (2005, April 5). Illegal immigrants are bolstering Social Security with billions. *New York Times,* pp. C1–C7.

Quinn, K. (2000). Working without benefits: The health insurance crisis confronting Hispanic Americans. The Commonwealth Fund. Retrieved on April 1, 2006, from http://www.cmwf.org/usr_doc/quinn_wobenefits_370.pdf

Raiz, L. (2006). Health care poverty. *Journal of Sociology & Social Welfare, 33*(4), 87–104.

Roslow Research Group. (2005). *U.S. Hispanic population projections.* Retrieved May 16, 2007, from http://www.roslowresearch.com/studies/102.pdf

Scheppers, E., van Dongen, E., Dekker, J., Geertzen, J., & Decker, J. (2006). Potential barriers to the use of health services among ethnic minorities: A review. *Family Practice—An International Journal, 23(3), 325–348.*

Schillinger, D., Bindman, A., Wang, F., Stewart, A., & Piette, J. (2004). Functional health literacy and the quality of physician-patient communication among diabetes patients. *Patient Education and Counseling, 52,* 315–323.

Seipel, A., & Way, I. (2007). Culturally competent social work practice with Latino clients. *The New Social Worker, 13*(4), 4–7.

Shah, N. S., & Carrasquillo, O. (2006). Twelve-year trends in health insurance coverageamong Latinos, by subgroup and immigration status. *Health Affairs, 25*(6), 1612–1619.

Sherraden, M. S., & Barrera, R. E. (1997). Culturally-protective health practices: Everyday pregnancy care among Mexican immigrants. *Journal of Multicultural Social Work, 6*(1/2), 93–115.

Spiegel, J. M., & Yassi, A. (2004). Lessons from the margins of globalization: Appreciating the Cuban health paradox. *Journal of Public Health Policy, 25*(1), 85–110.

Sundquist, J., & Winkleby, M. (2000). Country of birth, acculturation status and abdominal obesity in a national sample of Mexican American women and men. *International Journal of Epidemiology, 29*(3), 470–477.

van Ryn, M., & Burke, J. (2000). The effect of patient race and socio-economic status on physicians' perceptions of patients. *Social Science & Medicine, 50*(6), 813–828.

Vidal de Haymes & Kilty, (2007). Latino population growth, characteristics, and settlement trends: Implications for social work education in a dynamic political climate. *Journal of Social Work Education, 43*(1), 101–116.

Weech-Maldonado, R., Morales, M., Elliott, L. S., Spritzer, K., Marshall, G., & Hays, R. D. (2003). Race/ethnicity, language and patients' assessments of care in Medicaid managed care. *Health Services Research, 38*(3), 789–808.

Woloshin, S., Bickell, N. A., Schwartz, L. M., Gany, F., & Welch, G. (1995). Language barriers in medicine in the United States. *Journal of the American Medical Association, 273*(9), 724–728.

World Bank. (2007a). *Latin America & the Caribbean—Key issues in Central America health reforms: Diagnosis and strategic implications.* (Report No. 36426). Washington, DC: World Bank.

World Bank. (2007b). *Brazil—Governance in Brazil's unified health system (SUS): Raising the quality of public spending and resource management.* (Report No. 36601-BR). Washington, DC: World Bank.

CHAPTER NINE

Violence and Latino Communities

Erin A. Casey

Reba Brown

Diana Rowan

Ana Cisneros Howard

Kris Taylor

Introduction

Violent acts contribute to the loss of 1.6 million lives worldwide each year. Violence is among the leading causes of death globally, accounting for 14 percent of deaths in males and 7 percent of deaths in females (World Health Organization, 2008). Almost everyone in the United States, from infants to the elderly, is touched either directly or indirectly by violent acts. As with other ethnic communities, violence is a significant factor within Latino communities. Violent crimes, gang violence, intimate-partner violence (IPV), sexual violence, and other forms of violence rob individuals, families, and their communities of a capacity for health and well-being.

This chapter will explore several key factors related to violence in the Latino community. First, the incidence of three types of violence is reviewed, followed by an exploration of these types of violence and how they specifically impact the Latino community. Next, the impact that culture, assimilation, and immigration have upon how violence is expressed and experienced in the Latino community is explored. Third, some of the key practice issues for social workers to consider when addressing problems involving violence are discussed. A case study and related questions are then presented for consideration to illustrate many of this chapter's themes.

Incidences of Violence

VIOLENT CRIME

The Centers for Disease Control and Prevention (CDC), report that in 2005, 18,124 people in the United States died as a result of homicide. These numbers relate only part of the significance of violence as a social problem, however. Many more people survive violent crime and are left with permanent emotional and physical scars (Centers for Disease Control and Prevention, 2008). In Latino communities, estimates of victimization range from 25.6 per thousand for assault to 3.5 per thousand for robbery, rates that are higher across the board for Latinos than for white individuals (U.S. Department of Justice, 2005).

Two trends are apparent in violence against Latinos. According to a summary of findings by the U.S. Department of Justice (2002), there appears to have been a recent reduction in overall victimization of "Hispanics" (the descriptor utilized by the U.S. government on all federal forms and documents (Hispanic.com, 2007). Between 1993 and 2005, the rate of victimization of Hispanics fell 55 percent, from fifty-five to twenty-five victimizations per one thousand people. This is consistent with a nationwide decrease in many forms of violent crimes during this time. According to the report, persons of Hispanic descent experienced about 690,470 violent crimes, the majority of which were simple assaults (59%), followed by robbery (20%), aggravated assault (19%), and rape or sexual assault (2%) (U.S. Department of Justice, 2002). Within the Hispanic community, those most likely to experience these violent acts were males, juveniles, single people, and those reporting a yearly family income of less than $7,500. As with all statistics, reliability and validity are dependent on the methods of data collection, and it is likely that many violent crimes go unreported because of shame, pressure for secrecy, and fear of deportation.

At the same time, hate crimes against Latinos have increased markedly. Racially motivated crime against both Latino immigrants and U.S. citizens of Latino descent increased 35 percent between 2003 and 2006 (Southern Poverty Law Center, 2007), perhaps reflecting growing racism and anti-immigrant sentiment within U.S. discourses. Hate crimes are typically defined as offenses intended to intimidate someone based on his or her race, gender, national origin, etc., or crimes that are motivated by hatred of a victim's identity (Wallace, 2007). Such crimes carry the dual impact of the trauma of victimization and the psychological harm, fear, and stigmatization caused by the intense discrimination inherent in the attack.

Other interesting trends relate specifically to homicide rates and population density. Homicide rates tend to be positively correlated with population density (Martinez, 2000), with higher rates of homicide in more densely populated areas. Conversely, there appears to be a negative relationship between the affluence of a city and its homicide rates (Martinez, 2000). Governmental data show that through 2000, Hispanics in urban areas were victimized at a rate lower than the rates for blacks and whites. However, in suburban settings, Hispanics were victimized at a rate higher than that for whites, but lower than that for blacks. And, in rural areas, Hispanics sustained violent victimizations at a rate higher than those for whites and blacks (U.S. Department of Justice, 2002).

GANGS

Gang violence has gained popular attention within the past decade in areas outside of the traditional hot spots for gang activity. As Latinos became the largest ethnic minority group in the nation in 2003 (Malec, 2006), there appears to have been a concomitant increase in Latino gang affiliation and activity. Approximately one in six Latino males in U.S. urban centers is a member of a gang (Malec, 2006). Latinos were also more likely to be victims of crimes committed by gangs than non-Latinos (U.S. Department of Justice, 2005).

INTIMATE-PARTNER VIOLENCE

Intimate-partner violence (IPV) is also called domestic violence. The term IPV is a more encompassing way of including various types of intimate partnerships and the violence that can be experienced within these relationships. Defined as physical, sexual, or psychological abuse of a romantic partner, researchers and social workers are still learning about IPV in Latino communities (Adames & Campbell, 2005). Estimates of the incidence of IPV among Latinos vary widely, perhaps because of the heterogeneous nature of this population (Denham et.al., 2007) or because of a lack of culturally sensitive assessment approaches. Across community-based and convenience samples, approximately 19 to 34 percent of Latina women report experiencing violence in an intimate relationship at some point in their lives (Hazen & Soriano, 2007; Swan & Snow, 2006). Data from the U.S. Department of Justice (2007) suggest that between 1993 and 2005, the rate of nonfatal IPV declined for Latinos by two-thirds. It is important to note that this statistic would only reflect those incidences of IPV that were reported to authorities, and may reflect, in part, a decrease in willingness among victims to seek assistance.

Latinas in the rural southeastern United States have a higher risk of experiencing intimate-partner violence (IPV) than non-Latino women in the region (Denham et al., 2007). This particular area of the country experienced an approximate increase in the Latino population of 50 percent from 2000 to 2005 (Pew Hispanic Center, 2007). Owing to this rapid increase, these states are not as equipped to accommodate Latino women experiencing IPV as states in other areas of the country that have had a large Latino population for decades. Further, these states may have a less-established Latino community in place for these women to turn to for assistance regarding domestic violence (Denham et al., 2007), making it imperative that particular attention be paid to the issue of IPV in Latino communities in this region.

Impact on Latino Communities

VIOLENT CRIMES

Violence is a multifaceted issue that is further complicated by the effects of immigration, acculturation, and disproportionate poverty faced by Latinos. According to Martinez (2000), the majority of new immigrants to the United States are Latinos who are at risk for experiencing higher rates of violence because they settle primarily in more violent urban areas. Within these urban centers, poverty rates are higher, incomes are lower, and there remains a competition for stretched resources. However, in U.S. political discourse, Latinos may be identified as the reason for the increase in crime in an area, despite research and statistical evidence to the contrary (Martinez, 2000). The seminal work of Shaw and McKay (1931) discusses the link between immigrants, homicide, and violent crime. They argue that the relationship is based primarily on the breakdown of the community and the lack of social control that can emerge in under-resourced urban centers, not the immigrants themselves. Nonetheless, stereotypes regarding immigrants may form and be coupled with a backlash against immigrant communities, further raising their risk for experiencing discrimination or violence. National events such as the attacks of 9/11/2001 may further exacerbate stereotyping and scapegoating of immigrant communities (Claffey, 2006).

Other factors potentially related to Latino individuals' risk for experiencing or perpetrating violence are acculturation and assimilation. *Acculturation*, which is handled uniquely by each new Latino immigrant, can be defined as the process by which someone with more than one cultural identity works to be a part of each cultural group simultaneously (Holleran & Jung, 2005). Youth, in particular, may struggle with staying true to their culture of birth while learning the new American culture. Youth face complications in this process because of increased family responsibilities such as acting as an interpreter, translator, and possible buffer between their family culture and the culture of the society in which they live. These youth may also experience some stress related to academic achievement and assimilation into the culture of their peers. *Assimilation* occurs when one leaves behind his or her culture of origin and adopts the dominant culture. Multiple stressors related to pressure for academic achievement and difficulty negotiating acculturation may cause some youth to use violence, choosing aggression as a way to prove themselves (Holleran & Jung, 2005).

Also, as stated previously, violence occurs more often in areas that lack economic resources and where the rates of poverty are higher. Studies have repeatedly suggested that youth living in areas of high poverty are exposed to violence at a higher rate than their peers living in neighborhoods of greater advantage. This exposure has also been linked to mental health concerns for these children and to decreased educational success (Galster & Santiago, 2006).

GANGS

Gang membership within the Latino community can be linked to several factors including, but not limited to, poverty and identity crises generated by acculturation. Just as poverty plays a role in violent crime in the Latino community, it is also associated with gang membership. According to Galster and Santiago (2006), children and youth living in disadvantaged neighborhoods are more vulnerable to recruitment by gangs. Needs of these youth often go unmet because of economic disparity. Some common characteristics of gang members include overwhelming poverty, lack of social status, and lack of skills that would allow them to find gainful employment (Malec, 2006). Gangs offer mobility, advancement, and an opportunity for income that some Latinos, and others, in gangs need in order to survive.

Developing a sense of identity is a core task of adolescence. The stresses of acculturation and negotiating a new or different culture can render finding one's identity particularly challenging for some Latino youth. Identifying as Latino while fitting into a culture that sees Latinos as outsiders may prevent some Latino youth from positive identity formation. Gang membership offers one avenue for satisfying this need to belong. Malec (2006) states that the need to belong is central and is woven into our beings as much as love, respect, control, or physical well-being. Becoming a member of a gang gives one an identity, often even marked physically through tattoos and brandings. The process of initiation may mean that members must perform acts of violence in order to be accepted and to gain the respect of the other members (Malec, 2006). Gangs can offer a "surrogate family" that addresses some of young people's unmet needs (Malec, 2006).

INTIMATE-PARTNER VIOLENCE

Evidence is mixed about whether Latino communities are at lower or higher risk of IPV than other racial or ethnic communities. Latinas may face some unique risks for IPV victimization, however, including disproportionate exposure to poverty, lack of culturally relevant resources, and vulnerability due to immigration status (Klevens, 2007). Lisa Aronson Fontes (1995) points out that every cultural community holds values, beliefs, and behavioral patterns that both protect its members from intimate violence and that may exacerbate, excuse, or obscure it. Thus, it is important to explore how some common cultural patterns within Latino communities may increase risk for IPV, as well as how strengths within the community protect its members from violence or can be marshaled within interventions. At the same time, it is critical to avoid overgeneralizations about the extent to which heterogeneous Latino groups, or the individuals within them, ascribe to particular cultural beliefs and practices.

Some common values within the Latino community that may be related to the occurrence of IPV include *machismo, marianismo,* and *respeto. Machismo* is the valuing of male "virtue, courage and fearlessness" (Fontes, 1995, p. 40), but can also involve emphasis on traits such as physical aggressiveness, sexual prowess, and alcohol abuse, which can serve as risk factors for domestic violence. *Marianismo,* the counterpart role for Latinas, places a high value on virginity, purity, and sacrifice for family and children, which may decrease women's perceived options in the face of abusive treatment. Finally, the critical cultural value of *respeto* may serve as both a protective and a risk factor for IPV. *Respeto* is an emphasis on respect and deference to authority based on age, gender, and social position. Some evidence suggests that expectations for *respeto,* coupled with gendered cultural values, are associated with risk for IPV (Edelson, Hokoda, & Ramos-Lira, 2007). At the same time, cultural emphases on mutual respect and the importance of family may serve as factors that render intimate abuse unacceptable within Latino families and communities.

Several other IPV risk factors may be relevant for Latinas. In a southeastern sample of Latinas, half of women who lacked social support experienced IPV, while only one-fifth of women with supports reported victimization (Denham et al., 2007). The same study found that Latinas with a greater degree of acculturation were at greater risk of victimization. Processes of acculturation may challenge or stress traditional family arrangements, increasing the risk of men reinforcing familial power structures through the use of violence (Swan & Snow, 2006). Other risk factors for Latino communities include an undocumented legal status, which may reduce women's willingness to report abuse, and language barriers that prevent accessing services (Acevedo, 2000). Latina women share risk factors such as men's alcohol use, witnessing abuse as a child, pregnancy, and levels of a partner's jealousy with women of other ethnic backgrounds (see for review, Klevens, 2007).

Implications for Practice

Social workers will more than likely work with families or individuals of Latino descent. As mentioned in previous chapters of this book, Latinos are a heterogeneous group, and interventions for one subgroup may not be effective for other subgroups. Social work professionals must aim to be culturally competent and take responsibility to seek information when they lack knowledge about a particular culture.

Statistics from the U.S. Department of Justice (2002) suggest that crime experienced by Latinos may go underreported to the authorities. Although there were various reasons cited in the report, Latinos mentioned fear of reprisal and feeling as if their victimization was unimportant to the authorities as reasons they had not reported crimes. Social workers in agencies that come into contact with these victims should be aware of this barrier to service and clearly communicate the need for safety and protection of all clients. Having bilingual and bicultural staff members available to work with this population is one way to lessen this challenge. Following are implications for serving Latino clients in the context of gang membership and IPV involvement.

Although gang affiliation is viewed as a negative identifier, social workers serving this population should be aware of the positive aspects that gang membership affords an individual. In a 2006 article, Malec suggests that most programs aimed at working with individuals with gang affiliation focus on the delinquency of the individual and their rehabilitation after gang life. The article stresses the importance of replacing gang sources of income and power with alternative forms of these elements so that those individuals will not have to return to the gang for survival (Malec, 2006).

In regard to IPV, several intervention implications should be considered. Agency staff are encouraged to understand how immigration intersects with IPV for Latino populations. A Latina who is undocumented is more likely to experience separation from the local community and social supports than documented or U.S.-born Latinas

(Denham et al., 2007). Further, perpetrators of IPV may use the fear of being deported as a tactic of control and to prevent women from reporting abuse or from participating in a prosecution (Swan & Snow, 2006). Knowledge of immigration law as it relates to intimate-partner violence and of legal remedies available to immigrant victims is therefore essential to serving Latina survivors of abuse.

Efforts to reduce barriers to help-seeking are also critical. Barriers to IPV services specific to the Latino population include a lack of Spanish-speaking service providers and a lack of resources and transportation to services, as well as little knowledge of what services are available (Ingram, 2007). As social justice advocates, social workers can encourage the expansion of culturally and linguistically relevant services, as well as culturally specific community education about IPV and the services available to address it. Additionally, social work practitioners, regardless of setting, should consider screening for IPV. This should occur in the language preferred by the client and should involve the use of behaviorally specific questions (such as "Have you ever been in a relationship where you felt controlled/hurt by your partner?") rather than questions that require women to label themselves as "victims" (Wrangle, Fisher, & Paranjape, 2008). Screening should be followed by an open, nonjudgmental response to disclosure, a knowledge of available, culturally relevant community resources, and immediate attention to the safety needs of the client. Finally, it is critical to note that culturally specific batterer-intervention is more effective for Latino perpetrators than nonculturally tailored programming (Alianza Latina Nacional, 2007).

Social workers can also capitalize on the considerable strengths of Latino families and communities in mobilizing against IPV. Many Latinas are members of extended, close-knit families whose members could provide support, encouragement, and safety. Further, cultural emphasis on the importance of families and on respect (Fontes, 1995), can serve as a protective factor against violence and can be used as a point of departure in organizing and supporting Latino communities in their efforts to end IPV. Finally, the Church plays a central role for many Latino families and communities, and should be considered as an avenue for education, support, and services.

With regard to macro-level social work interventions of community action and mobilization, social workers can be powerful organizers and advocates for combating malaise toward violence in Latino communities. David Gil (1996) explores the reasons why communities become violent. He suggests that violent acts occur within poor communities when social structures and institutions thwart a community's capacity to meet their psychosocial needs. In following his assertion, social workers should be aware that prejudice, economic and health disparities, immigration, globalization, and the clash of cultural values can all affect how violence occurs in the Latino community. These factors need to be acknowledged and addressed if the change effort is to be made successful through buy-in from the local Latino community. Social work interventions aimed at the individual, family, group, organizational, and community levels must be culturally relevant, sensitive, and include Latino community stakeholders as much as possible.

CASE STUDY

Jesica Luna is a twenty-eight-year-old Nicaraguan woman living in the northeastern United States. Jesica, along with her two children, currently lives in the home of her sister's family. Jesica's story is one of strength and resilience and demonstrates how a woman can find it within herself to overcome sexual and domestic violence.

Jesica first experienced sexual violence at the age of fifteen, when one of her uncles asked her to perform oral sex on him. He stated that if she did not, he would tell her family that she had tried to seduce him, and he said that her parents would shun her. Afraid of being kicked out of her home, she submitted to her uncle's request. This event had a profound effect on Jesica. She internalized her uncle's insistence that Jesica was to blame. He told her that she teased him with the way she dressed, and that she was inherently a "whore." From that day onward, Jesica experienced episodic periods of depression and anxiety. Jesica, who had been an excellent student, began to fail her classes. She dropped out of school, believing that she would not ever "amount to anything." She began to work in her uncle's restaurant, the only job available to her. To protect herself from the pain she felt at his abusing her, she pretended that the event did not happen. From this time forward, she began to lose the ability to experience any joyful emotions. Jesica worked hard to help her family. Her father, who had been a journalist, had been unable to find work for many years. Her mother, who had heart problems and diabetes, worked when she could, making a living as a seamstress. Once middle class, her family became rather poor. Jesica worked long hours to support her family.

Two years later, Jesica met Jose, a Guatemalan man fifteen years her senior. Jose lived in Costa Rica and worked as a truck driver. While Jesica did not love Jose, she thought that he could provide her with stability and help her family. A year after they met, Jesica married Jose and moved to San Jose, Costa Rica. While the idea of being away from her family was painful, the economy of Nicaragua was not good, and this way she could send money home. Even though she had not lived in Nicaragua for many years, she was still deeply connected to her family and felt responsible for their well-being. Over the next several years, Jesica and Jose had three children. Having learned the skills to be a seamstress from her mother, Jesica made extra money to send to her family by sewing at home. Jesica and Jose's family was mostly happy until Jose's company closed. He was not able to find another job and within a few months, the family had little money and few options. Jesica took in as much sewing work as she could and got a poorly paying part-time job late at night at a factory. Jose began to drink. One night, he came home drunk and hit Jesica for no reason. Over the next several weeks, the couple argued, and Jose became more and more violent. Jesica tried not to take it personally, believing that once Jose found a job, things would get better. She worked, comforted her children, and forged on.

Jesica's sister, who lived in the United States, said that she could find them both work if they could find their way there. Over the next month, the family made plans to come to the United States. Jose went first, which gave Jesica some time away from Jose's increasingly violent temper. Jesica brought her children to Nicaragua to stay with her mother, and made the trek to the United States. Jose made the arrangements for her travel, which would cost the couple all the money they had left. She was able to get to Guatemala by bus, as her husband was a Guatemalan citizen. However, to get through Mexico, she had to be hidden in the back of a truck belonging to a man that Jose knew. Once at the border of the United States, "coyotes" (smugglers of people across borders) brought her into the United States in crowded vans, pickup trucks, and on foot. The journey was painful and frightening. Once on the other side of the border, she was brought to a safe house.

When in the safe house, Jesica was told by one of the coyotes that she had to repay "extra" costs of getting her safely to the United States. Jesica said that she would pay the additional costs when she got a job. However, the coyote informed her that she would have to earn the money before she could leave, and that the only way to do so was to have sex with men who came to the house. She was told that if she left the house without repaying her debt, they would find and hurt her children. This thought was horribly painful to her. She decided to submit, rather than risk her children's safety. For three weeks, Jesica was compelled to have sex with dozens of men. On the day she finally was told her debt was repaid, she was raped by two of the coyotes.

Jesica finally was given a bus ticket and arrived at the bus station several days later. Her anxiety and depression were the worst they had ever been. She was crying constantly, sobbing silently during most of the bus ride. When she arrived, her husband was furious with her. He could not believe that she had been unable to call. Jesica felt stuck; she worried that if she told her husband what had happened, he would not believe her and would think that she prostituted herself by choice. She also knew that she would need to come up with some reason why she was three weeks late. At her sister's home, Jesica began to cry uncontrollably. She began to shake and wail. Her husband, feeling angry and out of control, began to shake her. Jesica's sister and her husband opened the door and a scuffle ensued. Jesica's brother-in-law hit Jose on the head with a board. He physically removed Jose from the house, and told him to leave.

Jesica lay on the floor, crying and screaming. A wave of grief and pain shot through her body. Jesica's sister, who had been receiving help from a local social service agency for her own depression, called her counselor and told her what had happened. The counselor, a Mexican social worker who had worked with Jesica's sister for over a year, asked if they would like her to come to the house to talk to Jesica. Jesica, who for years had resisted talking with anyone about her history of abuse, agreed.

Over the course of several months, Jesica began to work through her feelings. Her counselor helped her understand that talking about her abuse was not a betrayal of her family, but a sign of strength. After several sessions, she told Jose, who was living in a hotel, that he would have to get help for his anger if he wanted to be with her. Jose refused. Jesica had a difficult time setting limits with him but began to feel empowered. When Jose would blame her for what had happened, she would tell him that he was the one who had the problem and that she would not tolerate any more blame and abuse. She came to see that if her own daughters were going to be strong and able to resist abuse, she would need to change her own sense of self-blame. While Jesica missed her children terribly, she knew that the family needed money to survive. After several months away from her children, she was able to arrange for a family member to bring them to the United States. Over the next year, Jesica began to attend a group for Latina women who were victims of violence. Jesica eventually became a leader and gained a sense of pride and purpose. She began to see that helping Latina women overcome violence, and making changes in her community, were going to be her new life's purpose.

For Writing and Reflection

1. As her social worker, how would you support Jesica in pursuing her new sense of purpose?

2. What does Jesica's story suggest about the services Latina immigrants may need?

3. As you read the story, what stereotypes do you notice coming up for you? How might this impact your work with Latina survivors of violence?

4. What strengths are evident in Jesica or in her family and community that would be important to incorporate into your work with her?

The end of this chapter concludes this section of the book. The following section explores interventions, programs, and methods that are applicable to various subgroups of Latinos. The first chapter of this section explores culturally competent assessment. Assessment is a part of all social work processes and is applied at the beginning, middle, and end of the helping relationship. The authors of the next chapter use case vignettes throughout as a means of exploring the importance of cultural competence to the assessment process and to the helping relationship as a whole. This practice-based exploration of cultural competence serves as a foundation for subsequent chapters.

References

Acevedo, M. (2000). Battered immigrant Mexican women's perspectives regarding abuse and help-seeking. *Journal of Multicultural Social Work, 8,* 243–282.

Adames, S. B., & Campbell, R. (2005). Immigrant Latinas' conceptualizations of intimate partner violence. *Violence Against Women, 11,* 1341–1364.

Alianza Latina Nacional.(2007). *Domestic Violence affects families of all racial, ethnic, and economic backgrounds: It is a widespread and destructive problem in Latino communities.* Factsheet from Alianza; The National Latino Alliance for the Elimination of Domestic Violence. Retrieved June 12, 2008, from http://www.dvalianza.org/resor/factsheet_dv.htm

Centers for Disease Control and Prevention.(2008). Violence prevention at CDC. Retrieved June 13, 2008, from http://www.cdc.gov/ncipc/dvp/prevention_at_CDC.htm

Claffey. J. E. (2006). Anti-immigrant violence in suburbia. *Social Text, 24,* 73–80.

Denham, A., Frasier, P., Hooten, E., Belton, L., Newton, W., Gonzalez, P., et al. (February 2007). Intimate partner violence among Latinas in eastern North Carolina. *Violence Against Women, 13,* 123–140.

Edelson, M. G., Hokoda, A., & Ramos-Lira, L. (2007). Differences in domestic violence between Latina and non-Latina women. *Journal of Family Violence, 22,* 1–10.

Fontes, L. A. (Ed.) (1995). *Sexual abuse in nine North American cultures.* Thousand Oaks: Sage Publications.

Galster, G. C., & Santiago, A. M. (2006). What's the 'hood got to do with it? Parental perceptions about how neighborhood mechanisms affect their children. *Journal of Urban Affairs, 28,* 201–226.

Gil, D. (1996). Preventing violence in a structurally violent society: Mission impossible. *American Journal of Orthopsychiatry, 66*(1), 77–84.

Hazen, A. L., & Soriano, F. I. (2007). Experiences with intimate partner violence among Latina women. *Violence Against Women, 13,* 562–582.

Hispanic.com, (2007). Hispanic vs. Latino, Hispanic or Latino, Hispanic & Latino, or neither . . . What's the difference? Retrieved June 17, 2008, from http://www.hispanic.com

Holleran, L. K,. & Jung, S. (2005). Acculturative stress, violence, and resilience in the lives of Mexican-American youth. *Stress, Trauma and Crisis, 8,* 107–130.

Ingram, E. M. (2007). A comparison of help seeking between Latino and non-Latino victims of intimate partner violence. *Violence Against Women, 13,* 159–171.

Klevens, J. (February 2007). An overview of intimate partner violence among Latinos. *Violence Against Women,* 13, 111–122.

Malec, D. (2006). Transforming Latino gang violence in the United States. *Peace Review, 18(1),* 81–89

Martinez, Jr., R. (2000). Immigration and urban violence: The link between immigrant Latinos and types of homicides. *Social Science Quarterly, 81,* 363–374.

Pew Hispanic Center (2007, December 14). *A statistical portrait of Hispanics at mid-decade.* Retrieved December 14, 2007, from http://pewhispanic.org/reports/middecade

Shaw, C. R., & McKay, H. D. (1931). Social factors in juvenile delinquency. *Report on the causes of crime, 13(2).* Washington, DC: U.S. Government Printing Office.

Southern Poverty Law Center (2007). Immigration backlash: Hate crimes against Latinos flourish. Retrieved December 10, 2008, from http://www.splcenter.org/intel/intelreport/article.jsp?aid=845

Swan, S. C., & Snow, D. L. (2006). The development of a theory of women's use of violence in intimate relationships. *Violence Against Women,* 12, 1026–1045.

U.S. Department of Justice. (2002). Hispanic victims of violent crime, 1993–2000. *Bureau of Justice Statistics.* Retrieved on February 29, 2008, from http://www.ojp.usdoj.gov/bjs

U.S. Department of Justice. (2005). Violence by gang members, 1993–2000. *Bureau of Crime Statistics Crime Data Brief.* Retrieved on February 29, 2008, from http://www.ojp.usdoj.gov/bjs

U.S. Department of Justice. (2007). Intimate partner violence in the United States. Retrieved on February 29, 2008, from http://www.ojp.usdoj.gov/bjs

Wallace, H. (2007). *Victimology: Legal, psychological and social perspectives.* New York: Pearson Publishing.

World Health Organization (2008). Violence and injury prevention. Retrieved June 13, 2008, from http://www.who.int/violence_injury_prevention/violence/en/

Wrangle, J., Fisher, J. W., & Paranjape, A. (2008). Ha Sentido Sola? Culturally competent screening for intimate partner violence in Latina women. *Journal of Women's Health,* 17, 261–268.

PART III

Interventions, Programs, and Methods

CHAPTER TEN

Culturally Competent Assessment of Latinos

Luis H. Zayas
Luis R. Torres
Stavroula Kyriakakis

Introduction

Assessment is a fundamental first step in providing services to our clients. A thorough, well-guided, culturally competent assessment will not only yield information that will serve as the basis for a comprehensive service or treatment plan, but will also help build rapport and trust between client and social worker. An assessment that fails to bring client and social worker closer may yield incomplete or inaccurate information, do little for the relationship, and very likely lead to the client dropping out or prematurely terminating services. One reason why assessments often falter is the social worker's failure to understand and skillfully handle elements of a client's culture that may be impacting the presenting problem, may filter how the client takes in the worker's recommendations, and may mediate the client's level of involvement in the service plan.

Our social work profession has a long history of assisting U.S.-born citizens and foreign-born immigrants and refugees. As our country witnesses the growth of the Latino population, social workers will once

Support for work on this chapter was provided by NIMH Grant R01 MH070689 and the Center for Latino Family Research, George Warren Brown School of Social Work, Washington University in St. Louis.

again be increasingly supplying the "frontline" social services for this population group. Because the social service workforce does not presently reflect the demographic profile of our diversifying population, it becomes imperative that we strengthen our skills in culturally competent assessment and treatment planning. This professional responsibility applies to social work practice across all settings, from mental health to adoptions to corrections and victims' rights, to name a few. Social workers need to understand culture and its function in human behavior and society; recognize the strengths that exist in all cultures; possess a knowledge base of their clients' cultures; demonstrate expertise in providing culturally competent services; and seek to understand the nature of social diversity and oppression with respect to race, ethnicity, national origin, color, sex, sexual orientation, age, marital status, political beliefs, religion, and mental or physical disability (National Association of Social Workers, 1996).

In this chapter, we discuss how to conduct culturally competent assessments of Latino clients across service settings. We begin with a brief discussion of cultural competency and assessment, and of the domains of culturally competent social work assessment. We then go on to discuss pre-encounter preparations for engaging Latino clients in social work practice. Much of this chapter is devoted to factors to consider in conducting a culturally competent social work assessment with Latino clients, including the heterogeneity of U.S. Latinos; language considerations; concerns of racial and ethnic identity; Latino cultural values; length of residency in the United States and acculturation; gender; and social class. The chapter ends with some guidelines on how to pursue cultural competence.

Cultural Competency and Assessment

The term *cultural competency* has gained considerable currency over the past twenty or more years. Its operationalization has progressed from being "aware" of the ways in which our clients might be different, to being "sensitive" to how those differences might impact a presenting problem and course of treatment. The current standard, "competency," implies both awareness and sensitivity to culture, but goes beyond this passive stance to evoke a more active involvement by the practitioner at the level of acquiring knowledge, competencies, and skills to serve diverse populations. Social workers can achieve this through readings, continuing education, supervision and consultation, immersion in cultural events, group discussions, and through interacting with individuals of diverse backgrounds within and outside of service provision settings. Cultural competency entails taking these experiences and knowledge and *putting them into effect* in the social work encounter, while remaining self-reflective and open to learning from clients and colleagues. In short, our functioning definition of cultural competency for this chapter is the active engagement of social workers learning about their clients' culture, acquiring knowledge and intervention skills, and refining those competencies in their interaction with and for clients.

Assessment typically refers to the practitioner listening to the client's story and reaching some conclusion. This conclusion might be a diagnosis, a formulation of the presenting problem, or a list of problem areas, and will be used to guide the elaboration of a service or treatment plan. Absent from this view of assessment are key social work values such as client self-determination, acknowledgment of individual human dignity, and recognition of the unique life-situations of the client. In this view of assessment, the client is a passive participant who is limited to relating a story. In a culturally competent social work assessment, on the other hand, the client is an active participant, bringing to the encounter not only a life story but a rich collage of cultural experiences that will impact how that story will be remembered and related by the client, how it will be co-interpreted by the client and social worker, and how recommendations will be shaped and acted upon. The emphasis in a culturally competent social work assessment is to reduce the hierarchy of the client-worker relationship or even "flatten" it (Dyche & Zayas, 1995). The social worker takes on the responsibility of facilitating client empowerment, giving audience to clients' voices, and engaging them as active and sincere participants in their own care (Aldarondo, 2007).

Domains of Culturally Competent Social Work Assessment

An essential first component in the process of becoming a culturally competent social worker is curiosity about oneself. This involves the study and examination of one's own cultural background and family history. It is through this process of exploring our own culture, family history, life experiences, and the values that have guided and resulted from our ancestry, that we are able to be open to the entirety of the persons we work with. Awareness and knowledge of our own cultural values and worldviews allows us to more accurately assess and interpret our clients' behavior, concerns, and needs within the context of genuine curiosity about others. We each have our own cultural lenses through which we view the world; knowledge of self may help prevent us from tinting the image of our clients or distorting entirely their experiences and attributes.

Knowledge of our own culture is also important in attuning us to how our clients might see us, to the concerns and perceptions they may project onto us based on what we look like and what they are able to assess about our own ethnic, racial, educational, and class background. Although we cannot always control how our clients assess and perceive us, especially in the initial encounters, awareness of our clients' potential perceptions of us is a critical component in the facilitation of safety, trust, and openness on the part of our clients.

Engaging Latino Clients in Social Work Practice: Pre-encounter Preparations

The initial encounter has important implications for assessment and the subsequent work to be done. This is especially true when working across cultural, linguistic, gender, socioeconomic, or other barriers. Whenever possible, social workers must take the time to review the information they have about their client, determine what knowledge, skills, and attitudes they possess for working with Latino clients, and examine any biases or stereotypes they may hold about the population. If necessary, they should seek supervision in preparation for the initial contact. The following vignette illustrates what this pre-encounter preparation might look like with a Latino client.

CASE STUDY

Preparations for Initial Encounter with a Latino Client

Jorge, a thirty-nine-year-old Latino male, called for an appointment after consulting his union's employee assistance program. He was looking for a therapist with offices convenient to both his work and home, and left a message for the social worker requesting that the return call be to his home and not his workplace. During the initial phone contact, Jorge stated that his reason for seeking services was depression. He mentioned he was of Puerto Rican descent; was married to a Puerto Rican woman from New York of the same age as him; and that together they had four children: a daughter (age fifteen) in high school, a son (eleven), named after his father, and two other boys (eight and four). The family lived in subsidized public housing and supported themselves on Jorge's modest salary. Over the phone, Jorge was accommodating and deferential, seemed eager to fit into the social worker's schedule, and easily agreed on a date and time for the initial appointment. His voice evinced traces of anxiety, and he came across in a gentlemanly, almost self-effacing manner. He spoke unaccented English, an indication that he had spent most of his life in the United States. From the referral source (an office and service workers union), the social worker surmised that Jorge worked in a nonprofessional occupation.

After scheduling the appointment, the social worker carefully reviewed the phone conversation and highlighted aspects of the referral and of Latino clients that might be important to the assessment and subsequent work. Jorge's deferential attitude over the phone might be common to other Latinos, but owing to his level of acculturation—suggested by his unaccented English but yet to be determined—he might be more assertive in person. As a group, Latino men seek services infrequently and most often come to the attention of service providers in the context of services to children, spouses, and families, typically under coercion from employers, courts, or family. This often results in awkward encounters with clients who do not want services. Was Jorge's treatment-seeking completely voluntary, or was there some coercion involved? In addition, Latino men frequently feel *verguenza* (shame) when they do seek help, whether coerced or voluntarily. Gender differences can be a concern, and often male Latino clients seem relieved to encounter a male provider. The therapist also made a mental note to be vigilant not to fall back on the one-sided stereotype held by society at large of the *machista* Latino, particularly when providing services to a blue-collar worker from a poor background.

In the brief vignette above, the social worker was careful to examine the few stated facts of the referral before the initial meeting, paying particular attention to both cultural and clinical aspects that might play a role. The social worker considered his preexisting knowledge of Latinos and how much of these preconceptions might actually apply to Jorge. This pre-encounter preparation will likely increase the odds of a successful assessment, and more importantly, of a positive connection between client and social worker.

Culturally Competent Social Work Assessment with Latino Clients

In addition to genuine curiosity and knowledge of self and others, there are several factors that are critical to the culturally competent assessment of Latino clients. These include understanding the heterogeneity of the Latino population; navigating language barriers and varying levels of English-language proficiency; knowledge, comfort, and skill when discussing racial and ethnic identity; issues of education and social class; and knowledge of Latino cultural values and how these might play a role in the presenting problems and course of treatment. We will now proceed to discuss these in more detail.

HETEROGENEITY OF U.S. LATINOS

Greatly complicating the challenges of conducting a culturally competent social work assessment with Latinos is the fact that they are a broadly heterogeneous group. Latinos have their cultural origins in nineteen independent countries in Latin America plus Puerto Rico, a U.S. territory. (Latin America has a combined population almost double that of the United States.) Not surprisingly, immigrants from Latin America come with different sociopolitical histories and varied social-class distributions and racial, ethnic, and linguistic backgrounds, cultures, and rituals. Each Latin American country has a different social-political relationship and history with the United States, which may affect the immigrant's perceptions and beliefs about the United States in general and about service providers specifically (Organista, 2007). Latinos also vary in terms of when their family migrated to the United States. The heterogeneity of Latinos may be reflected in their language, country of origin, former and current social class, education, reasons for and chronology of migration, ethnic and racial identity, and other factors that may contribute to their uniqueness. The following vignette illustrates this.

CASE STUDY
Latino Heterogeneity

Frieda is an eight-year-old female receiving services in a community mental health clinic to help her cope with her parents' recent divorce. Her parents came to the United States as young adults, her father from Ecuador and her mother from Germany. Frieda has two older maternal half-siblings, an eighteen-year-old brother and a sixteen-year-old sister, both half African American. The social worker initially met with Frieda's mother, Gertrude, to get a family history, with particular emphasis on the various ethnic/racial/cultural influences that might be contributing to Frieda's sense of identity. This was especially important as it might color Frieda's experience of her parents' divorce.

Prior to the separation, Frieda's father, Juan, was the primary caregiver while her mother worked. Juan's problems with alcohol were a contributing factor to the divorce. Although his drinking led to considerable marital conflicts, it did not interfere with his caregiving of Frieda. In fact, Gertrude acknowledged that Juan was a warm, affectionate, and attentive father, and Frieda had great affection for him. Although Frieda did not experience any behavior problems or decline in her academic performance following her parents' separation, she at times would appear sullen. Gertrude also noticed that Frieda had not discussed her father at all following the separation.

The social worker asked about Gertrude's family life prior to and following the divorce. Gertrude grew up in a home that was economically stable, but very violent. Her father, who also drank heavily, was frequently physically abusive toward Gertrude, all three of her siblings, and her mother. Gertrude finished high school in Germany and left when she was eighteen years old, primarily to get away from her family. She met her first husband several years after arriving in the United States, and they had two children together. He passed away suddenly from a heart attack seven years into their marriage. Gertrude reports that this was a very happy marriage, and her deceased husband remains the love of her life. She met Juan shortly after he arrived in the United States from Ecuador, which he left for economic reasons. Juan completed primary school in Ecuador, although Gertrude shared that he was very intelligent and was able to learn English very quickly. At the time they met he drank, but not heavily. When they married, Juan was working in a service sector job and Gertrude was employed as an entry level office worker. She became pregnant with Frieda shortly after their marriage. Juan lost his job when Frieda was two years old, so he became her primary caregiver and Gertrude became the sole household earner. At this time, Juan's drinking increased and became more problematic. Gertrude was laid off from her job shortly after her divorce and is currently receiving public assistance to support her family. Gertrude feels shame about the drop in her economic status. She stated that applying for public assistance was the most difficult thing she had to do in her life, but she said she did it for the sake of her children.

The social worker asked how everyone communicated in the household. Gertrude spoke to her husband and all three children in English. She stated that she does not speak German much because she really does not have anyone to speak it with. She did add, however, that the English she speaks with her children is "sprinkled with German words." Juan speaks Spanish only to Frieda, but she typically responds to him in English. Gertrude makes efforts to keep her children connected with their cultures because she feels it is important to their identity. She is still very close to the family of her first husband, who passed away ten years ago. She makes sure her two older children spend as much time as possible with their cousins, aunts, and uncles. They also continue to regularly attend a church she joined with Juan, a mostly immigrant Latino congregation from Central and South America. Gertrude proudly shared how the congregants speak to Frieda in Spanish and how she responds politely in Spanish.

As we can see, Frieda's family is quite culturally complex. To fully assess the impact of the divorce on Frieda, including how she understood and was experiencing the divorce and how it affected her own sense of identity, it was necessary to conduct a full assessment of the family. This included her parents' immigration history, the ethnic background of all family members, languages spoken at home, and contact with members of their German, African American, and Latino extended families and communities. We must always consider and inquire about the heterogeneity of Latino clients when conducting a culturally competent assessment.

LANGUAGE

Language barriers can be a formidable challenge to providing services to Latino clients. The heterogeneity of Latin America extends to its languages: many languages are spoken in Central and South America, including Spanish, Portuguese, French, Italian, English, German, Welsh, Dutch, Cantonese, and Japanese, as well as scores of indigenous languages including Quechua, Aymara, Nahuatl, Mayan languages, Guaraní, and Garífuna, among many others. Furthermore, while earlier waves of Latino immigrants were mostly Spanish-speaking, service providers are now frequently encountering immigrants from indigenous groups in Latin America who have no English skills and limited Spanish skills.

It is also important to keep in mind that there is a continuum of English-language proficiency for Latino clients. While some Latinos may be monolingual Spanish speakers, others may simply be more comfortable speaking in their mother tongue. Furthermore, many U.S.-born Latinos have limited Spanish-language proficiency, or are monolingual English speakers, and they might take offense at being addressed in Spanish simply because they have a Spanish surname. The key is to ask rather than assume.

While providing services in the client's language of choice is best, this is not always possible. Spanish-dominant Latinos might feel more comfortable having someone translate while speaking to an English-only social worker, particularly with legal, medical, or technical matters, even if they have some ability to understand and communicate in English. In these cases, the standard of care is to use professional (i.e., medical, legal) translators rather than friends or family members, to ensure accurate translation and safeguard confidentiality. If this is not possible, the social worker must pay special attention to how the use of a nonprofessional translator will impact the assessment. The following vignette illustrates how a social worker navigates the difficulties associated with having an adolescent son serve as a translator for his mother.

CASE STUDY

Language

Omar, a seventeen-year-old adolescent male, entered the Homelessness Diversion Unit of the public assistance office with his mother, Olga. The Homelessness Diversion Unit was set up to prevent people eligible for benefits from becoming homeless. Olga was responding to a letter sent to her home regarding concerns about the rent arrears on her apartment and pending eviction notice. Omar came along with his mother to the appointment to serve as her translator. His mother appeared to understand English, because she was responding nonverbally to what the social worker was saying. While maintaining a natural mode of speaking, the social worker made sure to speak clearly and slowly to make it as easy as possible for Olga to understand what was being said in English.

As much as was possible, the social worker wanted to maximize Olga's role in the discussion while minimizing Omar's. Conscious that Omar was still a minor, the social worker was also very careful not to inquire more than was necessary to help Olga and her family resolve the current crisis. During the conversation, the social worker made sure to look at Olga while asking her questions and while Omar was translating. The social worker also explained to Olga that her main role was to prevent homelessness by assessing whether or not Olga's family qualified for available public entitlements or emergency assistance.

The social worker sought only the information that was needed to assess the reason for the arrears and whether Olga qualified for a special grant to pay back her arrears. Olga did qualify for a grant that would pay her arrears as well as the portion of the rent not covered by Section 8. She needed to return to the office within a week with certain documents. The social worker wrote down the name of each document she needed on a piece of paper, and described each one to Olga with Omar translating. Olga returned the following week with Omar and the documents.

The social worker's awareness that Olga understood some English led to her speaking slowly and clearly, so that Olga could understand as much as possible. The more Olga understood the worker directly, the less she would have to rely on her adolescent son, and the more at ease she would be with the worker. This would in turn increase Olga's trust and how forthcoming she would be with the information the social worker needed in order to help. Although the social worker might typically have asked questions that went beyond assessing qualification for benefits, for instance, to assess for psychosocial issues that might be contributing to the housing problems, in this case she chose not to create a situation that would have exposed Omar to information that his mother may not have wanted him to know about.

RACIAL AND ETHNIC IDENTITY

Another important factor to consider in conducting a culturally competent social work assessment with Latino clients relates to the diversity of racial and ethnic identity among Latinos. In most Latino cultures, race is secondary to ethnicity. For instance, one is first Dominican, and only secondarily a black or white Dominican. Similarly, among Puerto Ricans race matters less (in most instances) than identifying oneself as Puerto Rican or of Puerto Rican heritage. However, along the Caribbean coast of Guatemala, Nicaragua, and Honduras, where there are large populations of Garífunas or Black Caribs, race is a more important social construct. When Garífunas migrate to the United States they are often confronted with a dilemma: to identify as black or as Latino; this often has implications for assessment and treatment. Through most of Latin America, however, ethnicity is the more prevailing factor, with many indigenous cultures that have endured hundreds of years of oppression, first by Europeans and later by the United States. When these indigenous peoples migrate to the United States, their history of oppression by the "white man" will certainly play a role in how they view systems of service provision, and will impact if, when, and how they seek services.

Many, if not most, Latinos in the United States have experienced racial discrimination and structural and institutional racism because of their mixed ethnic and racial backgrounds. The assessment process requires inquiry into clients' racial and ethnic identity and into their experiences of racism. They may have experienced race-based discrimination in their job searches; employment or promotions; romantic relationships; when entering stores to purchase goods; in service settings; and in everyday life. The combination of racial and language issues (e.g., darker skin and limited English or speaking with a heavy accent) may have caused them to experience great discrimination. An abundance of prior experiences of prejudice may lead clients to expect discrimination when seeking services. This may cause them to be guarded and not forthcoming with the necessary information to conduct a comprehensive assessment. The social worker must be able to ask skillfully, comfortably, and directly about these experiences, and offer validation, support, and reassurance.

Because of the varied and often mixed racial heritage of people from many Latin American countries, it is not unusual to see various skin complexions even among members of the same family. Unfortunately, racism that is pervasive in society may also be internalized within a family where individual members have different complexions. It may be possible that a family member who has a darker complexion is treated differently or labeled as the "less attractive" sibling. Similarly, a fairer-skinned sibling or parent may be treated in a special manner. Social workers must be aware of the attitudes and beliefs about race held by their Latino clients and their clients' families. Our next vignette illustrates this situation and how the social worker handled it.

CASE STUDY

Race and Racial Identity

Jessica, a twenty-six-year-old Puerto Rican mother, went to see a social worker because she was having trouble dealing emotionally with her eight-year-old daughter's behavior. Her daughter was abused by another family member, and although Jessica responded by protecting her daughter and pressing legal charges, her daughter expressed a tremendous amount of anger toward her. Most painful for Jessica was when her daughter called her "ugly, you are dark and ugly." Noticing the acute pain she felt when her daughter said these things, Jessica's social worker decided to explore further. She asked Jessica about skin color and what it meant to Jessica.

Jessica then revealed that although her parents treated her and her younger siblings the same, she always felt like the ugly one because she had a darker complexion. Her daughter's words made Jessica feel as she did in her childhood, when she did not look like her siblings, and many of their friends called her siblings "pretty," but not her. The disclosure of this experience prompted her to talk about her experiences of racism in the general community, particularly how she was treated by the child welfare system when she disclosed the abuse of her daughter to the authorities.

For Jessica, her daughter's angry words about how her dark skin made her "ugly" caused a resurfacing of the pain produced in the past by her own family's internalized racism as well as the institutional racism she experienced when seeking services. The social worker's ability to identify Jessica's pain and to ask about it comfortably and skillfully helped Jessica verbalize her feelings, connect them to the experiences of her childhood, and begin the process of exploration and healing.

LATINO CULTURAL VALUES

There are many cultural values common to Latinos. An examination of the literature will yield references to *dignidad, familismo, machismo, marianismo, personalismo, respeto, fatalismo,* and *simpatía,* among others (González -Ramos, Zayas, & Cohen, 1998; Cauce & Domenech Rodriguez, 2002). A comprehensive discussion of these values is beyond the scope of this chapter. Instead, we wish to highlight how a social worker might consider some of these values in conducting a culturally competent assessment.

In our role as social workers, we may be required to work with the entire family. A value common to many Latinos is *respeto*, the expectation that children obey and show deference and respect to their parents and elders in general. Thus, when working with families, we must be careful not to unwittingly undermine parental authority. It is important to avoid contradicting or correcting parents in front of their children. Social workers may inadvertently do this out of kindness, to place parents at ease who may be worried about their children making a bad first impression. It can, however, have the appearance of disrespecting a parent's authority. When working with Latino families and children, many social workers have lost their clients' respect when they have attempted to reduce hierarchy by using first names with parents, encouraged children to speak up assertively to their parents, or encouraged greater disengagement from extended family members who may be perceived as sources of irritation. *Familismo*, a strong allegiance and dutifulness to one's family even at the expense of individual needs, is an enduring cultural value that protects families and assures individuals of safety and security (Lugo-Steidel & Contreras, 2003). To have an outsider threaten this might propel the family to forge closer ties to keep the worker at arm's length.

There may be times, however, where the rules and policies of the agency come into direct conflict with cultural values. Our next vignette illustrates how a social worker addressed a situation where the policies of the agency came into direct conflict with the client's cultural values and practices.

CASE STUDY

Cultural Values: Corporal Punishment

Maribel entered a domestic violence shelter with her four-year-old daughter, Olivia. During the assessment process, the social worker explained the rules all shelter residents were expected to comply with. One of the shelter rules prohibited corporal punishment. The reason this rule was enacted was because some of the children in the shelter were experiencing post-traumatic stress symptoms due to the violence they had witnessed and experienced directly. Thus, watching a child being hit for some children who were severely beaten or had witnessed their mother being beaten had the potential to produce tremendous anxiety and distress.

When informing Maribel about this rule, the social worker was careful to explain that she and the shelter understood that corporal punishment, such as spanking, was a common and potentially effective form of discipline. However, because of the history of abuse and trauma many children and mothers in the shelter had experienced, corporal punishment was prohibited within the residential facility.

The social worker also suggested that Maribel attend the parenting support group offered in the shelter, where mothers often shared their parenting struggles and learned and explored alternative disciplinary techniques in place of corporal punishment. The group was put in place to assist mothers in maintaining their parental authority and children's respect while complying with shelter rules and regulations.

It is not unusual for many Latino parents to use corporal punishment with their children. In fact many parents view stern discipline as a sign that they care deeply about their children. In the vignette above, the social worker was careful not to judge corporal forms of punishment or suggest they were inferior in any way. This may require social workers to put aside their own values regarding the merits and effectiveness of corporal punishment. The social worker also explicitly explained the reasons for the rule, so that Maribel understood that it was not an arbitrarily imposed, value-determined rule meant to supersede or forever replace her own parenting practices. Finally, the social worker provided Maribel with the option of participating in a parenting support group, where she could learn other disciplinary techniques and openly express her feelings and struggles with parenting.

Clients will often seek out social workers when they are in crisis or in need. A thorough and culturally competent assessment is required not only to determine appropriate interventions and assistance, but also to ensure the client's safety and well-being. Social workers, especially when they lack knowledge of Latino culture, must take care not to presume a given behavior is necessarily problematic. It is also important, however, not to assume that because a behavior may be rooted in the clients' culture it is *not* problematic or interfering with functioning. Social workers must be aware of our learned, stereotypical characterizations or impressions of individuals from cultural groups other than our own, as they may lead us to make erroneous assumptions. When conducting assessments of Latino clients it is important to be aware of, ask about, and take into consideration cultural values. A culturally competent approach will help us determine whether the client's behavior is indeed culturally *syntonic*, or whether it is a problem behavior even when taking the client's culture into consideration. Our next vignette illustrates a conflict that arises when the cultural values of the social worker differ from those of the client.

CASE STUDY
Cultural Values: Female Socialization and Domestic Violence

Maricela, age twenty-five, entered a domestic violence shelter the previous month with her seven-year-old son and five-year-old daughter. Maricela's husband of nine years became abusive as soon as they came to the United States five years before from Mexico. Her husband would become very violent when he drank. Maricela urged her husband to get help many times, but he refused to get help even as his drinking worsened and his violent behavior toward Maricela increased in frequency and intensity. Maricela decided to enter a shelter after a serious violent incident when her husband struck her so hard that she fell unconscious. She awoke to see her two children hovering over her terrified and in tears.

Since entering the shelter, Maricela's children performed well in school and were very well-behaved. She took a tremendous amount of pride in being a good mother. She also shared with her social worker how hard she tried to satisfy her husband and how she now feels like a failure as a wife. In many of her sessions Maricela sadly talked about all the things she has lost, including her family back in Mexico, her husband, and the home they shared. She no longer felt like a wife, daughter, or sister, aspects of her identity that were very important to her. During one session she expressed shame for uprooting her children and bringing them into a shelter. She felt as though she was being selfish and that "a good mother puts the needs of her children over her own needs and happiness." The social worker challenged Maricela by pointing out how the value placed on a woman's ability to sacrifice and endure for the sake of her children creates conditions where women endure abusive behavior because they feel it is what a good woman should do.

Maricela strongly disagreed with this assertion and confronted her social worker. She stated that after losing her status as a wife, the pride that she felt in being a good mother to her children was her only source of self-worth. She added the she needed to hold on to this "traditional identity of being a woman" to experience the self-confidence she needed to move forward. Recognizing that she was challenging an important aspect of Maricela's cultural and gender identity, the social worker changed directions in her approach to addressing Maricela's feelings of selfishness. She pointed out to Maricela all the ways in which she was a good mother to her children now in the shelter, and all the opportunities she continued to provide for them. The worker also reminded Maricela of the danger she and her children faced remaining in the home with her violent husband, and how the difficult decision to leave her husband was also for the sake of her children's emotional and physical well-being. By focusing on aspects of Maricela's identity that she took pride in, and highlighting how her decision to protect her children by leaving her husband was consistent with her values and sense of identity, the social worker was able to help Maricela work through her feelings of selfishness. Maricela also felt more confident in her ability to take on the challenges of finding a home, learning English, and securing stable employment to support her family.

The vignette above demonstrates how assumptions about cultural values can be misleading to social workers. Perhaps out of concern that feelings of guilt would result in returning to her abuser, the social worker in this case was only able to see the adverse consequences of Maricela's values about "being a good Mexican woman." The literature refers to this Latino value of a woman's selfless sacrifice and abnegation to her family as *marianismo* (Cauce & Domenech Rodriguez, 2002), and many workers see it in a negative light. Most cultural values, however, have both positive and negative—or functional and dysfunctional— aspects. Social workers must be open to examining the full complexity of each value with the client, rather than focusing automatically on the negative connotations. As our skills in cultural competence continue to grow, we will be better able to do this. In the meantime, openness and assuming a nonjudgmental stance, attitudes we are trained to assume with all clients, will allow us to avoid a potentially damaging misstep.

Maricela was able to point out to her social worker how her values were also a source of strength and were integral to her identity and feelings of self-worth. This provided the social worker with a fuller understanding of Maricela's own gender identity, shaped largely by her cultural values, which the social worker then used to provide support in a manner that was consistent with Maricela's values. While Maricela and her worker had developed a relationship that allowed Maricela to confront her worker, such a misstep on the part of a social worker might have resulted in client reticence, if not termination of the work altogether. Thus, social workers must continuously assess and strive to more fully understand Latino clients' cultural values in order to provide quality services.

LENGTH OF RESIDENCY IN THE UNITED STATES AND ACCULTURATION

Many Latino groups emphasize the virtue of deference to the professional as an authority, causing the client to be reluctant to establish less-hierarchical, pro-active, or more familiar interactions with the professional. Indeed, these clients will see it as a sign of disrespect to assume a familiar stance too early in the relationship. Often, one must earn *confianza* (trust) before one can engage in *relajo* (a relaxed, tacitly

agreed upon bantering). For other Latinos, however, initiating an informal stance with a service provider will be quite acceptable. Social workers seeking to discern which approach to pursue might pay attention to
the client's level of acculturation and length of residency in the United
States, particularly as these factors interplay with the client's level of
education. Thus, we might expect a more deferential stance from a less-
educated, recently immigrated client than we would of an educated,
newly arrived immigrant who held a professional position in his or her
country of origin. The latter might readily welcome a non-hierarchical
relationship, while the former might be more acquiescent to persons
in authority. A second-generation, English-dominant Latino of modest
means will likely be more assertive with the social worker because of a
higher level of acculturation. In contrast, her immigrant mother who
has lived in this country for twenty years and still speaks limited English
might not understand quite as well why the provider is working on
empowering her to be assertive in her relationships with family, merchants, or telemarketers.

GENDER AND SOCIAL CLASS

Working at the intersection of cultural values, gender, and social class
can be extremely challenging. Knowledge of Latino cultural values and
comfort with discussing issues of class and gender can aid the social
worker in understanding the context of interactions with clients and
charting a course of action. The following two vignettes illustrate this.

CASE STUDY

Gender and Social Class in Social Work Practice

A middle-aged male social worker was assigned two female clients, one
Puerto Rican and the other Mexican, of different socioeconomic levels.
The first client, Patricia, was a forty-year-old wife and mother of two preadolescent children, who held a graduate degree in a health profession.
She had sought help at the family agency for two concerns: her professional transition into a supervisory position in a new area of work and
her husband's level of alcohol use. Regarding the promotion, Patricia had
begun to feel less confident in her abilities as the promotion neared. With
regard to her husband's alcohol use, she stated that his drinking had
begun to trouble her at about the same time as her professional transition
was occurring. Her husband was seen by the male worker for two couple's
sessions, and the husband's drinking was acknowledged by the couple as
not problem-drinking. In subsequent sessions, Patricia's concern with

her husband's drinking was connected to her loss of self-confidence during the professional transition. Specifically, Patricia was afraid he would not be available to support her in her promotion.

Since her social work appointments were late in the day, Patricia raised concern that the social worker was "working too hard" and should rest, while offering to surrender her session for him. It was clear that she had both professional and social-class affinity with the worker and a high level of acculturation, and thus felt comfortable directly verbalizing her concern for the worker's well-being. With exploration, Patricia came to understand that her reactions to both her husband and the social worker were related to the sense of abandonment she had felt as a young girl when her father had divorced her mother. Throughout her life, major transitions had caused her anxiety because she wanted the help and support of her father. Now in her adult life transition, her reactions were being repeated in her worries that the two men in her life whom she depended on (her husband and her therapist) would not be available to support her during a critical time period.

The second client, Marta, was a shy, timid woman in her mid-thirties who had completed high school. She had married at age twenty-five, and had two children, a preschooler and a third-grader. Her husband worked as a telephone repairman. Marta also shared her home with her mother, who was very traditional and fervently religious and very helpful in the home. Marta sought social work services at the family agency to discuss the dysthymic feelings she had experienced all of her life. This was her first time seeking help outside of her family, and Marta was uncertain about what she should say in the sessions. However, she became quickly engaged in trying to understand her shyness and low-grade depressive symptoms.

At one point in the early stages of the relationship with the social worker, the discussion turned to how comfortable she felt speaking to a male worker. Marta quickly and suddenly shifted the discussion to other topics. The social worker discerned that some anxiety had been aroused that caused the interruption in the flow of the conversation. The worker considered gender, social class, and acculturation differences as contributing factors to Marta's anxiety, but decided not to explore these yet. Later, Marta asked why the worker did not have curtains on his windows, an unexpected question but one that seemed relevant to the process of their work. Together, Marta and the social worker examined where her question came from. In time, it became apparent that the question about the curtains reflected Marta's growing sense of familiarity and intimacy with her worker. "I have never spoken to another man about my deepest thoughts and feelings as I have with you," Marta noted. "It makes me nervous to feel this way but at the same time I feel safe." Curtains represented symbolically the privacy and security of confidentiality that the sessions provided her.

The social worker clearly had knowledge of Latino cultural values, a sense of the client's levels of acculturation, skill in discerning issues of gender and social class in the context of culture, and comfort with discussing these issues. This allowed for a skillful handling of the situation and a successful resolution. Observation and knowledge of the broad heterogeneity of Latino clients prepared the social worker to serve in a more culturally competent manner, and engendered the skills to know when to pursue one approach instead of another. In culturally competent social work assessments, the impact of generation, acculturation, length of residency, education, race and ethnicity, and culture of origin are the issues that will elucidate the assessment process, guide the course of treatment, and result in a successful outcome.

INTEGRATIVE PSYCHOSOCIAL ASSESSMENT

In the social work assessment, we gather as much information as possible from our clients, empirical research and theory, evidence-based practice guidelines, and clinical wisdom. We then synthesize this information into a meaningful write-up, and we articulate an integrative formulation of the problems our clients are facing, possible etiologies, and potential courses of action. In a culturally competent assessment of Latino clients, we observe the principle that facts must be separated from assumptions and that all conclusions we arrive at must be supported by facts. This is how we keep stereotypes, myths, and common perceptions about Latino clients at bay to conduct a balanced, useful assessment.

In the following case involving clients with HIV (human immunodeficiency virus), the worker collected considerable information about the individuals in the family and their individual and collective functioning. Cultural aspects that influence male-female relationships, definitions of masculinity, fatherhood, and motherhood, and the vicissitudes of practicing in real-world circumstances over which neither worker nor clients have any control come together in the ongoing assessment of the family and ultimate outcomes.

CASE STUDY
Integrative Assessment and Practice

Carmen, a thirty-five-year-old Dominican mother of three, tested positive for HIV. She did not fit into any high-risk group for infection and had had three serial monogamous relationships. The social worker in the community health clinic where she was tested suspected that the cause of the infection was her live-in boyfriend of several years, Rafael. Carmen described Rafael as a loving man who was an excellent surrogate father to her three children (ages thirteen, ten, and eight) by her first husband, whom she had divorced because of domestic violence. After some deli-cate conversation with the male social worker, Carmen deduced that only her boyfriend could be the source of the infection. She was fearful and hesitant, since confronting him about this possibility would threaten their relationship and Rafael's status as the man of the house, and might bring shame with the extended family. Also, to inform him that she was HIV-positive might lead to accusations of her infidelity. With much trepida-tion, she agreed with the social worker that the best course of action was to disclose her seropositive status to Rafael first; the children would be informed later. Through the children's words and behaviors, the social worker was aware that they were already becoming concerned about the frequent medical visits their mother had been scheduling.

The social worker was faced with competing issues. On the one hand, Carmen preferred not to disclose her status to her boyfriend, children, or other family members. On the other hand, state and federal mandates dictated that the source of the infection must be traced, and those who may be in danger of infection alerted. In addition, initiating treatment would mean more medical visits, which would further increase the chil-dren's and family's concerns. Over the course of three assessment ses-sions, the worker engaged in a review of the entire family situation and short-term future family activities, discussed partner notification require-ments with Carmen, and played out various scenarios. Carmen finally agreed there was no choice but to inform Rafael. They planned the disclo-sure to take place at the next visit, with a sympathetic physician and the social worker present to facilitate and provide medical information.

As expected, Rafael was taken aback by the disclosure, but he was not angry. He allowed for the possibility that Carmen's previous boyfriend might have infected her, and agreed to be tested. Later, his test returned showing that he was also HIV-positive and was further along in the course of the illness than Carmen. It appeared that he was the source of her infection. Before any other intervention was taken, the social worker returned to the assessment process. The information to be gathered from this assessment was abundant, but several salient issues had to be addressed first. Identifying how and when Rafael was infected might shed light on the course of his illness, but might also reveal some delicate infor-mation (e.g., the possibility of infidelities) and invoke further partner notification mandates. Rafael reported no intravenous drug use and was likely infected through sexual relations with another person, woman or man. How might these disclosures impact Rafael and Carmen's relation-ship? They clearly shared a mutual love and respect and had formed a stable family life. Despite more than a decade of living in the United States, they spoke only Spanish and maintained all or most of the culture of their native country. The couple preferred to be led or instructed by the social worker rather than to question or assert themselves in the work process. They feared that their extended family, in many ways culturally typical in their past support of Rafael and Carmen, would reject them because of stigma if they told them they are HIV-positive. The children were happy and healthy, and consideration would have to be given as to how to best inform them of the situation, whether all at once or in small quantities, and only once the couple had assimilated the knowledge, and trust was restored to their relationship.

A plan was discussed with the couple as to what to tell the children and how to help them understand the information. Before informing the social worker, however, the couple told their families in the Dominican Republic that they had each acquired a serious, terminal liver ailment that may have come from their apartment environment or things they had eaten. The social worker would now have to incorporate this communication that the couple had had with their kin into his assessment and intervention planning.

As the above vignette illustrates, our clients often present with extremely challenging and complicated circumstances. Deference to authority and a willingness to collaborate with the social worker will not necessarily preclude clients from acting on their own. Knowledge of the culture, skill at making culturally based formulations and interventions, and a genuine openness to diversity, will enable the worker to conduct culturally competent assessments and to set the stage for a truly collaborative venture.

Becoming a Culturally Competent Social Worker

There is no shortcut to conducting culturally competent assessments. Inasmuch as culture is dynamic and changes constantly, cultural competency is in fact a journey, not a destination. However, there are many things beginning social workers can do to enhance their culturally competent assessment skills with Latinos. We list here some that the authors have found useful, without implying that these are the only ones, or that the list is comprehensive. It is most important to genuinely embrace diversity, to approach differences with authentic curiosity and respect, to ask questions comfortably and matter-of-factly, and to seek input from one's supervisors when working with a population different from us.

1. *Be comfortable with not knowing about all Latino cultures.*
The social worker must be comfortable "not knowing" and asking clients about their culture, race, ethnicity, socioeconomic status, migration history, previous life in their country (or countries) of origin, and other factors. With undocumented Latinos, some of these questions may be sensitive ones, as they raise the fear of being revealed to authorities, but the sincerity expressed in our demeanor will, in time, erode

any mistrust. Asking questions comfortably will set the stage for an open discussion about how cultural factors may be impacting the client's presenting problems, and to explore differences in the context of the client–social worker relationship. Even without being able to speak Spanish, for example, a social worker's effort to pronounce the client's name correctly, or to say a few words in Spanish, can go a long way toward placing the client at ease and demonstrating interest in the client and his or her culture.

2. *Engage in active listening without reaching premature conclusions.*

With all our clients, we are wise to remain open to new information and new sources of information. However, when cultural traditions differ from our own, it is the worker's ability to remain open and active in the interaction before making conclusive statements that earns the work credibility and trust. Thus, for example, assuming that your Latino adolescent client will benefit from greater degrees of autonomy because this is developmentally appropriate in our middle-class, mainstream perspective, may run counter to Latino families' expectations that family comes first and interdependence rather than independence is paramount. It is essential then that the social worker pay close attention to both verbal and nonverbal information, and keep in mind Latino cultural features. In one case known to the authors, an experienced clinician, working with a highly acculturated Puerto Rican woman whose sessions were spent discussing her intense conflicts and intense ties to her parents and siblings, suggested a break from the family. The client responded negatively to this suggestion because separation from family was unthinkable; what she wanted was the opportunity to vent and to find ways of negotiating the family system she lived in, one with several levels of acculturation across multiple generations.

3. *What you read about Latinos—including in this chapter—are just helpful suggestions and guidelines, and stereotypical portrayals may occur.*

To be sure, there are many excellent resources to learn about Latinos. Keep in mind, once again, that Latinos are not a homogeneous group, so the information in these resources may not apply to all Latinos. Furthermore, the information that *is* applicable might be mediated by social class, education, or acculturation, or may be a gross over-generalization. Remember that in the end, you are working with an individual, not an entire ethnic group, race, or culture. Rather than generalizing from something you have read or seen in a media outlet, ask questions, meet Latinos, participate in their cultural activities, and become involved in their communities. We are not suggesting that social workers abandon their core knowledge about human behavior, family functioning, community and group processes, and psychosocial assessment. What we are suggesting is that by taking this core knowledge and integrating it effectively into the evaluation process, while maintaining a flexible stance about the information gathered, social workers will be able to conduct culturally competent assessments.

4. *Observe important interpersonal processes often associated with Latino cultures, and demonstrate genuine curiosity and respect.*

Most clients can sense when you are genuinely interested in them and respect them (such as when you sincerely try to understand them, their culture, and their families), and this is likely to enhance their trust in you. Latino clients are prone to forming individual rather than institutional transferences. In other words, they are likely to be more connected to the social worker than to the agency setting. *Personalismo,* or the preference for a more personal, warm relationship over an impersonal businesslike one, is an important cultural value for Latinos. Taking a few minutes to engage in some meaningful small talk (e.g., asking about something that was previously discussed, like an ill relative or a recent trip) before plunging into "business mode" will foster a more comfortable working relationship and demonstrate *personalismo.* We will all make a mistake sooner or later, and a client is more likely to forgive us a blunder if they know we have made it in a genuine effort to get to know them and help them. A balanced level of self-disclosure may also help facilitate the interpersonal exchange with Latino clients.

Conclusion

We have outlined in this chapter some important considerations in conducting culturally competent assessments of Latino clients across diverse service settings. This must begin with the critical first component of self-exploration in the context of genuine curiosity of self and others. Social workers must then take into account a number of factors, chief among them being the broad heterogeneity of Latinos in the United States. Country of origin, education, previous and current social class, migration history, and length of residency in the United States will be different for each client and will differentially impact their life history and presenting problem. Language proficiencies will add to this heterogeneity, existing along a continuum from monolingual-English to monolingual-Spanish speakers, but also including clients who may speak neither. The impact of race and racial identity, both in their countries of origin and in the United States, and the clients' experience of internalized and societal racism and discrimination will also be important components of a culturally competent assessment. There are also important cultural values common to most Latinos, which will impact the relationship with service providers. These include deference to authority, *familismo, machismo, marianismo, personalismo*, and *respeto*, among others.

In the end, the client–social worker relationship, inasmuch as it is reflective of the client's life, will be an excellent forum to address differences between the worker and the client *in vivo*, and thus begin to help the client acquire the skills to address differences in their everyday life.

Speaking Spanish, or even being a member of a Latino group, will not automatically confer upon the social worker the capacity to conduct culturally competent assessments. Sharing our clients' race, ethnic background, socioeconomic status, gender, or other commonalities is not necessarily a shortcut to bonding, an error many beginning social workers make. We are all complex and not easily defined, and many providers have found themselves in trouble because they assumed "they knew where the client was coming from." There is no shortcut or substitute for "working through" a relationship with our clients and building it moment by moment.

Building upon this chapter's focus on cultural competence, Chapter Eleven helps the reader understand precisely how Latino cultural variables can be successfully applied in practice. In the next chapter the author deconstructs therapeutic constructs that were developed for practice with Americans of European descent, and demonstrates their limits with Latino faculties. He shows how systems theory and social constructionist practice can be used with Latinos, and how a liberation-based lens can help connect micro, meso, and macro practice.

References

Aldarondo, E. (Ed.). (2007). *Advancing social justice through clinical practice.* NJ: Lawrence Erlbaum Associates.

Cauce, A. M., & Domenech Rodríguez, M. (2002). Latino families: Myths and realities. In J. Contreras, A. Neal-Barnett, & K. Kerns (Eds.), *Latino children and families in the United States: Current research and future directions* (pp. 3–25). Westport, CT: Praeger Publishers.

Dyche, L., & Zayas, L. H. (1995). The value of curiosity and naiveté for the cross-cultural psychotherapist. *Family Process, 34*, 389–399.

González-Ramos, G., Zayas, L. H., & Cohen, E. V. (1998). Child-rearing values of low income, urban Puerto Rican mothers of preschool children. *Professional Psychology: Practice and Research, 29*, 377–382.

Lugo Steidel, A., & Contreras, J. M. (2003). A new familism scale for use with Latino populations. *Hispanic Journal of Behavioral Sciences, 25*, 312–330.

National Association of Social Workers (1996). *Code of Ethics of the National Association of Social Workers.* Retrieved June 21, 2007, from http://www.social workers.org/pubs/code/code.asp

Organista, K. C. (2007). *Solving Latino psychosocial and health problems: Theory, practice, and populations.* Hoboken, NJ: John Wiley.

CHAPTER ELEVEN

Direct Practice with Latino Families

Jason J. Platt

Introduction

A Venezuelan colleague frequently jokes that "what Freud might call an enmeshed relationship, I call a close relationship with my mother." His comment is humorous but nevertheless hints of a trend in which mental health theories are at odds with the values and needs of members of Latino communities. This includes many of the dominant theories guiding clinical approaches to mental health, which even outright pathologize some aspects of Latino culture. This is becoming increasingly significant given the seismic demographic shifts in the United States in recent decades, including an estimated growth of the Latino population to 42.7 million (León, 2007). The Latino population includes families with ties to such varied cultural contexts as Mexico, Colombia, Brazil, and El Salvador. If professional training in the mental health disciplines is to keep pace with the changing demographics, there is a need for shifting our frame of reference. Regrettably, mental health approaches have often remained rooted in a foundation of European and U.S. theories and also continue to be primarily individual rather than systemically focused (Martín-Baró, 1994; Sloan, 2003).

Clinical work with Latino families may also be limited in its effectiveness by an all-too-common bifurcated focus on the micro system of the family as opposed to a focus on the macro system of the larger societal context in which the family exists. Dean (1997) observes that ". . . social work's guiding principle of person-in-environment has often led to an emphasis on *either* the environment or the person" (p. 7). Fortunately, recognition that clinicians must balance competencies in addressing the complexities of both families and society is growing. As Constable & Lee (2004) observe, "Rather than segmenting a focus on one or the other, as social and behavioral sciences tend to do, social workers need to account for persons and social structures and for the interactions between them" (p. 15). This need demands that clinicians consider theories and interventions more critically as we apply approaches to an increasingly diverse client population.

A Framework for Therapy with Latino Families

The application of models that may not be culturally appropriate and the use of an individual approach with a largely collectivistic community may contribute to why Latinos underutilize mental health services and have high early termination rates (Snowden & Cheung, 1990). First sessions are often the last session for many Latino clients given that 50 percent never return for a second appointment (Dingfelder, 2005). Effective treatment for most mental health disorders exists, yet many in Latino communities face barriers in connecting with competent mental health services. The lack of correspondence of clinician's theoretical models with the cultural values and needs of the Latino population is one factor that contributes to this barrier. This chapter suggests several theoretical perspectives clinicians may draw upon that provide a useful framework to address this need—social constructivism, systems theory, and the concepts of Paulo Freire and the liberation psychology movement.

Social Constructionism

Social constructionism is a paradigm that helps social workers to be clinically sensitive and open to the multiple worldviews found within our pluralistic society. Social constructionism posits that social and historical contexts shape and circumscribe the possible ways in which people can understand themselves and others (Hedges, 2005). Historically, professionals were expected to be the holders of specialized knowledge that they would dispense or use on nonprofessionals. Social constructionism counters this view and challenges the idea that anyone can know anything with absolute certainty. Given this, it evokes a clinical stance of unknowingness among social workers and openness to the idea that there are infinite alternative ways of being in the world. As such, this tentative stance is also an intervention in that it creates space for clients to safely explore their different cultural legacies and the interactions that they have with those from other cultural backgrounds. The power of creating such a safe space for Latino clients, bombarded with not-so-subtle messages that aspects of their culture are not acceptable, should and cannot be underestimated.

All humans, therapists included, are born into a sociocultural context that profoundly influences their thoughts and behaviors. "Societies, including their institutions and professions (e.g., teaching, parenting, family life education, therapy), all are organized to greater or lesser degrees within the parameters of the prevailing worldview of the members of that society" (Becvar, Canfield, & Becvar, 1997, p. 3). The dominant ways of viewing the world slip into almost every aspect of what we do, even when we believe ourselves to be acting without influence. Alan Watts (1972) proposed that "our most private thoughts and emotions are not actually our own. For we think in terms of language and images which we did not invent, but which were given to us by society" (p.72). Ethically, clinicians must strive to develop greater consciousness of the constructions they have developed, in particular in regard to cultural and ethnic groups. Falicov (1998) suggests that "racial groups have been historically linked with positive and negative social constructions." Therapists are not above being influenced by the varied messages found in society regarding different ethnic groups, but they have an ethical duty to examine the clinical implications of the stories they have picked up.

A natural outgrowth of considering the tenets of social constructionism is the need for self-reflection as an important first step for therapists working with Latino families. This would be important for both non-Latino and Latino clinicians. It is fairly easy to underestimate the force of our own sociocultural context as we advance through the process of gaining an education, choosing the theories on which we will base our therapy, and later commence the process of assessing, interpreting, and intervening in the lives of clients. For example, as someone from a Danish family background, with its cultural values of stoicism and individualism, the fact that I was initially drawn to theories that emphasized cognition over emotion and individualism over interdependence makes sense. A lack of awareness of the influence of my sociocultural background on my clinical work though could lead to me to evaluate families from a different sociocultural background as less healthy or functional. A main push from the social constructionism perspective is to avoid what Gergen (1991) argues is the natural tendency for humans to forget that many social notions are socially and culturally created. Values and cultural legacies left unconscious and unexamined can quickly evolve into influences on a clinician's assessment methods, evaluations of health and normalcy, and intervention strategies. Michel Foucault suggests that constructionism helps avoid the limitation of more modernist approaches by helping clinicians remember "that explanatory theories about the world and humankind, far from representing objective truths, are essentially instruments of social power and are inherently imperialistic" (Doherty, 1991, p. 40). This realization can leave clinicians wondering about the best way to proceed when working with families. In some ways, this is the point of the social constructionism perspective. An acceptance that we honestly do not know "the truth" helps us avoid the temptation to force people into ill-fitting models, permits an openness to unique ways of being in the world, and unlocks a universe of possible new ways of working with families. As Paulo Freire (1998) explained, "education does not make us educable. It is our awareness of being unfinished that makes us educable" (p. 58). As social workers embrace being unfinished, it is like shifting from having the capacity of a teaspoon to that of an ocean. The flow of the fountain of knowledge isn't restricted by a container already full.

As a clinician begins working with a family, useful information can be gained by observing the stories held by the family members. In the interaction between different members of a family, what is communicated and what is received are influenced by the lenses of those involved. Bateson (1979) explained that "Evidently, the nature of 'meaning,' pattern, redundancy, information and the like, depends upon where we sit" (p. 407). It is not enough to identify what words come out of one individual's mouth into the ears of another, the meaning given and received must be understood. Becvar and Becvar (1993) expands this view, noting that, "Each of us punctuates our reality in different ways; that is, behavioral sequences are understood and meaning is experienced relative to the epistemology of the observer" (p. 217). An example could be a case with a bicultural couple in which one partner is of German heritage and keeps an "appropriate" personal distance in public from his or her Latino partner. The Latino partner may experience appropriate German boundaries as being cold or distant given that public affection is quite standard in most Latino cultures. Therapy, guided by a social constructionist paradigm, can assist the couple in developing a greater understanding of the influence of their different cultural systems. Conversations about these can provide opportunities to clarify the intentions of each individual, how their messages are being sent and received, and the impact this communication is having on their relationship.

A second reason for utilizing a social constructionist lens is the vital role that cultural stories have in the lives of Latino clients. Hernández (2002) observes social constructions or "stories speak of characters, contexts, and plots: Questions of who, when, where, what, and how are intertwined in the stories logic" (p. 2). There are powerful stories guiding the lives of Latino clients that are held at individual, familial, and community levels. These social constructions have direct clinical implications for families. As DiNicola (1997) states, "the family culture will shape its beliefs about how to define the foregoing problems, how and where to seek help, and what solutions are culturally sanctioned and acceptable to them" (p. 75). An example can be found in the account given by Lucille Marmolejo Romeo (2002) of the childhood messages she was sent by her mother, who would say *"Ay hija, no corras afuera. Tienes que aprender como cocinar porque cuando te cases, puedes cuidar a tu esposo y hijos."* (Oh daughter, don't run outdoors._You need to learn how to cook because when you marry, you will be able to take care of your husband and children) (p. 16). Effective clinical work will draw out such stories, and the clinician will seek to learn how these stories influence presenting problems the family members are experiencing. Sensitivity to the power of such stories will also lead to interventions that are respectful of the cultural context such stories create.

A basic step clinicians can take is to simply invite family members to talk about how being Latino has impacted their lives. "Race," Toni Morrison explained, has functioned as a "metaphor" necessary to the "construction of Americanness" in the creation of our national identity (Takaki, 1993, p. 2). Clinical conversation could involve opening up a dialogue about race and its impact on an individual client's life. Other conversations might involve dialogues about the cultural messages Latino clients have been given and which ones they have embraced or discarded. Therapists who do not share a cultural context with their client may also wish to make a space for openness by asking direct questions about what the client thinks could be missed in therapy, given cultural differences. They may wish to say something direct such as "As a white male, what types of questions might I not think to ask?" or "If you were working with a Latino therapist, how do you think the conversations we have might be different?" The social worker should then listen, nonreactively, and dialogue with family members about ideas to address any potential limitations stemming from being a non-Latino clinician. Discussion about ethnicity, race, and culture in general opens up important dialogues. It provides a chance to explore how a client's sense of self as a Latino informs him or her and how it contributes to the stories the client holds and the way he or she deals with any given presenting problem. As Mair (1988) suggests, "We inhabit the great stories of our culture. We live through stories. We are lived by the stories of our race and place. It is this enveloping and constituting function of stories that is especially important to sense more fully" (p. 127).

Utilizing a Systems Lens in Clinical Work with Latino Clients

The peculiar use of Spanish in the phrase "taking care of numero uno" is discussed by cross-cultural expert Ilya Adler (2006), who shares his experience of training groups of Latinos. He recounts "I tell them about this 'strange gringo' expression, and then I ask them if they can guess who that famous (or infamous) 'Number One' is. Typical answers include 'parents,' 'spouses,' 'children,' but rarely, if ever, does it cross their mind that the person is actually talking about her/himself" (p. 3). Clinical approaches based on individualistic theories can be experienced as similarly bizarre by Latino clients, given that on the whole Latinos typically are embedded within a cultural context of interdependence. Systems theory, with its focus on relationships, offers an alternative. What concepts guide a clinician coming from a systems perspective? The field of family therapy and the clinical literature on the application of systems theory is immense, but most systemic approaches include some common core concepts. Four systemic concepts that seem particularly relevant for work with Latino clients are isomorphism, homeostasis, the tenet that one cannot not communicate, and the idea of context.

ISOMORPHISM

An idea of significant clinical utility is the concept of *isomorphism*, which describes the phenomenon of structures, patterns, and content being replicated at all levels of a system. For Latino clients there is a cultural tendency to consider these multiple levels as being interrelated. "The basic social unit in Latino culture is the extended family" (Falicov, 1998, p. 161). Naturally then, isomorphism is a foundational system concept, or framework, under which the complex process therapy with Latino families can be understood. Perhaps the greatest rationale for discussions of isomorphism is "that the important point is not merely the notion of replicating transactional patterns or the observed concept itself, but that these patterns can be altered consciously via interventions" (Rothberg, 1997, p. 167). In creating change, isomorphism is a hopeful concept. Clinicians do not necessarily need to change an entire system, but may bring about changes by working with one part of the system. The idea is that if a pattern occurring in part of the family is altered, isomorphically other parts can be influenced. An example might be if a clinician were able to assist a daughter-in-law to find her voice in negotiating boundaries with her in-laws, this new pattern of clear boundaries has an increased chance of appearing in other parts of the system, such as between her spouse and their teenage son.

HOMEOSTASIS

All systems function according to a number of different rules. One of the main rules described by the communication theorists is that of *homeostasis*, the tendency for a system to attempt to maintain a steady state of being (Bateson, 1979; Watzlawick, Bavelas, & Jackson, 1967). In families, patterns of relating develop, and once they are developed, the system acts to maintain them. This occurs even when a current way of relating causes pain and suffering. When a challenge to the current pattern occurs, the system responds in a way that protects itself from being altered by the challenge. The founding father of family therapy, Don D. Jackson, proposed that the role of the social worker is one of participant observer in which the objective is to develop a hypothesis of the homeostatic patterns and system maintaining the client's problem. (Jackson, 1949). For example, parents from a Cuban background might bring in a daughter who has been caught acting out sexually. A cultural rule for many from Cuban backgrounds is the traditional expectation that women will remain sexually inexperienced until marriage (McGoldrick, Pearce, & Giordano, 1982). A clinician might observe homeostasis occurring if, say, the daughter attempted to return to culturally consistent behavior but was then inadvertently punished by the parents by their reminding her of her past behavior and/or treating her as a lost cause. This punishing might cause the daughter to feel hopeless about regaining her parents' respect and lead her to seek connection outside the family, including by further sexual acting out behaviors. Therapists can be helpful by observing the homeostatic ways the system maintains such consistencies and can intervene by helping facilitate new patterns through in-session interruptions and redirections and through the use of prescriptive and proscriptive homework assignments.

ONE CANNOT NOT COMMUNICATE

Clients often come to therapy with complaints about the lack of communication in their relationships. This would be challenged by many systems theorists because of the premise that *one cannot not communicate*. That doesn't mean that the intended message may be lost. This may be particularly common for Latino clients who have been taught to speak in a way that maintains harmony, including the use of indirectness, impersonal third person, or use of humor in order to make a statement (Falicov, 1998). Therapy can assist them in recognizing how they are communicating and to help them find ways they may wish to alter their patterns in order to reach their communication goals. Communication takes many forms, such as one's verbal expressions, body language, silences, and behaviors. Communication theorists particularly focus on what is communicated at a digital level (report, i.e., the words actually said) and what is communicated at an analog level (command, i.e., information on how the digital information should be used). When these two are not congruent, communication is experienced as confusing and limits individuals from knowing how to best respond. A goal of therapy may not be for Latino clients to discontinue layered ways of communicating, but to increase understanding among important relationships of the messages being sent.

CONTEXT

In the song "Fire Door" by singer Ani Difranco (1997) is the lyric "taken out of context I must seem so strange." This single lyric succinctly sums up a major concept that guides clinicians utilizing a systems theory approach, which is that to understand behavior clinicians must understand their client's context. This aptly applies to clinical cases in which client's behaviors may seem illogical or ill-conceived. Early family therapy theorists Watzlawick, Bavelas, & Jackson (1967) elucidated this idea in this way:

> A phenomenon remains unexplainable as long as the range of observation is not wide enough to include the context in which the phenomenon occurs. Failure to realize the intricacies of the relationships between an event and the matrix in which it takes place, between an organism and its environment, either confronts the observer with something "mysterious" or induces him to attribute to his object of study certain properties the object may not possess. (pp. 20–21)

Therapists guided by systems theory assume that "all behavior makes sense, or is logical, within a given context" (Becvar & Becvar, 1999, p. 19). Therefore systems therapists must take on the role of detective and seek to discover in what context their client's behaviors, attitudes, and interpersonal interactions make sense. An example might be the impact that the increasing media coverage of anti-Latino messages may have on the mental health and relationships of Latino clients. "In a diverse society there are inevitable collisions between family members and families and the larger society" (Constable & Lee, 2004, p. 21). This is particularly apparent for Latino families who are increasingly being slandered in the ways groups such as Jews and Irish have been in the past. Dehooded klansmen have had significant success in repackaging themselves as patriots, and racist ideas about Latinos are increasingly being accepted in the cultural mindset of Middle America. For example, Gonzalez (2000) recounts an incident in a routine child custody case in Amarillo, Texas, where state district Judge Samuel Kiser ordered U.S. citizen Martha Laureano to stop speaking to her daughter in Spanish, stating "[you are] abusing your child and relegating her to the position of housemaid . . . It's not in her best interest to be ignorant" (p. 206). Fortunately, many national Hispanic groups denounced the remarks as bigoted and offensive. Unfortunately, Judge Kiser's mindset is not that different from many within the dominant culture. As the immigration debate heats up, Latinos and components of their culture are progressively being treated as suspect. This creates a context for acculturation stress, as many Latinos feel a growing pressure to completely relinquish their cultural mores and adopt those of the dominant culture (Institute for Hispanic Mental Health, 2005).

Issues such as depression, substance abuse, gang affiliation, domestic violence, anorexia, suicidal ideations, and others make more sense within a context. Opening up a dialogue with clients about the influence of their context also allows an opportunity to diminish their sense of isolation, brainstorm about alternatives, and help connect them with community resources. Engaging in these types of conversations is difficult if clinicians have not done the work to learn about the contexts impacting Latino clients. Although it is impossible to know every cultural value and belief within the rich and varied Latino communities, clinicians should be seeking an increasingly complex understanding of the communities they serve. "The social worker offers the possibility of an informed helping process that can assist family members to come to terms with and find some resolution for some of the differences and dilemmas inherent in their situation (Constable & Lee, 2004, p. 21).

A Source of the Random

How do we as individuals working in the mental health field find better ways to meet the needs of Latino clients? There is a need to think beyond the standard ways of treating problems in any effort to develop improved approaches. Gregory Bateson (1979) suggested that ". . . *creative* thought must always contain a random component. The exploratory processes—the endless *trial and error* of mental progress—

can achieve the *new* only by embarking upon pathways randomly presented" (p.182). Ross Ashby (1963), a pioneer in cybernetic thinking
made a similar observation, stating that, "No system (neither computer
nor organism) can produce anything new unless the system contains
some source of the random." (p. 26). The origins of many of the theories
commonly used by clinicians have their roots in addressing the needs
of upper-class Caucasian clients. For example, Freud developed many
aspects of his theories based mainly on his work with the middle class
in Vienna. The foundations of feminist approaches have also been criti-
cized as being focused on the needs of white women. The movement
largely originated to fight for the right to work, despite the fact that
some women, such as most Latina women, have been working all along
(Hooks, 1984). Liberation psychology and its concepts may offer a
needed source of the random.

Liberation psychology is an attempt to start from a different foundation. Ignacio Martín-Baró was a Jesuit and liberation psychologist who
was murdered for articulating how the context of El Salvador impacted
the psychological health of its people. He argued that "What is needed
is for our most basic assumptions in psychological thought to be
revised from the bottom up. But this revision cannot be made from our
offices; it has to come from a praxis that is committed to the people"
(Martín-Baró, 1994, p. 23). Social workers may be professionally positioned to bring this vision about if they truly bridge both the micro and
macro systems of clients. Martín-Baró offered mental health workers a
challenge saying ". . . to achieve a psychology of liberation demands
first that psychology be liberated" (Martín-Baró, 1994, p. 25). Whether it
is psychology, social work, marriage and family therapy, or other mental health disciplines, the need remains. Prilleltensky (in press) echoes
Martín-Baró with his comments that "Time is short and the suffering
vast. . . . If we continue to use our limited community psychology
resources only to ameliorate conditions and to tend to the wounded,
who will work to transform the very conditions that create exploitation
and distress in the first place?" (p. 1). The answers are not yet clear.
Liberation psychology may be one way to access a source of the random
in an effort to better meet the needs of Latino clients, drawing on ideas
originating in Latin America. Only a brief introduction to the liberation
psychology concepts that may be useful for clinical work can be offered
here. These include avoiding the banking concept of therapy, dialogue
and *concientización*, and true practice over theory.

THE BANKING CONCEPT OF THERAPY

Paulo Freire (2007) wrote primarily for educators, but his concepts have
significant relevancy for clinicians. A crucial critique he offered was of

the banking concept of education. This is the idea that those we work with are empty and our job is to download important data. He explained that "in the banking concept of education, knowledge becomes a gift bestowed by those who consider themselves knowledgeable upon those whom they consider to know nothing. Projecting absolute ignorance onto others, a characteristic of the ideology of oppression, negates education and knowledge as a process of inquiry" (p. 72). It would be wise for therapists to avoid the same error as that of educators, which is to not recognize that clients already possess knowledge that can be applied in addressing their problems. Avoiding the banking notion of therapy means avoiding the temptation to be the only expert in the room and to trust more in the client's own knowledge. The fear of most beginning students of therapy is "What if I don't know how to help my clients?" It may, however, be that therapists are most helpful before they believe they know it all. This success may be tied to the avoidance of the banking notion. Seeking to be informed, but approaching therapy from a not-knowing position is the most honest. Could the brief courses in any diversity training program, no matter how good, help us know fully the complexities of lives of Latino families? Will we truly know the experience of families who fled to the United States from Nicaragua during the repressive Somoza dictatorship; the struggles of a transgendered Latina from Guanajuato, Mexico, who crossed the border illegally after contracting AIDS; or the Latina teenager dealing with being the only minority in her all-Caucasian school? Not knowing, but creating a holding space is a more truthful approach to a hierarchical claim of expertise.

DIALOGUE AND CONCIENTIZACIÓN

Dialogue is the alternative to banking therapy, and its aim is to bring about *concientización*, a form of consciousness-raising. An underlying philosophy of *concientización* is humanism, and the goal is to help people have more options for expressions of their humanity. "The 'Freire method' has provided a model of work in which outsiders—that is, people who are not themselves poor—can go to the popular classes in a nonpaternalistic way" (Berryman, 1987, p. 36). A successful early example of this method being used was with a literacy program for rural farmworkers in Angicos, Brazil. Peasants identified generative words that were relevant to them, and themes evolved. The work that evolved from this process was initiated and connected to their lived experiences. The participants became collective agents of change, and in forty-five days, three hundred rural farmworkers learned to read and write (McLaren, 2000). This model has significant potential for both group work and family work. One potential structure could be to bring groups of Latino families together to engage in dialogue and *concientización*. Headlines relating to U.S. Latinos could be presented with minimal commentary, to initiate a dialogue. Participants could be encouraged to comment on the struggles they perceive Latino families to face. Words that arise from these conversations could be noted, and eventually themes will evolve. The themes could then be fed back into the dialogue as the group's focus shifts to ideas for creating change. Through this process all members could have the chance to develop greater consciousness of the complexities and possibilities of their situations. "A deepened consciousness of their situation leads people to apprehend that situation as an historical reality susceptible to transformation" (Freire, 2000, p. 85).

TRUE PRACTICE OVER THEORY

Ignacio Martín-Baró (1994) said that true practice recognizes that "Actions are more important than affirmations . . . in this context, everything becomes meaningful that mediates the possibility of people's liberation from the structures that oppress and impede their life and human development" (p. 26). Social workers using this model would not seek to simply reframe the meaning of difficulties in the lives of Latino clients, because this could help maintain the problem. Simone de Beauvoir (1963) explains, ". . . the interests of the oppressors lie in "changing the consciousness of the oppressed, not the situation which oppresses them" (p. 34). Clinicians using a liberation framework would acknowledge the reality of oppression and join with clients in efforts to change to structures limiting the expression of their humanity. Perhaps this concept is summed up best by Freire (1998), who argued that "critical reflection on practice is a requirement of the relationship between theory and practice. Otherwise theory becomes simply 'blah, blah, blah,' and practice, pure activism" (p. 149).

CASE STUDY

Ulises and Vania are a couple in their early thirties who have been together for nine years. They have two children, Guillermo (age eight) and Laura (age six) and currently live in Santa Ana, California. Ulises immigrated to the United States from Mexico City with his father when he was seventeen and has a large family network in the States as well as many family connections in Mexico. He met Vania soon after returning from his mother's funeral in Mexico. Although he had been in frequent contact with his mother by phone, it was the first time he had returned to Mexico since crossing the border. Vania was born in Irvine, California. She had been told stories of how her grandfather had immigrated from Monterrey, Mexico, and met her Caucasian grandmother at a church function. She is unclear on many of the details of her family history because her mother (Elizabeth) had broken off contact with Vania's grandparents when she married Vania's father (Francisco). She also does not consider her Latino roots as her primary identity. Vania's parents divorced when she was two, and she has lost contact with her father. The couple initially presents for therapy because of Guillermo's constant conflict with teachers in his school and Laura's anxiety about beginning elementary school. It quickly becomes evident, though, that significant conflict exists between the couple about how to parent their two children.

This vignette likely sparks a number of stories about what therapy should focus on: Ulises' guilt about his mother's death, the history of cut-offs in Vania's family, or maybe concern that the school system is structured in ways that are biased against Latinos. When beginning from a social constructionist perspective, clinicians would put such prepackaged stories on hold and seek to be fully present in order hear the explanations given by the clients. This allows the social worker to learn which stories have the predominant influence on the behaviors of the different family members. For example, we might learn that Ulises holds a story about his mother having had no human flaws, which may be tied to the vital role of and societal social constructions regarding mothers in Mexican culture. This story could lead him to have a standard that his wife cannot meet. It may also come out that Ulises believes that Vania's disconnect from the Mexican culture he knows may limit her abilities to parent well. We might also learn that Vania holds a story that U.S. culture is more advanced than Mexican culture, which may lead her to reject any attitudes and methods of raising children she believes are too Mexican. This may lead her to disregard Ulises' ideas and concerns. Stories are powerful and influence behaviors and relationships. Stories are also the primary component of the worldviews held by clients. Clinicians who jump in too quickly to act on their own ideas regarding their clients' problems can easily be seen by clients as focusing on paths that seem irrelevant from their worldviews.

As the stories held by the clients are uncovered, the systemic implications become easier to detect. Continuing this illustration further, one can begin to form systemic hypotheses. Given the stories held by both Vania and Ulises, a fair hypothesis would be that each may be critiquing or undermining the other's parenting efforts because their stories do not seem to allow space for considering the strengths of their partner's parenting style. This recursive pattern of blaming and undermining may be creating the context in which the children's behaviors make sense. For example, a homeostatic pattern may exist in that when the children are behaving well, the parents are distant and disengaged from one another. One systemic story could be that the children's misbehavior requires the parents to engage and connect, and thus creates a solution for the problem of indifference. A clinically useful focus may be to discuss the differences in the couple's historical contexts and the parenting styles logical to them. This may help each person understand the logic of the other parent's ideas and behaviors.

Tuning into the influence of isomorphism may also be important. The stories that the clinician holds are as important to look at as the stories held by the clients. For example, clinicians should be aware of the impact of any story that places blame on only one member of this couple. If the social worker puts the source of the problem on Ulises, for example, his behavior may become the focus of therapy, and he may sense he is being blamed by the social worker, a likely outcome given the systemic tenet that one cannot not communicate (Fisch, Weakland, & Segal, 1982). Isomorphically, the pattern of blaming may be transferred from the social worker to the client (or vice versa). This is clinically problematic given that this is a process occurring in the system that likely needs to be altered. Isomorphism can also be used in a positive way. As the social worker is open and accepting, this pattern can also begin to be replicated in the couple's relationship.

Conclusion

A final way in which social workers might be uniquely positioned to assist Latino clients is by organizing Freirian dialogue groups. For example, one such group could be Latino parents who have children experiencing problems in school settings. The posing of problems is a typical initial step, and in this scenario it may just be an observation about some of the unique challenges Latino students face. From this initial dialogue, themes and ideas could be identified and fed back to the group. As *concientización* of the barriers facing Latino students increased, the possibilities for addressing them would enlarge. Such a process may feel less structured to social workers accustomed to traditional group therapy practices. This is largely because the structures are created more by the group, and to identify the actual needs requires greater initial vagueness. Also, in this kind of group, the social worker's role is as more of a facilitator and less of an expert. It involves a more in-depth involvement in assisting participants to liberate themselves from structures that limit the full expression of their human potential.

It may involve connecting them with other resources, as is typical in social work practice. In some instances, it may also involve increased effort in joining with clients to create the needed resources.

It is a time of hope for the field of social work and the impact that clinicians can have in Latino communities. Approaches to mental health include considerations of cultural complexities at levels never seen before. There are still many challenges ahead as clinical approaches are being further developed to be both culturally sensitive and effective. Systems theory, social constructionism, and liberation psychology offer some useful ideas for directions the field might take. Also hopeful is the realization that therapists can set aside the role of being all-knowing experts and that clients are being more empowered to be the source of change in their own lives.

This chapter presented work that links traditional concepts of family therapy to a more community-based type of work congruent with Latino values and needs. The following chapter presents a similar, cutting-edge intervention in child welfare practice. The authors demonstrate how a family-conferencing method developed for use in other service contexts can be used with Latino families involved with the child welfare system. The chapter carefully weaves together practice and policy issues, and demonstrates how both are intricately connected. Again, the importance of cultural competence is a key theme.

For Writing and Reflection

1. What are some of the contexts that impact Latino families, and what common presenting problems might make sense in those contexts?

2. Are there times when you feel that the banking approach to therapy is appropriate?

3. What are some examples of the ways in which the concepts of isomorphism and homeostasis can be occur in our attempts to assist Latino families?

4. "What is needed is for our most basic assumptions in psychological thought to be revised from the bottom up. But this revision cannot be made from our offices; it has to come from a praxis that is committed to the people" (Martín-Baró, 1994, p. 23). If we met this challenge, how would our clinical work look different?

References

Adler, I. (2006). About number one. *Mexconnect.*

Ashby, W. R. (1963). *An Introduction to cybernetics.* New York: John Wiley & Sons.

Bahar, R. (1996). *The vulnerable observer: Anthropology that breaks your heart.* Boston: Beacon Press.

Bateson, Gregory. (1979). *Mind and nature: A necessary unity.* New York: E. P. Dutton.

Becvar, D., & Becvar, R. (1993). *Family therapy: A systemic integration.* Boston, MA: Allyn and Bacon.

Becvar, D.S., & Becvar, R.J. (1999). *Systems theory and family therapy: A primer.* New York: University Press of America.

Becvar, R. J., Canfield, B. S., & Becvar, D. S. (1997). *Group therapy: Cybernetic, constructivist, and social constructionist.* Denver, CO: Love Publishing Company.

Berryman, P. (1987). *Liberation theology: The essential facts about the revolutionary movement in Latin America and beyond.* New York: Pantheon Books.

Carr, S., & Sloan, T. (Eds.). (2003). *Poverty and psychology.* New York: Kluwer.

Constable, R., & Lee, D.B. (2004). *Social work with families: Content and process.* Chicago: Lyceum Books.

Di Nicola, V. (1997). *A stranger in the family: Culture, families, and therapy.* New York: Norton.

de Beauvoir, S. (1963). La pensee de droite, Aujord'hui (Paris); ST, *El Pensamiento politico de la Derecha* (Buedos Aires, p. 34).

Dean, H. (1997). The "clinical" in *social work: A work in progress. Smith College Studies in Social Work, 67*(2), pp. 159–170.

Dingfelder, S. F. (2005). Closing the gap for Latino patients. *Monitor on Psychology, 36*(1), pp. 58–69.

Difranco, A. (1997). *Fire door* [Recorded by Ani Difranco]. On *Living in Clip* [CD]. London: Righteous Babe Records.

Doherty, W. J. (1991). Family therapy goes postmodern. *The Family Therapy Networker, 15*(5), 36–42.

Falicov, C.J. (1998). *Latino families in therapy: A guide to Multicultural practice.* New York: Guilford Press.

Fisch, R., Weakland, J., & Segal, L. (1982). *Tactics of change.* San Francisco: Jossey-Bass.

Freire, P. (1997). *Pedagogy of hope: Reliving pedagogy of the oppressed.* New York: Continuum.

Freire, P. (1998). *Pedagogy of freedom.* New York: Continuum.

Freire, P. (2007). *Pedagogy of the oppressed.* New York: Continuum.

Gergen, K. (1991). The saturated self: Dilemmas of identity in contemporary life. New York: Basic Books.

Gonzalez, J. (2000). Harvest of empire: A history of Latinos in America. New York: Penguin Books.

Hedges, F. (2005). *An introduction to systemic therapy with individuals. A social constructionist approach.* London: Palgrave Macmillan.

Hernández, P. (2002). Trauma in war and political persecution: Expanding the concept. *American Journal of Orthopsychiatry 72*(1), 1–12.

Hooks, B. (1984). *Feminist theory from margin to center.* Boston: South End Press.

Institute for Hispanic Mental Health. (2005). Critical disparities in Latino mental health: Transforming research into action. *NCLR*, 2–26.

Jackson, D. (1949). Unpublished transcript of a research discussion, Chestnut Lodge, Rockville, Maryland, involving Don Jackson and led by Harry Stack Sullivan, MRI, Palo Alto, CA.

León, D. J. (2007). Models of leadership institutes for increasing the number of top Latino administrators in higher education. *Journal of Hispanic Higher Education*, Vol. 6, No. 4, 356–377.

Mair, M. (1988). Psychology as storytelling. *International Journal of Personal Construct Psychology*. 1, 125–138.

Martín-Baró, I. (1994). *Writings for a liberation psychology*. Cambridge, MA: Harvard University Press.

McGoldrick, M., Pearce, J. K., & Giordano, J. (Eds.). (1982). *Ethnicity and family therapy*. New York: Guilford Press.

McLaren, P. (2000). *Che Guevara, Paulo Freire, and the pedagogy of revolution*. Lanham, MD: Rowman & Litchfield.

Prilleltensky, I. (In press). The role of power in wellness, oppression, and liberation: The promise of psychopolitical validity. *Journal of Community Psychology*.

Romeo, L. M. (2002). Growing up in two worlds—observations on gender. [Sidebar to D. L. Sollie (2002, July/August). Couples and gender: Exploring the real issues. *Family Therapy Magazine*, 1(4), 14–21.

Rothberg, N. (1997). Family therapist supervision: Philosophy and process. *Clinical Supervisor*, 15(1), 167–173.

Sloan, T. (2003). Globalization, poverty, and social justice: A basic introduction for students of psychology and social work. Retrieved April 24, 2007, from www.criticalpsych.org

Snowden, L. R., & Cheung, F. K. (1990). Use of inpatient mental health services by members of ethnic minority groups. *American Psychologist*, 45, 347–355.

Takaki, R. (1993). *A different mirror: A history of multicultural America*. New York: Back Bay.

Watts, A. (1972). *The book: On the taboo against knowing who you are*. New York: Vintage.

Watzlawick, P., Beavin, J., & Jackson, D. (1967). *Pragmatics of human communication: A study of interactional patterns, pathologies, and paradoxes*. New York: Norton.

Yeh, M., Hough, R., McCabe, K., Lau, A., & Garland, A. (2004). Parental beliefs about the causes of child problems: Exploring racial/ethnic patterns. *Journal of the American Academy of Child and Adolescent Psychiatry*, 43, 605–613.

CHAPTER TWELVE

Child Welfare Practice and the Use of Family Conferencing

A Culturally Responsive Intervention with Hispanic Children and Families

Maria Puig

Jim Drendel

Deb DeLuca

Introduction

In her short life, Mariela has experienced much change and turmoil. Only nine years old, she has witnessed her parents' verbal and physical fights much too frequently. Her father's bouts with alcohol and drug addictions have left the family homeless, as his inability to keep a job repeatedly results in yet another eviction. Like other Hispanic children, Mariela has lived in poverty and poverty-related conditions that have not been addressed because she lives in a resource-poor community. Both her mother and father generally are unable to provide Mariela with the care and stability she needs. This is the second time Social Services has been called. Mariela, a little older and more aware of her plight, now wonders: "What will happen to me and my family? Does anybody care?"

Although a hypothetical situation, Mariela's circumstances are quite common to cases that require the intervention of local child welfare agencies. Mariela's parents are poor, lack access to community resources, and only reluctantly and in an emergency contact available services because they are afraid to become more "visible." Afraid they will be charged with child neglect and abuse, Mariela's parents lack important information about how the child welfare system works, and the confidence to seek help or advocate for themselves and their child.

Child welfare is primarily concerned with the well-being of children and families and the many social problems they face. Historically, child welfare has responded to families in crisis from a "safety net" approach (Cohen, 2002), since American society, by and large, has not valued all children and families enough to help those most at risk. Cases like Mariela's have traditionally been handled by removing the child from the family and finding an out-of-home placement, such as foster family or kinship care, if available and appropriate. The decision to remove the child in situations like Mariela's has rested with a caseworker, who may or may not be prepared to provide needed services to the family based on his/her education, training, knowledge, experience, and skills. This same caseworker may also lack the prerequisite cultural competence to deal with the unique challenges Hispanic children and families bring to the already complex and challenging child welfare practice process.

As a means to responding to multifaceted problems and situations, and the growing demands child welfare workers face when making decisions about the lives of children and families, this chapter examines the use of family conferencing as an inclusionary and responsive child welfare practice method with Hispanics. The inclusionary nature of family conferencing promotes social equality and egalitarianism among family members and child welfare professionals. It also advances a more culturally fitting child welfare practice approach that promotes child safety and family responsibility, while making the most of family strengths. The concomitant power of the group decision-making process, a key component of family conferencing, is particularly effective when working with Hispanic families because it brings to the forefront the dynamics of culture such as language, speech, intonation, and emotional content (Lum, 2004).

This chapter also will provide a case vignette from a large child welfare agency in a western state, where family conferencing has been used as an alternate intervention with Hispanic families at imminent risk of separation. The case vignette involves a Mexican American family and illustrates the efficacy of family conferencing as a powerful, culturally affirming practice with Hispanics.

Problem Statement

During 2003 to 2004, there were more than 523,085 children involved with the child welfare system and living in out-of-home/family care

(Child Welfare League, 2003–2004). Of these, 53 percent were white, 36 percent were African-American, 16 percent were Hispanic, 2 percent were American Indian/Alaskan Native and 4 percent were children of other races and ethnicities (Child Welfare League, 2003–2004).

Underscoring the significance of these numbers is the fact that for ethnic minority children, there continues to exist cultural and racial bias in the manner in which the child welfare system responds to their needs (Hegar & Scannapieco, 1999). There is evidence to suggest that Hispanic children receive less comprehensive services and are overrepresented in substitute care, while their parents are afforded less support services (Kadushin & Martin, 1988). These facts are alarming as it is estimated that by 2010 Hispanic children will comprise the largest minority among the U.S. child populations (approximately 18 percent) and, by 2040, they will constitute one in four of all children in the United States (Delgado, 2007).

The heterogeneity of the Hispanic population, which is made up of Mexican Americans, Puerto Ricans, Cubans, Dominicans, and people from other Central and South American countries, is a dilemma child welfare workers face in providing culturally competent services. While to some practitioners it may appear that as a group, Hispanics have much in common, the reality is that each Hispanic subgroup is intrinsically different. Part of the dilemma lies in these obscure and, often, indiscernible dissimilarities, that further underpin the need for cultural competence in child welfare practice (Puig, 2002). For example, Cuban immigrants who came to the United States during the 1990s did not understand how family behaviors (leaving a young child at home in the care of an older sibling; physically punishing children) that were culturally coherent in Cuba, might result in a referral to a child welfare agency in this country. Although not unique to Cuban immigrants, similar situations involving the care and supervision of young children, along with parental discipline practices, continue to adversely affect newly arrived immigrant families whose unfamiliarity with U.S. child welfare policies often cause them to be brought to the attention of the child welfare system.

The increased diversity in the general population of the United States, along with the many problems Hispanics and other culturally diverse families face, creates serious concerns for child welfare practitioners. According to Puig (2002), cultural diversity is a reality of modern-day society, as are the problems Hispanics and other segmented members of cultural minorities face, including poverty, lack of education, teen parenthood, lack of health care, and limited employment and income. Hispanics who are recent immigrants also face additional problems, including how they are welcomed, received, and incorporated into the host society (Puig, 2002). For child welfare workers, knowledge and understanding of cultural diversity must be central to competent child welfare practice. It is this knowledge that will help clarify how inter- and intragroup differences impact Hispanics' definition of psychosocial problems and help-seeking behaviors (Puig, 2002). Child welfare services, therefore, must be provided with a person-in-environment, cultural "fit," where "ethnic knowledge," the understanding and use of ethnic information in daily practice becomes the norm and not the exception (Leigh, 1985).

Because of the increase in cultural diversity in the U.S. population, combined with the difficulties families face, child welfare agencies are turning to new and innovative ways to resolve family problems. Two innovative strategies that are proving to be effective and are being accepted are family conferencing and family group decision making.

Literature Review

The growth and progress of core child welfare services has been tempered by legislative mandates, beginning with the Social Security Act of 1935, CAPTA (Child Abuse and Protection Act of 1975), Title XX in 1975, the Indian Child Welfare Act of 1978, the Adoption Assistance and Child Welfare Act of 1980, MEPA (the Multi-Ethnic Placement Act of 1984), Family Preservation and Support, 1993, Welfare Reform via the Personal Responsibility and Work Reconciliation Act (PRWORA, 1996), ASFA, (Adoption and Safe Families Act of 1997), and the 2003 Adoption Promotion Act (Mather, Lager, & Harris, 2007). As these laws were enacted, policies and regulations soon followed that dictated how and when child welfare practitioners could and could not act. For example, after the Great Depression, the use of foster care increased and the institutionalization of children decreased (Cohen, 2002). However, it was later discovered that as more and more children were coming into care, they were also staying in foster care longer and longer. Quite often, children remained in out-of-home care until they reached eighteen years and aged out of the system (Cohen, 2002).

As a result, subsequent legislation attempted to not only reduce the number of children who come into care, through the provision of intensive family preservation or reunification services and service limits stipulated in the Personal Responsibility and Work Opportunity Act of 1996, but through even more aggressive legislation, such as the Adoption and Safe Families Act of 1997. This Act pushes for and mandates that alternative plans be made, within specific time frames, to facilitate the termination of parental rights, thus reducing the numbers of children experiencing foster care drift (Mather, Lager, & Harris, 2007). The new legislation has not been able to control the various and personally transforming problems children and families now face. One such example is the increased use of methamphetamines, and how this one problem has negatively impacted child/family well-being and child welfare practice because of the length of time it takes a parent to overcome methamphetamine addiction.

Family Conferencing

Family conferencing is an alternate approach for dealing with child welfare problems. The model is based on the belief that most, if not all families, seek help, hope, security, and a sense of belonging ("we're all in this together") when facing difficulties. Families can also include fictive kin, or people who are considered "family members" without the benefit of being related by blood or through marriage.

According to Pennell and Burford (2000) and Waites and colleagues (Waites, Macgowan, Pennell, LaNey, and Weil, 2004), family conferencing is rooted in the Maori culture and is similar to practices in many indigenous cultures. It was first used in New Zealand, when the indigenous peoples did not want child welfare "experts" dictating what would happen in their kinship structures or with interventions they felt ultimately marginalized their culture and cultural identity (Waites et al., 2004).

In 1989, the legislature in New Zealand mandated that when dealing with child welfare and juvenile justice issues, family group conferencing be used first; it was viewed as a way to rely less and less on legal proceedings, while advancing the rights of families and children and avowing cultural and community tradition, norms, and values (Hassall, 1996).

The basic premise of family conferencing appears to be simple, and it requires a basic recognition that "families know best." It is through the process of giving families the opportunity to formulate a plan of action to resolve whatever presenting problems are affecting the child/ren, that family members' voices are represented and accepted. Family conferencing also acknowledges the principle that there are strengths in numbers and that a family is a collection of multiples strengths.

Family conferencing returns the power to the family, but it also provides a safety net, since all plans ultimately must be approved by the child welfare authorities before they are implemented. According to Merkel-Holguin (2004), "it provides a forum for individuals to come together to exchange information, share ideas, and demonstrate their care and concern," and furthermore it "establishes a process by which families can work through their problems and devise their own solutions" (p. 156), as family members, including friends and other members of a family's support system, come together to create and arrange solutions by channeling their own resources and strengths. Rather than having child welfare workers make the decisions according to entrenched and often inflexible policies and procedures, family conferencing returns the decision-making power to the family. This process reinforces the family's need and ability to self-regulate. It also emphasizes and places in practice social work's value of clients' rights to self-determination, because family members are the ones who know the nature and frequency of the challenges they face, their strengths and weaknesses. As such, they should have the right to ascertain what is in the best interest of the child and family.

Family conferences are usually organized by a coordinator who is not responsible for the case; family members are invited to attend and are prepared for their participation in the process. Conference coordinators are in charge of arranging the date and time and location of the conference, developing the format for the conference, and for providing enough information about the situation so that everyone involved knows what is at stake. In addition, the family is accountable for developing the intervention plan, while they reflect and mull over alternatives in private. Finally, any negotiations between the family and child welfare officials are agreed upon before the final plan is accepted and implemented. It is also expected that the family will come together whenever any changes to the agreed-upon plan are necessary or as situations mandate.

Incorporating Cultural Diversity in Family Conferencing Practice

Cultural diversity and cultural competence are central components of child welfare practice. They require that child welfare practitioners change their frame of reference from, as Bennett (1993) describes it, ethnocentrism to ethnorelativism. Rather than assessing families (and risk to children) in relation to one's own cultural values and beliefs, ethnorelativism promotes the thinking that ". . . cultures can only be understood relative to one another and . . . that behaviors can only be understood within a cultural context." Bennett further states that "cultural difference is neither good nor bad, it is just different" (Bennett, 1993, p. 26).

Conceptually, this shift in thinking is akin to principles of family conferencing and family decision making. Who understands the family better than family members themselves? If behaviors can only be understood within a particular cultural context, then families must also be understood within particular family systems and circumstances.

According to Puig (2002), cultural competence requires that social work practitioners be able to alter and adjust the fundamentals of social work practice skills, knowledge, and competencies, learned as a generalist or advanced generalist practitioner, to culturally specific situations. Skills such as interviewing, assessment, problem definition, service provision and interventions, and practice evaluation must be carried out using a "person-in-environment," cultural "fit" approach (Puig, 2002).

Draguns (1981), likens cross-cultural practice and helping to being more "experiential, freewheeling, and bilateral" (p. 17). Draguns explains experiential practice as the work that will impact the worker more directly and emotionally, freewheeling practice as the ability of social workers to adapt practice interventions to the client's cultural needs, and bilateral practice as the collaboration between the client and the practitioner. Cross-cultural practice and competence, then, promotes self-awareness and greater recognition of the "dynamics of difference" (Cross, Bazron, Dennis, & Isaacs, 1989) so necessary for the culturally competent adaptation of professional social work practice skills when family conferencing methods are utilized.

Culturally competent family conferencing also recognizes that traditions, customs, and values inculcate behaviors that are generally normative to the group. When applying this idea to family conferencing, it supports what Ho (1995) has conceptualized as internalized influences that "(culturally) operate within the individual that shape (not determine) various aspects of psychological functioning" (p. 5). Similar to the Maori culture of New Zealand, where the family exerts a significant influence on all aspects of decision making concerning the well-being of children, in Hispanic culture, for example, the concept of family over individual, or familism, overrides all other values. It is the family that one turns to when experiencing difficulties; it is their counsel one seeks. Therefore, this value is incorporated into the family conferencing process when the family involves a *padrino* (godfather) or *madrina* (godmother) or a *comadre* (best female friend) or *compadre* (best male friend) in the family decision. Because families often include non-blood relatives, it is not unusual to have a close friend and confidant be part of the family conferencing process. These individuals are to be regarded and treated with the same respect and consideration one would give a family member.

Similarly, the cultural value of personalism, or the general orientation for close and warm relationships with people, is another important value for Hispanics. Personalism requires that one be social, and that individuals know how to relate to others. It encourages a strong personal commitment to one's family, friends, and people in general. In family conferencing, this may be evident by how aware Hispanic clients are of the distance (both spatially and in relation to the "personal" relationship, or lack thereof) they have with caseworkers. Hispanic clients may feel there is little warmth between them and caseworkers; in other words, little trust or confidence. They may compensate by having not only family members present at the family conference, but also by including other trusted members of their group to seek comfort, security, connection, and acceptance.

Family conferencing is also a culturally affirming intervention with Hispanics because it is problem-focused and reinforces their cultural view of the family and how families jointly make decisions. Hispanic immigrant families, particularly undocumented persons, may require more "specialized" methods of family conferencing. The undocumented family may fear the implied power and authority the social services agency represents and may also fear meeting in an agency setting. Many undocumented immigrant families come from countries where government officials are the primary abusers of basic human rights. A culturally competent child welfare practitioner will find another location for the meeting if this is a concern for the family. Preferably in the immigrant community, the family conferencing can safely take place at the local church, a community center, or in a trusted friend's home. This type of accommodation requires minimal effort on the part of the worker, and it is illustrative of culturally competent child welfare practice. Also, the inclusion and acceptance in the family conferencing process of culture-specific healers, such as a *curandero,* or folk healer, would be an example of culturally competent practice.

Cultural competence is not a skill social workers acquire because they attended school and earned a degree. Cultural competence is a life-long learning process that must be practiced and improved upon. No social worker, not even one who is bilingual and bicultural, is free of biases that impact how he or she views clients' cultures, beliefs, values, and behaviors.

The Agency Setting

Larimer County Department of Human Services, Children, Youth and Family Division, is located in the city of Fort Collins, in northern Colorado. The county-run agency uses a neighborhood-based, service delivery system aptly called Family Options. Believing that families should be included from the beginning and throughout the life of a case, Family Options makes use of many of the principles of family conferencing to bring families together to repair harm, reduce risk, and build community. The department's belief is that "family knows family best" and that family members should be part of the planning and decision making for themselves and their children.

When the agency receives a referral regarding a family, the first step taken is to have a Family Safety and Resources Team meeting. The purpose of this meeting is to identify family strengths, areas of concern, family support systems, and to begin the planning process for ensuring the safety and protection of the child(ren). At this initial meeting the agency caseworker, supervisor, a kinship/foster care worker, the parents, and other family member the parents have invited, including external members of their support system, are in attendance. The kinship/foster care worker is included in every family conferencing meeting so that family members, or others, can ask questions regarding foster care, kinship care, and how family members and agency staff can work together to find the best out-of-home placement for the child, if it becomes necessary. The initial family conferencing meeting is made possible by a trained agency facilitator, since the main focus of the meeting is to develop an immediate safety plan for the children and to identify the resources needed to implement said plan.

Following the first Family Safety and Resource Team meeting, an appointment date and time is arranged for a family conference. The same facilitator that participated in the first meeting "follows" the family, as the facilitator begins to help the family prepare for the conference. Preparation is the key to effective family conferencing, as it involves meeting with all the parties who will attend the family conference meeting and discussing the issues for which family must plan. The facilitator also collects needed information on other family members, friends, and members of the family's support system that parents or other family members have identified. During the preparation process, family members begin to consider how best they can provide for the safety and protection of the child. Often, Hispanic families will use this point in time to identify an elder family member as their guide and counsel, as this individual helps guide the process and other family members in planning for the welfare of the children.

Children are also included in the family conferencing process, which means the facilitator must also prepare them for the meeting and discussion. Children may be present at the family conference meeting, along with family members, friends, therapists, and others to help support them. They can also choose to be present by using other means such as letters, videotapes, and pictures. Having a child present during a family conference is extremely valuable in the planning, as it helps the family to stay focused; it helps the child to feel included, and to see everyone working together for them and for their family as a whole. In the past, there was hesitancy about including children in this process. However, the agency has recognized that the children have been living in the situation and are much more aware than any agency worker about what has happened. A phrase often used by agency staff is: "No decision about me, without me." For Hispanic families, these meetings often take place in a family member's home, as this provides comfort and a sense of the family owning their meeting. The family also is encouraged to follow any traditions they practice, including prayer, food, and other rituals that are unique to their family's culture, values, and belief system.

The Family Options model also takes into account the importance of culture, cultural values, and cultural norms as part of the family conferencing decision-making process. As previously stated, more and more ethnic minority children are coming to the attention of the child welfare system. The need for child welfare practitioners to be culturally sensitive and competent goes without saying. However, since cultural competence requires that social workers "think and behave in ways that enable members of one cultural, ethnic, or linguistic group to work effectively with members of another" (Samantrai, 2004, p. 32), that obligation is much easier said than done. Most child welfare workers do not have the prerequisite knowledge and related skills to effectively practice from a culturally competent place. The Family Options program provides the opportunity by having the family—the cultural experts—impart that expertise. One of the outcomes from using family members as cultural guides has been the increased numbers of brothers and sisters who have remained together while in kinship or foster placement (Winokur, 2007).

CASE STUDY
Family Options as Practice: The "O" Family

The "O" family consists of Gema (Mom), age twenty-eight, Jose (Dad), age thirty-one, and their five children: Jose Jr., age nine; Miguel, age seven; Lilly, age five; Carlos, age three; and Ennie, one year old. The parents have a large extended family with whom they share a loving and supportive relationship, as well as many friends they also regard as "family." The family came to the attention of the child welfare system when it was suspected that Lilly, Carlos, and Ennie were being neglected by their parents. Initially, the three children were removed from their home and placed in foster care.

After the three children had been in foster care for thirty days and as part of an administrative case review, agency staff recommended the case be transferred to the Family Options program. The former caseworker had not established a positive relationship with the parents, and family members were now asking for a change.

Believing the family could benefit from the Family Options program, the case was reassigned. Within seventy-two hours, the first family conferencing meeting was scheduled. A case review indicated the family's primary problems had been a history of neglect by young parents who had had too many children too soon, along with the parents not seeming to understand the seriousness of the situation. Compounding the family's circumstance was their total distrust of any government agency.

The first family conference did not go as well as intended because no extended family or friends attended. However, Mom and Dad were present and with the assistance of a certified translator, the family conferencing process was explained. Both parents reacted very positively to their new roles as participants and decision-makers, rather than passive spectators in a complicated process. The caseworker and facilitator had a lot of difficult work to do, as the extended family was very fearful of the agency. Several meetings with individual family members were held to assure them this was not an agency ploy. After gaining an understanding of the agency position, the family was ready to partially trust the concept of a family conference. The facilitator individually met with several key family figures to explain the role of the facilitator and to make sure family members knew they were going to be heard. During this process, the facilitator clearly identified a caring family, with a very strong aunt and grandmother figure. These two family members were crucial in getting the family to participate. (It is interesting to note that one of these two women had been identified by the former caseworker as too aggressive.) The facilitator then worked with the new caseworker and family to learn to trust each other. Most of the work by the new caseworker required following up with what the caseworker had indicated they would do. Gradually, trust developed.

Soon, two other family conferences were scheduled, in which aunts, uncles, grandparents, cousins, and friends all attended. The family conference was scheduled in the home of the assertive aunt. Again, using the services of a translator, the process was explained and family and friends expressed their gratitude for being consulted and asked to provide ideas about how to best take care of the children and help the young couple. The agency facilitator did an effective job making sure that all parties were heard, including the caseworker, who presented some "musts" for the family, along with other service providers who expressed their concerns about what they believed the family needed to do. All present acknowledged that their main goal was to ensure the well-being and safety of the children.

At the conclusion of the second family conference meeting one of the aunts and her husband agreed to take care of the two older children, allowing the parents time to address their needs. Part of the plan developed by family members included weekly visitations with all the children and the parents at jointly held family get-togethers. Family members also requested and received the services of an in-home therapist who would work for a period of sixty days with the parents and the children. The mother also decided to undergo a medical evaluation to determine the root cause of her depression, and to follow whatever medical treatment regime the doctor prescribed. The father made the decision to cut back his overtime hours, to provide more support to his wife and children. The grandparents were regarded as the arbitrators between family members and treated with great respect by all.

Ultimately, the family expressed that the family conferencing process respected their roles and insights and provided them with the means by which the children could return home. They appreciated being included in the planning and decision making, and felt they could openly discuss their ideas and opinions. By using their collective resources, family and friends helped the young parents to become more engaged in their roles and to understand the need to provide a safe and loving home for all their children.

The caseworker expressed great satisfaction from working on the case, but did point out that this type of case required much more time because the family did not know the "system" like a foster family generally does. The caseworker also had to devote more time to the family to answer questions and calls, including having to schedule more meetings to respond to individual questions from family members.

Conclusion

The use of family conferencing with Hispanic families, as presented by the case study, promoted family inclusion and cohesion, while recognizing the importance of cultural values (familism, personalism, *simpatismo*, respect) and behavioral norms (interdependence, cooperation, group cohesiveness). By partnering with family and friends, the Family Options program maximized the resources of the "O" family and utilized these to help the parents meet their family's needs. Family conferencing stresses that families can function as mentors for one another and as cultural guides to the professional staff. This team approach avoids making the caseworker the "expert" and provides the affected parties and their families with a much-needed and valued voice in the decision-making process. Family conferencing with Hispanics captures and uses the most important ingredient in the culture, *la familia* (the family), and acknowledges the pivotal role it plays in everyday life and in family decisions. It also recognizes that commitment to core family values "stands for respect for the worth and dignity of all people" (Healy, 2001, p. 101). Ultimately, it is the appreciation for participation and self-determination that family conferencing provides as a "move toward equal treatment for all as professional goals" (Healy, 2001, p. 101).

Children and youth who wind up in the child welfare system frequently are also influenced by substance abuse. Programs like family conferencing increase the likelihood that families and youth will be able to access services that best meet their needs. While the provision of these services is important, too little attention has been paid to substance abuse prevention. In the following chapter, the authors explore the key issues involved in preventing substance abuse with Latino youth and examine substance abuse prevalence, risk, and protective factors, as well as the importance of engaging in culturally sensitive practices designed for Latino youth. They present an ecodevelopmental perspective that provides the theoretical grounding for their work, and explores its application in key youth-servicing systems.

References

Bennett, M. (1993). A developmental model of intercultural sensitivity. In R. M. Paige (Ed.), *Education for Intercultural Experience*. Yarmouth, ME: Intercultural Press.

Child Welfare League, (2004). Children's Bureau AFCARS Reports #10 and #11. Retrieved on August 7, 2008, from http:www.acf.hhs.gov/programs/cb/pubs/stats_research/index.htm; nscan.

Cohen, N. A. (2002). *Child welfare: A multicultural focus.* Needham Heights, MA: Allyn & Bacon.

Cross, T. L., Bazron, B. J., Dennis, K. W., & Isaacs, M. R. (1989). *Towards a culturally competent system of care.* Washington, DC: Georgetown University Child Development Center.

Delgado, M. (2007). *Social work practice with Latinos: A cultural assets paradigm.* New York: Oxford University Press.

Draguns, J. (1981). Dilemmas and choices in cross-cultural counseling: The universal versus the cultural distinct. In P. B. Andersen, J. G. Draguns, W. L. Lonner, & J. E. Trimble (Eds.), *Counseling across cultures* (pp. 3–22). Honolulu: University of Hawaii Press.

Hassall, I. (1996). Origin and development of family group conferences. In J. Hudson, A. Morris, G. Maxwell, & B. Galaway (Eds.), *Family group conferencing: Perspectives on policy and practice* (pp. 17–36). Monsey, NY: Willow Tree Press.

Healy, L. M. (2001). *International social work.* New York: Oxford University Press.

Hegar, R. L., & Scannapieco, M. H. (1999). *Kinship foster care: Policy, practice and research.* New York: Oxford University Press.

Ho, D. (1995). Internalized culture, cultocentrism and transcendence. *The Counseling Psychologist, 23*(1), 4–24.

Hogan, P. T., & Siu, S-F. (1988). Minority and the child welfare system: An historical perspective. *Social Work, 33*, p. 493.

Kadushin, A., & Martin, J. A. (1988). *Child Welfare Services*. New York: Macmillan.

Leigh, J. W., Jr. (1985). The ethnically competent social worker. In J. Laird & A. Hartman (Eds.), *A handbook of child welfare: Context, knowledge, and practice* (pp. 449–459). New York: The Free Press.

Lum, D. (2004). *Social work practice and people of color: A process-stage approach.* California State University. Pacific Grove, CA: Thompson/Brooks/Cole.

Mather, J. H., Lager, P. B., & Harris, H. J. (2007). *Child welfare policies and best practices* (2nd ed.). Belmont, California: Thompson/Wadsworth.

Merkel-Holguin, L. (2004). Sharing power with the people: Family group conferencing as a democratic experiment. *Journal of Sociology and Social Welfare, 31*(1), 156.

Pennell, J., & Burford, G. (2000). Family group decision-making: Protecting children and women. *Child Welfare, 79*(2), 131–158.

Puig, M. E. (2002). The adultification of refugee children: Implications for cross-cultural social work practice. *Journal of Human Behaviors in the Social Environment, 5*(3/4), 85–95.

Samantrai, K. (2004). *Culturally competent public child welfare practice*. Pacific Grove, CA: Brooks/Cole/Thomson.

State of Colorado. (2004). Compass measures—children in out-of-home placements. Retrieved June 12, 2007, from http://www.co.laraimer.co.us/compass/children_in_placementdemographics.htm

Waites, C., Macgowan, M. J., Pennell, J., LaNey, I. C., & Weil, M. (2004). Increasing the cultural responsiveness of Family Group Conferencing. *Social Work, 49*(2), 291–300.

Winokur, M. (2007). Program evaluation final report on the Family Options Program, Larimer County, Department of Human Services. Unpublished report.

CHAPTER THIRTEEN

Substance Abuse Prevention and Latino Youth

Guillermo Prado
Hilda Pantin
Maria Tapia

Introduction

This chapter provides an overview of the literature on substance abuse among Latino adolescents in three areas: prevalence, etiology, and prevention. Extant research indicates that Latino youth are at particulary high risk of using illegal substances and that considerable within-Latino differences in prevalence rates exist. Culture and family processes play an important role in understanding the genesis of substance use among this population. Despite the elevated rates of substance use, few intervention programs have been found to be efficacious in preventing substance use among Latino youth. The literature reviewed and the recommendations provided in this chapter address how to reduce the health disparities between Latino youth and their non-Latino white counterparts.

As noted in previous chapters, Latinos are the largest and fastest-growing minority group in the United States (Ramirez & de la Cruz, 2003), accounting for 14 percent of the U.S. population. Moreover, Latinos accounted for approximately half of the population growth in the United States between 2000 and 2005 (Bernstein, 2006; Huntington, 2004). Latinos are also a youthful population, with almost 40 percent under the age of nineteen (Marotta & Garcia, 2003). Latino children and adolescents therefore represent a growing share of U.S. youth, and their well-being represents an important public health priority. In addition to their large and growing numbers, Latino adolescents are disproportionately affected by substance use (Johnston, O'Malley, Bachman, & Schulenberg, 2007). Research suggests that substance use, including alcohol, tobacco, and/or illicit drug use, may contribute to the health disparities between Latinos and non-Latino whites. For example, Latino adolescents are more likely to initiate substance use earlier than are their non-Latino white counterparts (Johnston et al., 2007). These disproportionate rates of early substance use initiation, in turn, contribute to the disparities observed between Latinos and non-Latino whites in the prevalence rates of HIV, assaults/homicides, intentional harm/suicides, and chronic lower respiratory disease (Arias, Anderson, Kung, Murphy, & Kochanek, 2003). The purpose of this chapter is to provide an overview of the state of Latino adolescent substance abuse research in the areas of prevalence, risk and protection, and prevention; it is divided into three sections, accordingly. A case vignette as well as recommendations for social work practice and for future prevention research with Latino youth are included at the end of the chapter.

Prevalence

Although substance use is pervasive among American youths of all ages and ethnicities, Latino youth are at particulary high risk of using illegal substances. Compared to non-Latino whites and African Americans, Latino eighth- and tenth-graders report the highest lifetime, annual, and thirty-day prevalence rates of alcohol, cigarette, and licit or illicit drug use (with the exception of amphetamines; Johnston et al., 2007). However, by the twelfth grade, Latino youth report less drug use (for most major drugs) than their non-Latino white counterparts. Johnston and colleagues conclude that the discordant positioning of Latinos at eighth and tenth grade versus twelfth grade in their school-based survey is accounted for by the fact that a disproportionately large number of Latino students drop out of high school before the twelfth grade and are therefore not included in the twelfth-grade prevalence rates.

Although Latinos as a group are at high risk for substance use, there are considerable differences in prevalence rates by nationality (i.e., country of origin) and nativity status (i.e., U.S.-born versus foreign-born). For example, according to the Monitoring the Future Survey, Cuban American eighth-graders report higher rates of marijuana and cocaine use and heavy drinking than do their Mexican American, Puerto Rican, and other Latin American counterparts in the United States (Delva et al., 2005). Differences in substance use by nativity have also been documented. For example, Vega, Gil, & Kolody (2002) found that U.S.-born Latino adolescents report higher drug use rates than do foreign-born Latinos.

The disproportionate rates of substance use among Latino adolescents, as well as the differences in prevalence rates within different Latino groups, suggest the need to identify risk and protective processes that are associated with substance use in the Latino population. Although many of these processes are similar to those that operate in other ethnic groups, some of them are specific to Latinos (Pantin, Schwartz, Sullivan, Coatsworth, & Szapocznik, 2003; Pantin, Schwartz, Sullivan, Prado, & Szapocznik, 2004). In the next section, we review research on risk and protective processes associated with substance use in Latino adolescents.

Risk and Protective Processes

The risk and protective factors paradigm proposed by Hawkins, Catalano, & Miller (1992) is one of the most widely endorsed frameworks for organizing the processes that predispose adolescents toward or away from substance use. Contemporary views of risk and protection, such as ecodevelopmental theory (Pantin, Schwartz, et al., 2003; Szapocznik & Coatsworth, 1999) take into consideration the multiple social contexts influencing development, the interrelations among those contexts, the changing nature of each context, and how these elements affect risk for the development of problem behaviors, including substance use (Cicchetti & Aber, 1998; Cicchetti & Richters, 1993).

ECODEVELOPMENTAL THEORY

Ecodevelopmental theory borrows from and extends Bronfenbrenner's social-ecological framework (see Schwartz, Coatsworth, et al., 2006, for a more extended discussion), which organizes the multiple influences on adolescent development, such as family, peers, and school. Ecodevelopmental theory suggests that cultural processes such as the discrepancy between the parents' culture of origin and that of the host country, produce a "trickle-down" effect by isolating parents from sources of parental support as well as their adolescent's peer networks (Leon & Dziegielewski, 2000; Pantin, Schwartz et al., 2003, 2004). Lack of social support for parents may result in less supportive and involved parenting (Simons, Lorenz, Wu, & Conger, 1993), which in turn increases the likelihood of adolescent behavior problems (Coatsworth, Pantin, & Szapocznik, 2002), association with deviant peers (Ary et al., 1999), and youth substance use (Pettit, Bates, Dodge, & Meece, 1999).

Understanding how cultural change in Latino families may set in motion and/or exacerbate a series of contextual processes that have been shown to be important predictors of problematic outcomes across ethnic groups (e.g., Barrera, Biglan, Ary, & Li, 2001) is an important step in preventing substance use in Latino adolescents.

CULTURAL RISK AND PROTECTIVE PROCESSES

Acculturation has been consistently linked with substance use among Latino youth. It occurs when one's cultural orientations change as one adapts to a new cultural context (Schwartz, Montgomery, & Briones, 2006). Acculturation, typically conceptualized as preference for English-language use and or endorsement of U.S. practices, has been shown to be associated with higher rates of substance use (Fridrich & Flannery, 1995; Gil, Wagner, & Vega, 2000; Turner, Lloyd, & Taylor, 2006). In Latin American countries, consistent with collectivist values, the family is given precedence over the individual (e.g., Sabogal, Marin, Otero-Sabogal, Marin, & Perez-Stable, 1987). When Latino families immigrate to the United States, important aspects of the parent-child relationship that are consistent with Latino culture (Santisteban, Muir-Malcolm, Mitrani, & Szapocznik, 2002), such as respect for adults, obedience to authority, and a sense of duty to parents, may conflict with those commonly endorsed in the more individualistic U.S. society. Youth acculturate more quickly to U.S. values than their parents do, which may result in increased family conflict and parental disinvestment from their "Americanized" adolescents. Research has shown that the relationship between acculturation and substance use may be mediated, both through acculturative stress and through erosion of the collectivist values and family connectedness that are so prominent in many Latino cultures (Gil, Vega, & Biafora, 1998).

FAMILY RISK AND PROTECTIVE PROCESSES

Families play a crucial role in child and adolescent development (Steinberg, 2001), including substance use (e.g., Broman, Reckase, & Freedman-Doan, 2006; Bahr, Hoffman, & Yang, 2005). Parental involvement, family support for the adolescent (Crosby et al., 2001; Rodgers, 1999), parent-adolescent communication (Brody & Ge, 2001; O'Sullivan, Jaramillo, Moreau, & Meyer-Bahlburg, 1999), and parent-adolescent connectedness (Miller, 2002; van den Bree & Pickworth, 2005) are strong protective processes against adolescent substance use. Parental disinvestment may be a particularly important risk factor for adolescent substance use in Latino families because of the influence of acculturation on the Latino family and because of the prominence of family in the Latino culture.

PEER RISK AND PROTECTIVE PROCESSES

Researchers have repeatedly found that adolescents who affiliate with substance-using peers are more likely to engage in substance use (Dishion, Capaldi, & Yoerger, 1999; Epstein, Botvin, Baker, & Diaz, 1999; Marshal & Chassin, 2000). Peers may play an especially salient role in the lives of Latino adolescents, whose parents are generally not able to socialize them about the receiving culture. Peers are often the vehicle through which Latino immigrant adolescents learn to navigate through and adjust to U.S. culture. As a result, given the especially high rates of substance use among Latino adolescents, whether or not Latino youths affiliate with substance-using peers is an important predictor of substance use in this population.

SCHOOL RISK AND PROTECTIVE PROCESSES

Schools play a significant role in the lives of children and adolescents of all ethnic groups. Research has shown that adolescents who lack interest in school are at heightened risk of substance use (Henry, Swaim, & Slater, 2005; Simons-Morton et al., 1999). Moreover, compelling evidence has shown that adolescents who drop out of school are at significantly greater risk for substance use than adolescents who complete high school (Ellickson, Bui, Bell, & McGuigan, 1998; Guagliardo Huang, Hicks, & D'Angelo, 1998). Given that 40 percent of Latino adolescents fail to complete high school (Greene & Forster, 2003), school may be a particularly salient factor for this population.

NEIGHBORHOOD RISK AND PROTECTIVE PROCESSES

Residing in a poor and disorganized neighborhood may exacerbate existing risks for substance use (cf. Sampson, Raudenbush, & Earls, 1997). A considerable proportion of immigrant Latino adolescents tend to live in poor, socially disconnected neighborhoods. Such neighborhoods are characterized by high crime rates and related problems such as substance use. The high rates of poverty and economic deprivation in the lives of Latino immigrants partially contribute to the high rates of substance use in this population (Coatsworth et al., 2002). Having briefly reviewed the risk and protective processes for substance use, we now turn to a review of prevention intervention models that have been found to be efficacious for Latino youth.

Four Preventive Interventions

In a recent review, Szapocznik and colleagues (Szapocznik, Prado, Burlew, Williams, & Santisteban, 2007) concluded that, to date, there are four drug use prevention interventions that have been found to be efficacious and/or to increase protection or decrease risk for substance use in Latino adolescents. Below, we briefly review each of these intervention models. More details about the methodology used to identify these interventions or about the intervention models themselves can be found in Szapocznik et al. (2007).

FAMILY EFFECTIVENESS TRAINING

Family Effectiveness Training (FET) was developed to correct maladaptive family interactions, resulting from intercultural conflict, in Cuban youth and their families. Working with the family, FET uses a combination of cultural change and strategic restructuring to reduce the adolescent's risk for substance use (Szapocznik, Santisteban, Rio, Perez-Vidal, & Kurtines, 1989). The intervention also aims to reduce intercultural conflict by reintroducing Latino adolescents to their heritage culture while simultaneously familiarizing parents with U.S. culture. FET aims to reduce family conflict and improve family collaboration and problem solving by promoting cultural understanding between generations.

FET was evaluated (Szapocznik et al., 1989) using a randomized controlled trial. The intervention consisted of thirteen weekly sessions. Seventy-nine Latino adolescents and their families were randomized to either FET or a minimal-contact control. The results of the study demonstrated that FET was efficacious (relative to control) in improving family functioning and decreasing youth behavior problems as reported by parents. The results were maintained at six-month follow-up. Substance use data were not collected as part of this study.

KEEPIN' IT REAL

Keepin' it REAL, a four-month intervention, is the only school-based intervention of the four prevention intervention models found to be efficacious for Latino youth. Keepin' it REAL, which is grounded on ecological risk and a resilience approach (Bogenschneider, 1996), was developed to incorporate Latino cultural values and practices that diminish intrapersonal risk for substance use (e.g., communication, competence, and drug-resistance skills) (Castro, Proescholdbell, Abeita, & Rodriguez, 1999; Kulis et al., 2005). The intervention aims to disseminate culturally grounded prevention messages (Kulis et al.,

2005). Keepin' it REAL promotes aspects of Mexican American, European American, and African American culture that protect against substance use.

Keepin' it REAL was evaluated using a pre-post randomized controlled trial design (Kulis et al., 2005). Thirty-five schools in Arizona consisting of 3,402 Latino seventh-graders were randomized into one of four conditions. The first, second, and third conditions consisted of three different versions of the Keepin' it REAL intervention: one based in Mexican American culture, another based in African American and European American culture, and a third that consisted of half of the lessons from the Mexican American version and half of the lessons from the African American/European American version (referred to as the "multicultural" version). The fourth condition was a no-intervention control group.

The study aimed to evaluate the efficacy of the three versions of the Keepin' it REAL intervention relative to the control in terms of (a) preventing and reducing substance use by enhancing cultural identification, (b) promoting personal antidrug norms, and (c) increasing decision-making and resistance skills. The results of the study indicated that relative to students in the control condition, students who participated in either the Mexican American or "multicultural" versions of Keepin' it REAL reported significantly less substance use and marijuana use in the past thirty days. Students in the Mexican American version of Keepin' it REAL also reported greater refusal confidence, fewer intentions to accept offers of substance use, and less peer use. There were no significant differences in any of the outcomes between the African American/European version of the intervention and the control group.

NUESTRAS FAMILIAS

Nuestras Familias (Martinez & Eddy, 2005) is a culturally adapted version of Parent Management Training (Forgatch & Martinez, 1999; Reid, Patterson, & Snyder, 2002), a substance abuse preventive intervention that uses dyadic instruction, modeling, role playing, and at-home practice to help parents acquire skills in encouragement, parental monitoring, discipline, and problem solving. Nuestras Familias is grounded in two theoretical frameworks: social interaction learning theory (Reid et al., 2002), and ecodevelopmental theory (Szapocznik & Coatsworth, 1999) and is also informed by acculturation processes salient to Latino families.

Nuestras Familias was evaluated using a pre-post randomized controlled trial design. Seventy-three adolescents and their families were randomized to either Nuestras Familias or a no-intervention control. Families randomized to the Nuestras Familias intervention participated in twelve weekly group sessions that focused on topics such as effective family communication, family problem solving, and monitoring and supervision for school success (Martinez & Eddy, 2005). The results demonstrated that, relative to the control condition, Nuestras Familias was efficacious in (a) increasing parental reports of general parenting, skills encouragement, and overall effective parenting, and (b) reducing adolescent reports of aggression, other externalizing behavior problems, and likelihood of smoking. Substance use data were not reported as part of this study.

FAMILIAS UNIDAS

Familias Unidas is based on ecodevelopmental theory and its application to the prevention of substance use in Latinos. Familias Unidas aims to prevent substance use (and HIV) by primarily targeting four family processes found to protect against substance use: positive parenting, parent-adolescent communication, parental involvement, and family support (Pantin et al., 2004; Prado et al., in press). Consistent with Latino cultural values, Familias Unidas places parents in positions of leadership and expertise to facilitate the prevention of substance use and unsafe sex in their adolescents. In most of the Familias Unidas intervention, parents meet in groups to discuss and role-play the specific parenting skills targeted in the intervention. This group format was designed to create social support networks for Hispanic immigrant parents by introducing them to other parents in similar situations. Not surprisingly, Prado and colleagues (Prado, Pantin, Schwartz, Lupei, & Szapocznik, 2006) have shown that active participation in the group sessions is predictive of initial and continued attendance in the intervention.

Familias Unidas has been evaluated in two separate randomized controlled trials, and a third is ongoing. In the first study (Pantin, Coatsworth, et al., 2003), 167 Latino adolescents and their families were randomized to either Familias Unidas or a no-intervention (treatment-as-usual) control. The results of the study demonstrated that Familias Unidas was efficacious (relative to control) in (a) increasing parental involvement, parent-adolescent communication, and parental support for the adolescent; and in (b) reducing adolescent behavior problems. The results also demonstrated that increases in the family processes were related to the decreases in behavior problems. Substance use data were not reported as part of this study.

In the second randomized trial, Prado et al. (in press) evaluated the combination of Familias Unidas and Parent Preadolescent Training for HIV Prevention (PATH; Krauss et al., 2000) in preventing both substance use and unsafe sex. Whereas Familias Unidas was originally developed as a family strengthening and substance abuse preventive intervention, PATH was developed to increase parent-adolescent communication about sexuality and HIV risk behaviors (Krauss et al., 2000). The combination of these two intervention modules therefore has the potential to address family functioning, substance use, and HIV risk.

In this second study, Prado and colleagues (in press) evaluated the efficacy of Familias Unidas + PATH relative to two control conditions: (a) English for Speakers of Other Languages (ESOL) + PATH and (b) ESOL + HEART, a family-centered adolescent cardiovascular health intervention. All three conditions were designed to deliver equivalent dosage and participant contact. The first aim of the study was to determine the relative efficacy of Familias Unidas in preventing substance use and unsafe sexual behavior, as well as increasing family functioning defined as parental involvement, parent-adolescent communication, positive parenting, and family support. The second aim was to examine whether, and to what extent, the effects of condition on substance use and unsafe sexual behavior are mediated by improvements in family functioning.

Two hundred and sixty-six Latino adolescents and their families were randomized to one of the three intervention conditions. The results from a three-year longitudinal follow-up demonstrated that Familias Unidas + PATH was efficacious in reducing illicit drug use relative to ESOL + HEART, and in reducing unprotected sex at last sexual intercourse relative to ESOL + PATH. The results also showed that Familias Unidas + PATH was efficacious relative to both control conditions in preventing and reducing cigarette use. Finally, the results showed as well that Familias Unidas was efficacious in improving family functioning (relative to both control conditions), and that the effects of condition on cigarette and illicit drug use were mediated by the improvements in family functioning.

The following case vignette illustrates the trickle-down or cascading effects of ecodevelopmental theory. The case is from one of the families that participated in the Familias Unidas intervention described above.

CASE STUDY

Sandra-Isabel is a fourteen-year-old Honduran girl who has been living in the United States for four years with both her parents. She prefers to speak English and has acculturated to the U.S. way of life, whereas her parents are monolingual Spanish speakers who have very limited understanding of U.S. culture. Sandra-Isabel's adolescent strivings for autonomy and individuation, which her parents view as deviant, have strained the family relationships. The parents have attempted to decrease her deviant behavior by increasingly setting harsher limits on her association with peers, which has resulted in decreased communication between Sandra-Isabel and her parents. The parents have not become acquainted with Sandra-Isabel's friends and have not had contact with her school because "in Honduras parents do not get involved in school activities." Sandra-Isabel's performance in school has progressively deteriorated, and her academic and conduct grades as well as her attendance are poor. Although she is not using alcohol or illicit drugs, the school counselor has been concerned that Sandra-Isabel is showing some of the precursors of substance use, such as poor academic achievement and poor family relationships. Concerned with her deviant behavior, the school counselor requested a meeting with Sandra-Isabel's parents, at which time the school counselor referred them to the Familias Unidas intervention.

The Familias Unidas intervention is designed to help families like that of Sandra-Isabel's. As previously mentioned, the Familias Unidas intervention targets processes such as parent-adolescent communication and parental involvement (Pantin et al., 2004; Prado et al., in press). Familias Unidas helped Sandra-Isabel's father develop skills to more effectively communicate his concerns with his daughter in a supportive fashion and to learn to listen and reflect what his daughter was saying to him. In addition, during the intervention, parents are encouraged to become involved in the adolescent's school and peer worlds. In the case of Sandra-Isabel's parents, her father could not understand how being involved would help Sandra-Isabel do well in school. "I don't think San-dra-Isabel would care if I met anyone at her school. My meeting with teachers or school counselors will not help Sandra-Isabel do better." The Familias Unidas facilitator replied that "If you are involved in San-dra-Isabel's school, then you can begin to better monitor her atten-dance. The teachers and school counselor can also keep you informed of Sandra-Isabel's attendance and grades." Another parent in the group chimed in and told Sandra-Isabel's father that "meeting with school personnel has helped me know how my daughter does in school and what I can do to collaborate with school personnel to improve my daughter's academic achievement." Sandra-Isabel's parents set up a meeting with the school counselor and developed a plan to help San-dra-Isabel get back on track at school. In the Familias Unidas interven-tion, parents are also encouraged to be involved in their child's peer world. During the session on peers, facilitators help parents understand the critical role that peers play in the development of their children's lives. Through these focused group discussions, parents come to value the importance of monitoring their child's association with peers and becoming acquainted with the peers' parents to form supervisory networks. In the case of Sandra-Isabel's father, he was a bit reluctant to understand the positive effects of getting to know his daughter's friends, and even in letting his daughter associate with friends. "If you think she is doing poorly in school now that I don't let her go out, imagine if I let her go out with her friends." One of the other parents in the group replied, "It is normal for a teenager to be able to get together with friends. You are being too harsh with your daughter, which is probably leading to her rebelling by doing poorly in school. As we discussed earlier today, you should get to know your daughter's friends and their families." Sandra-Isabel's father began to understand that his attempts to protect his daughter were backfiring and that he needed to develop new parenting skills to be effective in supporting his daughter's development. A few weeks after the peer monitoring session, Sandra-Isabel's father invited two of Sandra-Isabel's friends to the house. Sandra-Isabel was very appreciative of her dad's effort, and promised him she would do better in school. Additional details about the Familias Unidas intervention, including case vignettes, can be found elsewhere (Pantin et al., 2007; Prado et al., in press).

Recommendations for Social Work Practice and for Future Prevention Research with Latino Youth

Having reviewed the literature on prevalence, etiology, and prevention of substance use among Latino adolescents, we now provide recommendations for social work practice and for future prevention research with this population. First, we highlight the need and importance of attending to cultural processes when developing substance use preventive interventions for Latino adolescents. As reviewed above, all of the intervention models found to be efficacious for Latino youth incorporated culture in the intervention. For example, Keepin' it REAL (Kulis et al., 2005) and Nuestras Familias (Martinez & Eddy, 2005) were adapted from existing interventions targeting general-population adolescents, but they integrated culture within the intervention. Family Effectiveness Training (Szapocznik et al., 1989), Familias Unidas (Pantin, Schwartz, et al., 2003, 2004), and BSFT™ (Szapocznik et al., 2003) were developed specifically for Hispanics. Accordingly, an important consideration when developing and evaluating substance use preventive interventions for Hispanic adolescents is the controversy of whether culturally specific interventions are more efficacious than generic interventions. Because scant research has examined the relative efficacy of culturally specific versus generic interventions not designed or adapted for any specific cultural group or cultural adaptations of existing generic interventions, additional research is clearly needed in this area (Nagayama Hall, 2005).

Second, given that family processes play a major role in the prevention of substance use, it is important that future preventive intervention studies examine whether, and to what extent, family processes mediate the relationship between intervention and the observed outcomes. For example, as described above, the effects of Familias Unidas on cigarette use and illicit drug use were mediated by improvements in family functioning. Hence, it is recommended that those evaluating the efficacy of substance abuse preventive interventions for Hispanic adolescents include measures of family process to examine the degree to which it mediates the effects of the intervention.

Third, future studies should examine the heterogeneity in prevalence that exists within the Latino population. Although research has documented that nativity status (i.e., U.S.-born versus foreign-born) and country of origin (e.g., Delva et al., 2005; Vega, Gil, & Kolody, 2002) help explain the heterogeneity of substance use in Hispanic subgroups, these variables are not amenable to intervention. We have previously argued (Pantin, Prado, Schwartz, & Sullivan, 2005; Prado et al., 2006) that creating subgroups based on risk and protective processes that are amenable to intervention (as opposed to more traditional methods of subgrouping by such things as country of origin and nativity status) can both (a) help explain the heterogeneity of substance use within and across Latino subgroups, and (b) prevent substance use by targeting preventive interventions toward specific risk subgroups of Latino adolescents.

Finally, for the efficacious preventive intervention models reviewed above, it is important to conduct effectiveness trials that evaluate the impact of these intervention models outside of the laboratory setting. To date, no effectiveness trials have been conducted with any of the preventive interventions that have shown to be efficacious for Hispanic adolescents (Szapocnik et al., 2007).

Conclusion

This chapter has reviewed the literature on the prevalence, etiology, and prevention of substance use among Latino adolescents. The literature reviewed in this chapter demonstrates that despite the evidence that Latino youth are disproportionately affected by substance use, few intervention programs have been found to be efficacious in preventing substance use in this population. The literature on risk and protection suggests that culture and family processes are crucial factors in the genesis of substance use. Theoretical frameworks, like ecodevelopmental theory, that utilize the multiple influences on adolescent development to explain the etiology of substance use among Latino adolescents, are particularly salient. It is hoped that the literature reviewed and the recommendations provided above contribute to the reduction of the health disparities that exist in this large and fast-growing minority population.

In this and the previous chapter, the authors explore culturally competent practice with young Latinos and families. In the next chapter, the authors explore social work practice with older Latino adults. The profession of social work has put a great deal of energy into improving its training of gerontological social workers and developing new methods of providing services to older adults. At times, however, diverse groups of older adults have received less attention than other groups. This is true of Latino older adults, who have traditionally been cared for in the home. However, as the next chapter explores, Latino older adults are more frequently finding themselves in need of services, and social workers must learn the key methods and approaches for providing them.

For Writing and Reflection

1. How does ecodevelopmental theory integrate and expand upon the Hawkins, Catalano, & Miller (1992) risk and protective factors paradigm for adolescent substance use?

2. How does the "trickle-down" effect in ecodevelopmental theory explain how cultural mismatches between Latino families' cultural values and those of the host culture lead to adolescent substance use?

3. From a prevention perspective, why is it necessary to understand the role of cultural change and adaptation in Latino families and the sequelae of these changes?

4. What important family processes have been identified as protective against adolescent substance use, and how can acculturation negatively impact these processes?

5. What common characteristics do many of the efficacious substance use preventive interventions for Latino adolescents share?

6. How are the elements of ecodevelopmental theory interwoven in the case vignette?

References

Arias, E., Anderson, R. N., Kung, H. C., Murphy, S. L., & Kochanek, K. D. (2003). Deaths: Final data for 2001. *National Vital Statistics Reports, 52*(3), 1–116.

Ary, D. V., Duncan, T. E., Biglan, A., Metzler, C. W., Noell, J. W., & Smolkowski, K. (1999). Development of adolescent problem behavior. *Journal of Abnormal Child Psychology, 27*(2), 141–150.

Bahr, S. J., Hoffmann, J. P., & Yang, X. (2005). Parental and peer influences on the risk of adolescent drug use. *The Journal of Primary Prevention, 26*(6), 529–551.

Barrera, M. Jr., Biglan, A., Ary, D., Li, F. (2001). Replication of a problem behavior model with American Indian, Hispanic, and Caucasian youth. *Journal of Early Adolescence, 21*(2): 133–157.

Bernstein, N. (2006, May 21). 100 years in the back door, out the front. *New York Times.* Section 4, 4.

Bogenschneider, K. (1996). An ecological risk/protective theory for building prevention programs, policies, and community capacity to support youth. *Family Relations, 45*(2), 127–138.

Brody, G. H., & Ge, X. (2001). Linking parenting processes and self-regulation to psychological functioning and alcohol use during early adolescence. *Journal of Family Psychology, 15*(1), 82–94.

Broman, C. L., Reckase, M. D., & Freedman-Doan, C. R. (2006). The role of parenting in drug use among black, Latino and white adolescents. *Journal of Ethnic Substance Abuse, 5*(1), 39–50.

Castro, F. G., Proescholdbell, R. J., Abeita, L., & Rodriguez, D. (1999). Ethnic and cultural minority groups. *Addictions: A comprehensive guide,* 10, 499–505.

Chicchette, D. & Aber, J.L. (1998). Contextualism and developmental psychopathology. *Development and Psychopathology,* 10, 137–141

Cicchetti, D., & Richters, J. E. (1993). Developmental considerations in the investigation of conduct disorder. *Development and Psychopathology,* 5, 331–344.

Coatsworth, J. D., Pantin, H., & Szapocznik, J. (2002). Familias Unidas: A family-centered ecodevelopmental intervention to reduce risk for problem behavior among Hispanic adolescents. *Clinical Child and Family Psychology Review, 5*(2), 113–132.

Crosby, R. A., DiClemente, R. J., Wingood, G. M., Cobb, B. K., Harrington, K., Davies, S. L., Hook, E. W., & Oh, M. K. (2001). HIV/STD-protective benefits of living with mothers in perceived supportive families: A study of high-risk African American female teens. *Preventive Medicine, 33*(3), 175–178.

Delva, J., Wallace, J. M, O'Malley, P. M., Bachman, J. G., Johnston, L. D., & Schulenberg, J. E. (2005). The epidemiology of alcohol, marijuana, and cocaine use among Mexican American, Puerto Rican, Cuban American, and other LatinAmerican eighth-grade students in the United States: 1991–2002. *American Journal of Public Health,* 95 (4), 696–702.

Dishion, T. J., Capaldi, D. M., & Yoerger, K. (1999). Middle childhood antecedents to progressions in male adolescent substance abuse: An ecological analysis of risk and protection. *Journal of Adolescent Research,* 14, 175–205.

Ellickson, P. L., Bui, K., Bell, R. M., & McGuigan, K. A. (1998). *Does early drug use increase the risk of dropping out of high school?* New York: RAND.

Epstein, J. A., Botvin, G. J., Baker, E., & Diaz, T. (1999). Impact of social influences and problem behavior on alcohol use among inner-city Hispanic and black adolescents. *Journal of Studies on Alcohol, 60*(5) 235–238.

Forgatch, M. S., & Martinez, C. R., Jr. (1999). Parent management training: A program linking basic research and practical application. *Journal of the Norwegian Psychological Society, 36*, 923–937.

Fridrich, A., & Flannery, D. J. (1995). The effects of ethnicity and acculturation on early adolescent delinquency. *Journal of Child and Family Studies, 4*, 69–87.

Gil, A. G., Vega, W. A., & Biafora, F. (1998). Temporal influences of family structure and family risk factors on drug use initiation in a multiethnic sample of adolescent boys. *Journal of Youth and Adolescence, 27*, 373–93.

Gil, A. G., Wagner, E. F., & Vega, W. A. (2000). Acculturation, familism, and alcohol use among Latino adolescent males: Longitudinal relations. *Journal of Community Psychology, 28*(4), 443–458.

Greene, J. P., & Forster, G. (2003). *Public high school graduation and college readiness rates in the United States.* New York: Center for Civic Innovation at the Manhattan Institute.

Guagliardo, M. F., Huang, Z., Hicks, J., & D'Angelo, L. (1998). Increased drug use among old-for-grade and dropout urban adolescents. *American Journal of Preventive Medicine, 15*(1), 42–48.

Hawkins, J. D., Catalano, R. F., & Miller, J. Y. (1992). Risk and protective factors for alcohol and other drug problems in adolescence and early adulthood: Implications for substance abuse prevention. *Psychological Bulletin, 112*(1), 64–105.

Henry, K. L., Swaim, R. C., & Slater, M. D. (2005). Intraindividual variability of school bonding and adolescents' beliefs about the effect of substance use on future aspirations. *Prevention Science, 6*(2), 101–112.

Huntington, S. P. (2004). *Who are we?: The challenges to America's national identity.* New York: Simon and Schuster.

Johnston, L. D., O'Malley, P. M., Bachman, J. G., & Schulenberg, J. E. (2007). *Monitoring the future national results on adolescent drug use: Overview of key findings 2006.* (NIH Publication No. 07–6202). Bethesda, MD: National Institute on Drug Abuse.

Krauss, B. J., Godfrey, C., Yee, D., Goldsamt, L., Tiffany, J., Almeyda, L., Davis, W. R., Bula, E., Reardon, D., & Jones, Y. (2000). Saving our children from a silent epidemic: The PATH program for parents and preadolescents. In *Working with Families in the Era of HIV/AIDS* (pp. 89–112). Thousand Oaks, CA: Sage.

Krauss, B. J., Goldsamt, L., Bula, E., & Sember, R. (1997). The white researcher in the multicultural community: Lessons in HIV prevention education learned in the field. *Journal of Health Education, 28*(6), S67–S71.

Kulis, S., Marsiglia, F. F., Elek, E., Dustman, P., Wagstaff, D. A., & Hecht, M. L. (2005). Mexican/Mexican American adolescents and Keepin' it REAL: An evidence-based substance abuse prevention program. *Child and Schools, 27*, 133–45.

Leon, A. M., & Dziegielewski, S. F. (2000). Engaging Hispanic immigrant mothers: Revisiting the psycho-educational group model. *Crisis Intervention and Time-Limited Treatment, 6*(1), 13–27.

Marotta, S. A., & Garcia, J. G. (2003). Latinos in the United States in 2000. *Hispanic Journal of Behavioral Sciences, 25*(1), 13–34.

Marshal, M. P., & Chassin, L. (2000). Peer influence on adolescent alcohol use: The moderating role of parental support and discipline. *Applied Developmental Science, 4*(2), 80–88.

Martinez, Jr., C. R., & Eddy, J. M. (2005). Effects of culturally adapted parent management training on Latino youth behavioral health outcomes. *Journal of Consulting & Clinical Psychology, 73*(5), 841–851.

Miller, B. C. (2002). Family influences on adolescent sexual and contraceptive behavior. *Journal of Sexual Research, 39*(1), 22–26.

Nagayama Hall, G. C. (2005). Introduction to the special section on multicultural and community psychology: Clinical psychology in context. *Journal of Consulting and Clinical Psychology, 73*, 787–789.

O'Sullivan, L. F., Jaramillo, B. M. S., Moreau, D., & Meyer-Bahlburg, H. F. L. (1999). Mother-daughter communication about sexuality in a clinical sample of Hispanic adolescent girls. *Hispanic Journal of Behavioral Sciences, 21*(4), 447–469.

Pantin, H., Coatsworth, J. D., Feaster, D. J., Newman, F. L., Briones, E., Prado, G., Schwartz, S. J., & Szapocznik, J. (2003). Familias Unidas: The efficacy of an intervention to promote parental investment in Hispanic immigrant families. *Prevention Science, 4*(3), 189–201.

Pantin, H., Prado, G., Schwartz, S. J., & Sullivan, S. (2005). Methodological challenges in designing efficacious drug abuse and HIV preventive interventions for Hispanic adolescent subgroups. *Journal of Urban Health, 82.*

Pantin, H., Schwartz, S. J., Coatsworth, J. D., Sullivan, S., Briones, E., & Szapocznik, J. (2007). Familias Unidas: A systemic parent-centered approach to preventing problem behavior in Hispanic adolescents. In P. H. Tolan, J. Szapocznik, & S. Sambrano (Eds.), *Preventing substance abuse ages 3–14* (pp. 211–238). Washington, DC: American Psychological Association.

Pantin, H., Schwartz, S. J., Sullivan, S., Coatsworth, J. D., & Szapocznik, J. (2003). Preventing substance abuse in Hispanic immigrant adolescents: An ecodevelopmental, parent-centered approach. *Hispanic Journal of Behavioral Sciences, 25*(4), 469–500.

Pantin, H., Schwartz, S. J., Sullivan, S., Prado, G., & Szapocznik, J. (2004). Ecodevelopmental HIV Prevention Programs for Hispanic Adolescents. *American Journal of Orthopsychiatry, 74*(4), 545–558.

Pettit, G. S., Bates, J. E., Dodge, K. A., & Meece, D. W. (1999). The impact of after-school peer contact on early adolescent externalizing problems is moderated by parental monitoring, perceived neighborhood safety, and prior adjustment. *Child Development, 70*(3), 768–778.

Prado, G., Pantin, H., Briones, E., Schwartz, S., Feaster, D., Huang, S., Sullivan, S., Tapia, M., Sabillon, E., Lopez, B., & Szapocznik, J. (in press). A randomized controlled trial of a family-centered intervention in preventing substance use and HIV risk behaviors in Hispanic adolescents. *Journal of Consulting and Clinical Psychology.*

Prado, G., Pantin, H., Schwartz, S. J., Lupei, N. S., & Szapocznik, J. (2006). Predictors of engagement and retention into a parent-centered, ecodevelopmental HIV preventive intervention for Hispanic adolescents and their families. *Journal of Pediatric Psychology, 31*(9), 874.

Ramirez, R. R., & de la Cruz, G. P. (2003). *The Hispanic population in the United States: March 2002.* U.S. Dept. of Commerce, Bureau of the Census, Economics and Statistics Administration.

Reid, J. B., Patterson, G. R., & Snyder, J. (2002). Antisocial behavior in children and adolescents: A developmental analysis and model for intervention. Washington, DC: American Psychological Association.

Rodgers, K. B. (1999). Parenting processes related to sexual risk-taking behaviors of adolescent males and females. *Journal of Marriage and the Family, 61*(1), 99–109.

Sabogal, F., Marin, G., Otero-Sabogal, R., Marin, B. V., & Perez-Stable, E. J. (1987). Hispanic familism and acculturation: What changes and what doesn't? *Hispanic Journal of Behavioral Sciences, 9*(4), 397.

Sampson, R. J., Raudenbush, S. W., & Earls, F. (1997). Neighborhoods and violent crime: A multilevel study of collective efficacy. *Science, 277*(5328), 918–924.

Santisteban, D. A., Muir-Malcolm, J. A., Mitrani, V. B., & Szapocznik, J. (2002). Integrating the study of ethnic culture and family psychology intervention science. *Family Psychology: Science-Based Interventions, 28*, 331–352.

Schwartz, S. J., Coatsworth, J. D., Pantin, H., Prado, G., Sharp, E. H., & Szapocznik, J. (2006). The role of ecodevelopmental context and self-concept in depressive and externalizing symptoms in Hispanic adolescents. *International Journal of Behavioral Development, 30*(4), 359.

Schwartz, S. J., Montgomery, M. J., & Briones, E. (2006). The role of identity in acculturation of among immigrant people: Theoretical propositions, empirical questions, and applied recommendations. *Human Development, 49*, 1–30.

Simons, R. L., Lorenz, F. O., Wu, C. I., & Conger, R. D. (1993). Social network and marital support as mediators and moderators of the impact of stress and depression on parental behavior. *Developmental Psychology, 29*(2): 368–381.

Simons-Morton, B., Crump, A. D., Haynie, D. L., Saylor, K. E., Eitel, P., & Yu, K. (1999). Psychosocial, school, and parent factors associated with recent smoking among early-adolescent boys and girls. *Preventive Medicine, 28*(2), 138–148.

Steinberg, S. (2001). *The Ethnic Myth.* Boston: Beacon Press.

Szapocznik, J., & Coatsworth, J. D. (1999). An ecodevelopmental framework for organizing the influences on drug abuse: A developmental model of risk and protection. In M. Glantz & C. R. Hartel (Eds.), *Drug abuse: Origins and interventions* (pp.331–366). Washington, DC: American Psychological Association.

Szapocznik, J., Hervis, O.E., & Schwartz, S. (2003). *Brief Strategic Family Therapy for adolescent drug abuse.* [NIH publication no. 03–4751; NIDA Therapy Manuals for DrugAddiction Series]. Rockville, Maryland: National Institute on Drug Abuse.Szapocznik, J., Prado, G., Burlew, K., Williams, R., & Santisteban, D. (2007). Drug abuse in African American and Hispanic adolescents: Culture, development, and behavior. *Annual Review of Clinical Psychology, 3*, 77–105.

Szapocznik, J., Santisteban S., Rio, A., Perez-Vidal, A., & Kurtines, W. M. (1989). Family Effectiveness Training: An intervention to prevent drug abuse and problembehaviors in Hispanic adolescents. *Hispanic Journal of Behavioral Sciences, 11*, 4–27.

Turner, R. J., Lloyd, D. A., & Taylor, J. (2006). Physical disability and mental health: An epidemiology of psychiatric and substance disorders. *Rehabilitation Psychology, 51*(3), 214–223.

van den Bree, M. B. M., & Pickworth, W. B. (2005). Risk factors predicting changes in marijuana involvement in teenagers. *Archives of General Psychiatry, 62*(3), 311–319.

Vega, W. A., Gil, A. G., & Kolody, B. (2002). What do we know about Latino drug use? Methodological evaluation of state databases. *Hispanic Journal of Behavioral Sciences, 24*(4), 395–408.

CHAPTER FOURTEEN

Social Work Practice with Older Latino Adults

Blanca M. Ramos
Gary A. Wright

Introduction

As the twenty-first century continues to unfold, the number of older adults in the Latino population is growing rapidly (Villa & Torres-Gil, 2001). As a result, social workers are increasingly more likely to encounter older Latinos and their families in a variety of practice arenas. At the same time, research consistently emphasizes the importance of cultural contexts in understanding the aging experience (Sokolovsky, 2000), underscoring the need for social workers to be culturally responsive in their practice with older Latinos.

This chapter provides readers an opportunity to expand their understanding of the aging experience for older Latinos as it is profoundly impacted by ethnic and cultural factors. This chapter also offers strategies for culturally responsive practice with this population. We begin with a brief overview of the diverse nature and sociodemographic characteristics of the aging Latino subpopulation. This is followed by discussions of the life course perspective, cultural practices and norms, and historic and contemporary issues, which provide the context for social work practice with older Latinos. The closely related theme of support systems and family caregivers is addressed next, as well as practice strategies for the contact, assessment, and intervention stages of the helping process. In conclusion, a case vignette is provided to illustrate the case of older Latinos, as well as questions that are meant to generate discussion. Throughout, discussions on older Latinos draw primarily upon their similarities as members of this ethnic group, while still calling attention to individual subgroup differences.

The Aging Latino Population

DIVERSITY WITHIN THE OLDER LATINO POPULATION

The older Latino population is very diverse. Recognizing this variability is essential as it differentially shapes the sociocultural realities, and, thus, the aging experience of older Latino clients. Part of their heterogeneity is due to differences in national origin or Latino subgroup affiliation, ancestral and racial heritages, historical experiences in the United States, and some cultural elements such as speech patterns, music, and food (Ramos, 1997). Sociodemographic characteristics such as gender, age, income, education, religion, sexual orientation, acculturation, and immigration status also contribute to the diversity of older Latinos.

Aging Latinos also differ as a result of country of birth or time residing on the U.S. mainland. In the current cohort, some were born here and trace their descent to ancestors who settled many generations ago or were born to immigrant parents. Others arrived as children or young adults and are aging here. The cohort also includes Latinos who have come later in life as older adults along with younger kin or to reunite with immigrant family or friends (Ramos, Jones, & Toseland, 2005).

Despite these significant within-group differences, older Latinos also share some commonalities. These include language and other cultural traits drawn from their Hispanic legacy such as values, traditions, and social networks (Ramos, 1997). Although their social, cultural, and political histories in the United States differ, they all are ascribed ethnic minority status and exposed to its accompanying oppression. The ensuing social disadvantages are particularly apparent in the disturbing sociodemographic profile elderly Latinos exhibit as a group.

A Sociodemographic Profile

Latinos age sixty-five and over make up 6 percent of the total U.S. older adult population, and by 2030 the number of older Latinos is projected to grow dramatically (U.S. Census Bureau, 2001). This rise is expected to be significantly higher for Latinos than for white older adults whose numbers, estimates indicate, will increase by 81 percent compared to 219 percent for older Latinos (Administration on Aging, 2001). By the year 2050, older Latinos will comprise 16.4 percent, or 12.5 million, of the older adult population (Administration on Aging, 2000). This unprecedented growth is due primarily to greater life expectancy and international migration (Ramos et al., 2005).

Older Latinos are primarily of Mexican descent (50%), followed by those of Central and South American (22%), Cuban (17%), and Puerto Rican (11%) heritage.

Most elderly Latinos (61%) are young-old (ages sixty-five to seventy-four), while 30 percent are in the middle-old range (seventy-five to eighty-four), and 9 percent are over eighty-four years old.

Although some older Latinos are well educated and economically stable, as a group they present a fragile socioeconomic profile and are clearly disadvantaged when compared to white older adults. Specifically, while 10.2 percent of non-Latino older adults live below the poverty level (Administration on Aging, 2001), older Latinos experience significantly higher levels of poverty, with 18.8 percent living below the poverty line. While for older Latinas living alone or with nonrelatives, the rate is significantly higher at 38.3 percent. Older Latinos also tend to rely more heavily on Social Security and SSI payments than private pensions or savings for income (Torres-Gil & Moga, 2001). Similarly, only 35 percent have a high school education compared to 74 percent for white older adults.

Yet, these daunting circumstances occur within an environmental-structural setting that can either enhance or limit opportunities for an optimum aging experience (Morales & Sheafor, 1998). For older adults of color, the historical period in which they have lived continues to be marked by exposure to oppressive conditions, rendering old age particularly challenging.

As of 1997, U.S. life expectancy was 77.1 years for whites and 71.1 years for African Americans (Administration on Aging, 2002). This discrepancy in life expectancy is not surprising given the limited access of older adults of color to health care. The life expectancy for Latinas (77.1 years) is slightly lower than that for white women (79.6 years) and higher than that for Latino men (69.6 years) (Giachello, 2001).

The health status of Latino elders points to acute disparities. In particular, Latino elders are more likely than white elders to report poorer health, such as high rates of diabetes, hypertension, respiratory problems, disability, and functional dependency. Older Latinos are also at higher risk for several acute and chronic conditions such as stroke, obesity, and some heart diseases (Villa & Torres-Gil, 2001). Underutilization of formal services compounds the poor health outcomes of Latinos. Compared to whites, fewer older Latinos report receiving preventive care and/or using nursing care and in-home services (Administration on Aging, 2002; Mui & Burnette, 1994; Tennstedt & Chang, 1998). This underutilization of services has often been attributed to systemic language and cultural barriers (Dietz, 1997; Talamantes & Aranda, 2004; Tennstedt & Chang, 1998).

The Context of Social Work Practice with Older Latinos

A LIFE COURSE PERSPECTIVE

In this chapter we approach aging from a life course perspective, where old age, the last stage of a person's biological development, is viewed as a natural process that brings about age-related social roles and physical, emotional, and social changes (McInnis-Dittrich, 2005; Ramos et al., 2005). Although aging is a universal process, the way it is experienced varies considerably. Individual and larger social and cultural factors define elders' societal roles and influence how they adapt and respond to the biopsychosocial changes, making their life course unique. For aging Latinos, these include traditional cultural practices and sociopolitical, gender, and immigration forces associated with their historical oppression and resilience. Some of the differences between Latino and non-Latino white elders are discussed below.

CULTURAL PRACTICES AND NORMS

Traditionally, cultural norms associated with the key core values of familism, collectivism, and respect, discussed by Magaña and Ybarra in Chapter Five, have strongly influenced how the aging process and older people are viewed in Latin American societies. Together, these values define old age and prescribe the roles and status accorded to elders. For example, great value is placed on old age and, as a result, those who have reached this life stage are appreciated because of their wisdom and cherished life-long experience. Elders are considered to be vital members of their communities and are expected to actively fulfill essential roles such as those of mentors, cultural transmitters, providers of care for grandchildren, and civic and religious leadership. As a result, older adults are accorded an honorable high social status and are often perceived to have earned the right to be cared for and protected, as well as to be treated with respect and deference (Ramos et al., 2005). Although, the practice of these cultural norms varies on an individual basis, these key core values still influence the aging experience of older Latinos in the United States today, in the midst of a broader Western-values cultural context

Social workers must thus be able to understand the cultural norms present in their elder Latino clients lives but also be able to carefully evaluate Western middle-class–based theoretical models that have been traditionally used to explain the aging process and expectations about successful life stages. These Western models are often not inclusive of the cultural context of older Latinos' lives. For example, among older Latinos, enjoying a large intergenerational family in harmony may be a stronger, more powerful indicator of successful aging than the ability to retire and be free of work and familial responsibilities in order to pursue individual interests or hobbies. Those who have immigrated to the United States later in life may be negatively affected by the youth-obsessed culture of the United States and as a result may feel devalued in old age. Similarly, older adults who immigrated to the United States at a younger age may have difficulty reconciling the marked contrast between the status and treatment they accorded their own parents and grandparents with what they themselves are now receiving from their children and grandchildren. This occurs particularly when there are different levels of acculturation among family members. Thus, aging in U.S. society, where attitudes about old age and social roles are sometimes in sharp contrast to that of Latino culture, has a major impact on the psychosocial functioning of older Latinos. This experience of aging in the United States intersects with the multiple oppressions that Latinos as a group have historically experienced, and shapes how old age as a life stage of the life course is manifested and experienced.

HISTORIC AND CONTEMPORARY ISSUES

The history of the Latino ethnic minority group in this country, characterized by open conflict, social inequality, prejudice, and discrimination, has dramatically shaped the sociocultural realities of aging Latinos today. For example, the relocation of the U.S. borders into Mexico and to encompass Puerto Rico in the nineteenth century brought about drastically different cultural values and norms as well as oppressive structural systems to these already well-established societies. As a result, some older Latinos of Mexican and Puerto Rican descent may still carry the lingering effects from stories passed down through generations about the painful experiences associated with alienation, stigmatization, and subordinate status (Ramos et al., 2005).

Perhaps the most salient historic and contemporary sociopolitical factor that affects Latino's aging process is that of immigration. Throughout time, Latinos, even if born in the United States, have been the target of continuous anti-immigrant sentiments, which have negatively impacted their ability to experience old age successfully. Immigration status has also contributed to severely restricting access to health care and preventive treatment that could ameliorate some of the acute medical conditions that are compounded by old age. Many Latinos also often occupy the least desirable jobs in U.S. society, such as harvesting crops and laboring as domestics and in factories and sweatshops under distressful working conditions. Of utmost importance for Latinos as they age, these jobs typically offer very low pay and little or no health and retirement benefits.

Support Systems and Family Caregivers

Older Latinos tend to rely on family and informal networks for support and caregiving. For example, research with Mexican Americans and Puerto Ricans found that the family, particularly daughters, is the major source of social support and caregiving for older members (Clark & Huttinger, 1998; Delgado & Tennstedt, 1997; Ramos, 2004). Caregiving for older Latino adults then needs to be understood within its sociocultural context as culture and ethnicity greatly influence caregiving practices (Dilworth-Anderson & Anderson, 1994; Ramos, 2002).

Caring for elders can be especially challenging for Latino families, who often bring few social resources to caregiving and tend to provide care to more highly disabled elders compared to white caregivers (Tennstedt et al., 1998). For example, studies show that Puerto Rican caregivers juggle many competing responsibilities but tend to have limited formal education and incomes below the poverty level (Delgado & Tennstedt, 1997; Tennstedt et al., 1998). As a result, caregivers may not be able to afford the medical care and prescribed medicines needed by their older kin, or understand and follow the nutritional and medical regime of their older kin. At the same time, migration, immigration, smaller families, divorce, and more women joining the labor force often results in fewer available relatives to care for frail elders than in the past (McCallion, Janicki, & Grant-Griffin, 1997).

Given the multiple financial, physical, and emotional demands of caregiving, Latino family caregivers are at high risk for burden and stress (Cox & Monk, 1993; Calderon & Tennstedt, 1998; Purdy & Arguello, 1992; Tirrito & Nathanson, 1994). Yet, despite these seeming obstacles, Latino caregivers still perceive their caregiving role more positively than whites and view caring for aging family members as a responsibility that goes beyond obligation (Clark & Huttinger, 1998; Phillips, de Ardon, Komnenich, & Rusinak, 2000; Valle, Cook-Gait, & Tazbaz, 1993). Thus, it is crucial to recognize the role of family caregivers in an older Latino adult's psychosocial functioning as well as the many difficulties associated with caregiving that can affect the well-being of caregivers, some of whom are elders themselves.

Strategies for Practice with Older Latino Clients

INITIAL CONTACT AND ENGAGEMENT

During the contact phase, social workers should facilitate engagement and help launch a successful professional relationship, as this can be decisive as to whether an older Latino continues participating in the helping process. Since older Latinos rarely use formal services, when they do, every effort must be made to ensure continuity and to reduce the potential for dropout. Clients' reluctance to seek help outside their informal networks, and fears and concerns with issues of privacy and confidentiality should be explored and addressed clearly and sensitively. When the older adult is accompanied by the caregiver or another person, workers should take care to emphasize the client's presence, address the client directly, and seek his or her input at all times. This strategy holds even in situations where, because of a frail mental condition and level of functioning, a greater participation of the primary caregiver may be required.

To minimize communication barriers, the worker should promptly determine a client's linguistic preferences and English proficiency, phrasing questions and comments sensitively, and should not make assumptions solely based on family names or physical characteristics. This step requires considerable empathy and understanding of the multiple educational experiences (or lack thereof) that an older Latino may have encountered throughout the life course. At times, a client may decline the use of a translator because of pride or a desire not to inconvenience (Root, 1998). It is also important to use trained translators who are familiar with the client's language, culture, and the literature on the use of translators (Pine et al., 1990). In short, applying social work practice and communication skills in a culturally sensitive manner is vital, particularly in work with clients who speak little English and/or have limited education.

Practitioners should communicate with the client in a clear, simple, positive, and nonjudgmental manner. Workers must listen attentively, focusing on the elder's words and sounds and not let accented speech or external appearance distract them. Familiarity with a client's culturally sanctioned nonverbal communication is absolutely necessary. For example, some older Latinos may consider making eye-to-eye contact with the worker as intrusive or disrespectful and presumptuous, especially in situations where the worker is much younger. It is incumbent upon practitioners to closely watch their own posture and other nonverbal behaviors to ensure cultural appropriateness and to avoid communicating a power differential or transmitting a patronizing, condescending attitude toward a client (Cournoyer, 1996; Lum 2003;

Ramos et al., 2005). Lum (2000) warns practitioners of the risk of resorting to previously formed stereotypes about the client's ethnic group, which can inadvertently creep in and betray communication. This might lead workers to hear what they expect to hear and as a self-fulfilling prophecy make those stereotypes become a reality. Social workers should, then, consistently reexamine their own biases and stereotypes in their practice.

Familiarity with the protocols or codes of ceremonial courtesy and formality prescribed by Latino culture for social interactions is also very important. For example, consistent with s*impatia,* a cultural norm that promotes cooperation and smooth, amiable social interactions, some older Latinos may prefer to begin a session with a friendly, informal conversation rather than proceeding directly to the presenting situation (Ramos, Toseland, McCallion, & Smith, unpublished). Accordance with cultural protocol is important because it conveys respect for the client and guides appropriate ways to relate to an older adult, who should be addressed in a deferential, attentive, and solicitous manner. Overall, during engagement, social workers should work to create a comfortable atmosphere, which encourages openness and collaboration, as well as recognizes the client's strengths and expertise, which, in turn, helps build an effective professional relationship (Johnson & Grant, 2005; Miley, O'Melia, & Dubois, 2001).

ASSESSMENT

In practice with older Latinos, social workers should conduct a comprehensive assessment of the client's needs and resources using a dynamic, collaborative, strengths-oriented approach. Given the lifelong oppressive experiences of many older Latinos, an assessment that looks beyond liabilities to focus on personal and environmental assets is especially germane, as it can help them feel hopeful and gain a more positive insight into their current life situations. Information should be gathered on the expected biological, psychological, and social age-related life changes as well as on the contextual conditions that are not necessarily part of the course of aging but affect the older adult's ability to adapt and cope successfully (McInnis-Dittrich, 2005; Ramos et al., 2005). For example, an assessment of cognitive and physical ability must also seek information on the oppressive environments in which the client might have lived and may still be embedded.

Furthermore, social workers should recognize and validate potential feelings of distrust and anger due to previous experiences of prejudice and discrimination with formal services. Some clients might feel guilt and shame at seeking help from someone outside their informal network, which typically is not culturally congruent or may not be totally voluntary. Practitioners should then use communication skills that respectfully convey empathetic regard for the elders' hesitation in seeking services, as well as be open to answering any questions that would clarify both their role as a social worker and the therapeutic experience. For example, practitioners can encourage clients to tell their stories in their own words by asking open-ended questions and prompting clients to provide additional necessary information as needed. Closed-ended questions should be used with prudence, and avoided when seeking information of a sensitive, emotional nature.

A comprehensive assessment of older Latino clients and their presenting situations pays special attention to issues related to immigration and acculturation. For example, living in a society that has historically gone back and forth between acceptance and rejection of immigrants from Latin America may have resulted in a client's little or lack of retirement income, health benefits, and access to formal services. Clients who immigrated at an advanced age may be facing painful cultural value conflicts and difficulties adapting to a new environment at a time when they are undergoing major life stage changes that accompany the aging process. Moreover, for those who do not have proper immigration documents, fears of deportation may only exacerbate their risks for financial and emotional distress.

The presence of family members for support and care cannot be automatically assumed and must be carefully assessed. Although some older Latinos can and do rely on the family for support and care, for others this may not be an option. As discussed earlier, migration and immigration can place considerable geographic distance between adult children and parents, disrupting the continuity of family relationships. Changes in the structure and gender roles of Latino families due to acculturation and adaptation to mainstream society may further reduce the number of available and willing caregivers. Practitioners should then assess the role of other collaterals, such as informal networks or other service providers, in the life of the older adult to develop a comprehensive picture of available support networks.

Social workers should also look for relevant client information beyond the micro level, and the nature and availability of community resources should be jointly examined. These include experiences, if any, with organizational support offered by Latino-specific and mainstream agencies, churches, and neighborhood groups.

INTERVENTION

As is the case with older adults cross-culturally (Morales & Sheafor, 1998), in work with older Latinos, an intervention plan should include strategies geared to assist them to acquire resources to maintain quality of life, facilitate their effective interaction with others, promote their independence, and influence social policy on behalf of elders. Of utmost importance, these strategies should be congruent with the client's individual, ethnic, and cultural realities. For example, while workers should use interventions that promote clients' independence and empowerment, they should also recognize that some older adults may prefer, enjoy, and even expect to depend on family members as prescribed by traditional familism values (Ramos, 2001).

Health and mental health interventions to support, restore, or replace clients' levels of functioning should take into account the older adult's educational level and cultural and religious beliefs about well-being and healing. For example, the use of cognitive-behavioral strategies to address anxiety or depression may require extra steps to ensure the client's approval, comfort, and thorough understanding of both the condition and the intervention. Similarly, problem-solving strategies may run counter to fatalism, the belief that one has little or no control over life problems, which is not unusual among some older Latinos (Ramos, 2004).

Together, the worker and client can identify indigenous interventions or culturally bound alternative ways to effect positive change, thus incorporating options that are in harmony with the older adult's specific situation, life experiences, and sociocultural contexts (Lum, 1999). Using indigenous interventions, workers can draw effectively from the natural strengths of the client's own communities and traditions (Green, 1999). In work with older Latinos, practitioners can then develop and implement intervention plans that simultaneously address the micro, meso, and macro levels that affect the lives of older Latino adults.

CASE STUDY

Ms. Sonia Ruiz, a seventy-one-year-old Latina, moved to the United States from Ecuador six years ago to live with her daughter Luz and her family. Her daughter Luz has lived in the United States for over twenty years and is married to Pedro (who is of Puerto Rican descent). They have three children, ages twelve, thirteen, and sixteen. Ms. Ruiz did not complete high school and has no income of her own. She spends her day doing household chores and stays at home taking care of her grandchildren while Luz works in a factory and Pedro works odd jobs. Ms. Ruiz has been taking English classes at a neighborhood center and can somewhat speak and understand English. For the past few weeks, she has been experiencing a variety of body aches and pains including *nervios* and headaches, and has little interest in eating or doing things. She refuses to see a doctor, arguing that these are minor and come and go. Luz has also noticed that her mother cries more often than usual. Luz finally successfully persuades her mother to seek help from a Family Services agency recommended by their pastor.

Upon arrival at the agency, Ms. Ruiz and Luz are greeted by a social worker experienced in work with Latino families. She invites Ms. Ruiz into her private office and politely asks the two women if they would prefer to have Luz participate in the session. After some discussion, they respond that Luz will remain in the waiting area to join them if needed. The worker begins the session by sharing some personal information about her own children. She addresses Ms. Ruiz with deference and respect at all times.

Ms. Ruiz tells the worker about her other four adult children and her grandchildren, noting with a choked-up voice that they live in Ecuador and that she has not seen them since she came to this country. She also states that she did not feel "right" when she could not go to her twin sister's funeral last month and wants to go back "where she belongs." Unsuccessfully trying to hold back her tears, she apologizes profusely for crying and appearing to be ungrateful, especially when Luz and her family have been so good to her. She stresses how ashamed she feels about being such a bother to everyone. The worker acknowledges Ms. Ruiz's feelings and reassures her about the confidentiality of what is discussed and of her own genuine interest in Ms. Ruiz's well-being.

Recognizing Ms. Ruiz's low affect, the worker evaluates her for depression, which shows the client is moderately depressed. Here, Ms. Ruiz quickly described her somatic symptoms but showed difficulty in identifying those of a psychological nature. Even though she worries about her health, the thought of going to the doctor is overwhelming to her because of transportation, scheduling issues, and cost. She further worries about being a financial burden and taking away resources from Luz's family. Ever since Luz's husband lost his permanent job, they fight constantly over money, and he has even left the household for a few days and threatened Luz with divorce.

Ms. Ruiz only briefly talked about these things to her pastor the last time she attended church services. One of her two close friends is very ill and frail, and the other one moved back to Peru last summer.

Conclusion

This chapter has provided insights into some of the age-related experiences of the Latino aging subpopulation. Emphasis has been placed on how these experiences are strongly shaped by ethnocultural forces. A main thrust was to identify some of the knowledge and skills that are especially important when working with older Latino clients. It is hoped that this chapter will further motivate readers to continue broadening

Social Work Practice with Latinos

and updating their knowledge and practice skills to enhance/strengthen the cultural competence and effectiveness of their practice.

As have the other chapters of this book, this chapter has highlighted the collective, social nature of Latino life. This aspect of Latino culture and other cultural variables can be used successfully in group work and group therapy, the subject of the next chapter. There the author presents a careful discussion of the pitfalls and potentials for group work and explores the importance of careful planning throughout the life of groups.

For Writing and Reflection

1. What elements of the aging process appear to be universal across cultures? Discuss some of the defining sociocultural characteristics of aging Latinos and their implications for social work practice.

2. Given your own ethnic heritage, discuss your values, beliefs, and biases both positive and negative about older Latinos and about old age. How might these affect your practice with an older Latino client?

3. Discuss the special nature of the biopsychosocial needs and strengths of older Latinos. Compare and contrast how these are similar and dissimilar to those for Latinos at earlier stages in the life cycle.

4. Describe culturally relevant micro and macro strategies a social worker may draw upon in practice with an older Latino client.

5. What strategies could social workers use to take an active role in the pursuit of human rights and social justice, particularly as these relate to aging Latinos?

References

Administration on Aging. (2000, May). *A diverse aging population: Working toward a healthier, longer life.* Access: http://www.aoa.dhhs.gov/May2000/Fact Sheet.html

Administration on Aging. (2001). Profile of older Americans. Retrieved September 12, 2002, from http://www.aoa.dhhs.gov/aoa/STATS/profile/2001/11.htm

Administration on Aging. (2001). Profile of older Americans. Retrieved September 12, 2002, from http://www.aoa.dhhs.gov/aoa/STATS/profile/2001/11.html

Administration on Aging. (2002). The many faces of aging: Resources to effectively serve minority older persons. Retrieved September 12, 2002, from http://www.aoa.dhhs/gov/minorityaccess/stats.html

Calderon, V., & Tennstedt, S. (1998). Ethnic differences in the expression of caregiver burden: Results of a qualitative study. *Journal of Gerontological Social Work*, 30, 159–178.

Clark, M. & Huttinger, K. (1998). Elderly care among Mexican American families. *Clinical Nursing Research*, 7(1), 64–81.

Cournoyer, B. (1996). *The social skills workbook* (2nd ed.). Pacific Grove, CA: Brooks/Cole.

Cox, C., & Monk, A. (1993). Hispanic culture and family care of Alzheimer's patients. *Health & Social Work*, 18, 92–100.

Delgado, M., & Tennstedt, S. (1997). Making the case for culturally appropriate community services: Puerto Rican elders and their caregivers. *Health and Social Work*, 22, 46–255.

Dietz, T. (1997). Family and formal assistance limitations: Who helps Mexican American elderly? *Hispanic Journal of Behavioral Sciences*, 19(3), 333–352.

Dilworth-Anderson, P., & Anderson, N. (1994). Dementia caregiving in blacks: A contextual approach to research. In E. Light, G. Niederehe, and B. Lebowitz (Eds.), *Stress effects on family caregivers of Alzheimer's patients* (pp. 385–409). New York: Springer.

Giachello, A. (2001). The reproductive years: The health of Latinas. In M. Aguirre-Molina C. W. Molina, R. E. Zambrana (Eds.), *Health issues in the Latino community* (pp. 107–157). San Francisco: Jossey-Bass.

Green, J. W. (1999). *Cultural awareness in the human services: A multi-ethnic approach* (3rd ed.). Boston: Allyn & Bacon.

Johnson & Grant (2005). A multi-systemic approach to practice. In J. L. Johnson & G. Grant, Jr., (Eds.), *Domestic violence* (pp. 1–28). Boston: Allyn & Bacon.

Lum, D. (1999). *Culturally competent practice: A framework for growth and action.* Pacific Grove, CA: Brooks/Cole.

Lum, D. (2000). *Social work practice and people of color: A process stage approach* (4th ed.). Belmont, CA: Brooks/Cole.

Lum, D. (2003). Culturally competent practice. In D. Lum (Ed.), *Culturally competent practice: A framework for understanding diverse groups and justice issues* (2nd ed.) (pp. 3–33). Pacific Grove, CA: Brooks/Cole.

McCallion, P., Janicki, M., & Grant-Griffin, L. (1997). Exploring the impact of culture and acculturation on families caregiving for persons with developmental disabilities. *Family Relations*, 46, 347–357.

McInnis-Dittrich, K. (2005). *Social work with elders: A biopsychosocial approach to assessment and intervention.* Boston: Allyn & Bacon.

Miley, K., O'Melia, M., & Dubois, B. (2001). *Generalist social work practice: An empowering approach.* Boston: Allyn & Bacon.

Morales, A., & Sheafor, B. (1998). *Social work: A profession of many faces.* Boston: Allyn & Bacon.

Mui, A., & Burnette, D. (1994). Long-term care service use by frail elders: Is ethnicity a factor? *The Gerontologist* 34(2), 190–198.

Phillips, L., de Ardon, E., Komnenich, P., & Rusinak, R. (2000). The Mexican American caregiving experience. *Hispanic Journal of Behavioral Sciences*, 22(3), 296–314.

Pine, J., Cervantes, J., Cheung, F., Hall, C., Holroyd, J. Ladue, R., Robinson, L., and Root, M. (1990). *Guidelines for providers of psychological services to ethnic, linguistic, and culturally diverse populations.* Washington, DC: American Psychological Association, Office of Ethnic Minority Affairs.

Purdy, J., & Arguello, D. (1992). Hispanic familism in caretaking of older adults: Is it functional? *Journal of Gerontological Social Work*, 19, 29–43.

Ramos, B. (1997). *Acculturation and depression among Puerto Ricans and Puerto Rican veterans in the continental U.S.* Doctoral dissertation, University of New York, Albany.

Ramos, B. (2001). Culture, ethnicity, and caregiving stress among Latino family caregivers. Paper presented at the 54th Scientific Meeting of the Gerontological Society of America, Chicago.

Ramos, B. (2004). Culture, ethnicity, and caregiver stress among Puerto Ricans. *Journal of Applied Gerontology, 23*(4), 469–486.

Ramos, B., Jones, L., & Toseland, R. (2005). Social work practice with older adults of color. In D. Lum (Ed.), *Cultural competence, practice stages, and client systems* (pp. 320–358). Australia: Brooks/Cole.

Ramos, B., Toseland, R., McCallion, P., & Smith, T. (manuscript submitted for publication). A psychoeducational group intervention for Latino family caregivers.

Root, M. (1998). Facilitating psychotherapy with Asian American clients. In D. R. Atkinson, S. Morten, & D. W. Sue (Eds.), *Counseling American minorities* (5th ed.) (pp. 214–234). Boston: McGraw-Hill.

Sokolovsky, J. (2000). Images of aging. In E. Markson & L. Hollis-Sawyer (Eds.), *Aging: Readings in social gerontology* (pp. 6–11). Los Angeles: Roxbury Publishing Co.

Talamantes, M, & Aranda M. (2004). *Cultural competency in working with Latino family caregivers.* National Caregivers Alliance Monograph. Retrieved on September 17, 2008, from www.caregiver.org/caregiver/jsp/publications.jsp ?nodeid = 345&exp andnodeid = 443.

Talamantes, M., Lindeman, R., & Mouton, C. (2003). *Health and health care for Hispanic elders.* Retrieved February 2, 2004, from http://www.stanford.edu/ group

Tennstedt, S., & Chang, B. (1998). The relative contribution of ethnicity versus socioeconomic status in explaining differences in disability and receipt of informal care. *Journal of Gerontology, 53*B, S61–S70.

Tennstedt, S., Chang, B., & Delgado, M. (1998). Patterns of long-term care: A comparison of Puerto Rican, African-American, and non-Latino white caregivers. In M. Delgado (Ed.), *Latino elders and the twenty-first century: Issues and challenges for culturally competent research and practice* (pp. 179–200). New York: Haworth.

Tirrito, T., & Nathanson, I. (1994). Ethnic differences in caregiving: Adult daughters and elderly mothers. *Journal of Women and Social Work, 9*(1), 71–84.

Torres-Gil, F., & Moga, K. B. (2001). Multiculturalism, social policy and the new aging. *Journal of Gerontological Social Work, 36*(3/4), 13–32.

U.S. Census Bureau. (2001). *Hispanic population in the United States. Current population survey.* Washington, DC: U.S. Government Printing Office.

Valle, R., Cook-Gait, H., & Tazbaz, D. (1993). The cross-cultural Alzheimer/dementia caregiver comparison study. Paper presented at the 46th Scientific Meeting of the Gerontological Society of America, New Orleans, LA.

Villa, V. M., & Torres-Gil, F. M. (2001). The later years: The health of older adults Latinos. In M. Aguirre-Molina, C. Molina, & R. E. Zambrana (Eds.), *Health issues in the Latino community* (pp. 179–208). San Francisco: Jossey-Bass.

CHAPTER FIFTEEN

A Tale of Two Groups: Culturally Sensitive Group Therapy for Latinos

Margarita Leonor Díaz

Introduction

In order for group therapy with Latinos to be most effective, therapists need to incorporate Latino values into its development and implementation (Vasquez & Han, 1995). Most group therapy fails to incorporate Latino values because it is based on theories developed from Eurocentric ones (e.g., Ormont, 1992; Yalom, 1995). Nonetheless, the increase of Latinos in the United States has created a new challenge—to provide group therapy that is just as effective with people holding Latino values as with those holding Eurocentric values. As a result, there has been an ongoing effort to adapt traditional group therapy approaches to better fit Latinos (e.g., Olarte & Masknik, 1985; Organista, 2000; Torres-Rivera, Wilbur, Roberts-Wilbur, & Phan, 1999). The Counseling and Mental Health Center at the University of Texas at Austin has one of the strongest group programs at a university counseling center in the nation. However, in my role as program director for our group services, and with my expertise in clinical services to Latinos, it had become apparent

The author would like to express her appreciation to Dr. Neesha Patel and Dr. Mariela Fuenmayor for their support and assistance with this chapter.

to me that traditional group offerings that were successful with students of the majority culture were seldom attended by minority clients. Latino students are the largest minority at the university, and their numbers were not represented in the groups. Continuing in the effort to provide culturally competent group therapy to this population, my group work practice during the last decade at this institution has been aimed at addressing obstacles that may prevent Latinos from receiving effective therapy and at conducting therapy based on culture-specific values. In this chapter, I will discuss the need for culture-specific group therapy with Latinos and present examples and lessons learned from the groups that were developed.

The Need for Culture-Specific Group Therapy

When conducting group therapy with any minority population, it is important to acknowledge that traditional group therapies work under the assumption of European American values, which are not necessarily congruent with the values of many minority populations (Vasquez & Han, 1995). The most popular and traditionally taught approaches to group therapy, such as those of Yalom (1995) and Ormont (1992), are psychodynamic approaches. They are based on Eurocentric values such as individualism, independence, self-sufficiency, future-time orientation, and so on. As Vasquez & Han (1995) point out, "Group psychological approaches have Eurocentric assumptions about the primacy of the individual in treatment." The interventions and objectives of the group are grounded in these values. A group member may be encouraged to become more independent and self-sufficient. However, some of these values can be different than salient Latino values. Latinos, as a group, tend to be more oriented toward family and community than individualism. More specifically, Magaña and Ybarra, in Chapter Five, suggest that some of the most salient values in Latino culture include *familismo, personalismo, respeto,* and the importance of community. These values are very different from traditional, individualistic Eurocentric ones.

Despite the importance of individual differences and heterogeneity among Latinos, members of this population tend to differentiate themselves from the majority culture by the relative importance and relevance of these values in their lives. In order for groups conducted with Latinos to be effective, these differences in values need to be taken into account (Arredondo et al., 1996).

One way to address these value differences is to encourage the discussion of topics that are relevant to Latinos, such as family, Latino values, and so on. However, when support groups are formed to address issues specifically relevant to Latinos, their effectiveness may still be limited if their structure and interventions still reflect more traditional European American values. Therapist stances and boundaries that are effective and therapeutic in traditional groups may unwittingly challenge the members' cultural values and be ineffective with Latinos. For example, time has a different value in different cultures (Sue & Sue, 2003). In European American cultures, being on time may be seen as a sign of respect, consistency, predictability. In some traditional approaches to group therapy, time boundaries are used to create safety in the group (e.g., Yalom, 1995; Ormont, 1992). In Latino culture, however, time may sometimes be seen as flexible and secondary in importance to relationships. That is, someone keeping to a strict time routine at the expense of the conversation they are having may be seen as rigid, inflexible, not honoring the relationship, and even disrespectful. In a Latino treatment group, a clinician interrupting a member's painful disclosure in order to keep to a time boundary may be perceived as disregarding or shaming the group member. This perceived disrespect on the part of the clinician may actually reduce the sense of safety that the members feel in the group. Thus, the same intervention can result in an entirely different outcome in a group with different cultural values. As Vasquez and Han (1995) indicate "assertiveness and expression of negative feelings . . . may be curative for many members of the dominant society . . . [but] for the client whose ethnic heritage considers family or group belongingness primary and the individual secondary, such direct expressiveness could be considered impolite, presumptuous, and unacceptable." In this way, well-intended interventions that are not taking the values of the group members into account can interfere with the success of the group.

In addition to the structure of the group being based on Eurocentric values, the system in which the therapy is being conducted can also be based on Eurocentric values and can affect the outcome of a Latino group. Accumulated knowledge has shown that many times the underuse of therapy by minorities is the result of a Eurocentric system failing to match the needs of culturally diverse populations (Arredondo et al., 1996; Miranda, Azocar, Organista, Munoz, & Lieberman, 1996; Sue & Sue, 2003). Such systemic failures may be present in situations where access to groups or expectations for members do not take into account Latino values of *personalismo* or *familismo* and in their rigidity scare off potential members. Further examples will be given below. In order to have a successful group for Latinos, it is also important to be aware of the ways in which the system embodies Eurocentric values and how it may be impacting the success of a group.

Content, Structure, and Systemic Considerations in Conducting Groups with Latinos

In order to create a culture-specific group that is successful with Latinos, Latino values need to be incorporated not only at the level of content but more importantly in the infrastructure of the group and in the system in which it is run. These values of *familismo, personalismo,* and *respeto* should be at the center of the treatment from beginning to end and from recruitment to termination.

Based on this belief, for the past few years, in conjunction with student trainees at the center, I have conducted a series of groups for Latinos and other minorities that tried to follow this model of infusion of the core cultural values mentioned above. Curses and Blessings of Navigating between Cultures (also called Between Cultures) (Díaz, Perez, & Craig, 2004) ran for seven years and En Español (Díaz, Fuenmayor, & Piedrahita, 2007) ran for two years at the UT-Austin Counseling and Mental Health Center. We will use adapted examples from these groups to illustrate how this model can be used to incorporate Latino values into group therapy. Even if therapists conduct groups in a different type of setting and the specific situations that arise are different, the principles behind the cultural interventions described below can be generalized to accommodate those differences, and specific techniques can be adapted.

Groups in the Counseling Center Setting

Group therapy in counseling centers is affected by the university system. It is worth noting some of the basics of how the majority of groups ran at our center, as they can affect the applicability and generalizability of this model. The center ran twenty or more groups each semester. The members were undergraduate and graduate students. Group therapy was the primary long-term therapy modality at the center, so students who saw individual therapists for short-term therapy were referred to group therapy usually after only a few sessions. Clients met with group leaders for an interview to determine fit with the group and learn group therapy rules. Assignments to the group were made, and groups would start at the beginning of each semester as soon as there were enough members (usually six). They would take breaks during the usual academic breaks. Members usually commit to try the group for four sessions; after that they are committed to being part of the group for the entire semester, and they have the option of returning in following semesters. Sometimes students' class schedules do interfere with group time, and they are unable to return to the same group. This resulted in a mix of different group members each semester throughout the years that the groups ran.

These system procedures have worked pretty effectively with the majority of process and support groups at the center. However, as you will note in the case examples, some of these had to be adapted as well in order to match cultural needs.

FORMING THE GROUP

One of the most challenging parts of leading a group that serves Latinos can be having enough group members to form the group. Latinos are an underserved population when it comes to mental health services, partly because it can be harder for them to seek therapy than for those in the mainstream culture. This is believed to occur for many reasons, some of which have not been empirically supported, such as beliefs about therapy, and others which have been supported, such as negative experiences with a mental health system that has a history of overpathologizing minorities, language barriers, and too few service providers with cultural expertise, among others (Miranda et al., 1996). Hence, identifying and tackling the barriers to access is a crucial part of having a successful group.

If it is difficult for Latinos to come to therapy, it can be even more difficult for them to enter into group therapy. It is common for clients to be hesitant to join a group out of fear that their privacy is at stake. Unlike individual therapy, where the therapist can legally protect the confidentiality of clients, there is uncertainty whether other group members will keep their confidence. In joining a group, clients have to be willing to assume the added risk of other community members knowing that they are in therapy. They may worry that others might think that they are "crazy." The Latino client's concern about being perceived as "crazy" is legitimate given the stigma associated with therapy prevalent in the Latino community. The popular Latino saying, *"los trapos sucios se lavan en casa"* (dirty laundry is washed at home), highlights the cultural belief that personal problems are not to be dealt with outside the home.

For instance, a Latina client was appropriately referred to the En Español group when she had expressed a desire to have therapy in Spanish. This was a unique opportunity for the client owing to the lack of resources for this type of therapy. Surprisingly, the client adamantly refused the group in Spanish, even though she cautiously agreed to interview for a general psychotherapy group in English. The client felt that even though she would have to make more of an effort to communicate in English, her chances of running into someone she knew would

be significantly less in that group. Here, the client chose a higher guar-
antee of confidentiality over the ease of her native language with people
who understood her culture.

In my experience, the obstacles to joining a group may be gradually
decreasing in the Latino community as the notion of therapy being
exclusively for "crazy" people is challenged. This seems to be happening with younger generations, such as college students. Even so, it is
common for these younger clients to seek therapy without the knowledge of their parents or older family members because they are afraid
of their judgment or disapproval.

Because of these obstacles for Latinos, it is very important that therapists plan for countering these barriers to accessing group therapy. It
can require great effort from the group therapists, in terms of time,
patience, flexibility, and creative problem solving to do so. The following are examples of strategies to help therapists in providing group services to Latino clients.

THERAPIST BELIEFS ABOUT GROUP

In order for therapists to encourage Latino clients to participate in
group therapy, they need to ask themselves, "Do I believe my group
will truly help my clients and be worth the risk of being exposed to
others as a person seeking therapy?" When done well, groups can have
many benefits over individual therapy for Latinos (McKinley, 1987). If
you, the therapist, are not convinced of this, however, it will be next to
impossible to convince a client.

Group, for Latinos, is not simply helpful, in some cases it can be the
primary treatment of choice. Because group forces have been especially
detrimental to minorities because of prejudice, group can be a powerful
corrective experience (Fenster, 1996). Furthermore, groups are an
important means for empowering Latinos (Gutiérrez & Ortega, 1991). If
a client is experiencing cultural marginalization, the mere fact that he
or she becomes a part of a group of peers can directly reduce the individual's isolation in a way that one-on-one therapy cannot. Moreover,
the sharing that occurs in group can create strong validation that is
essential when clients are questioning an experience of discrimination
or their reaction to it. Therefore, it is important to be clear on the benefits your group can offer a client, if you expect him or her to risk joining
it.

In the Between Cultures group, we often noted that within a few sessions there was a noticeable shift in marginalized clients. In one case,
we questioned whether a client would be able to benefit from group
because of the level of depression she presented in individual therapy.
Within a couple of group sessions though her mood was significantly

improved. Even though her conflicts hadn't been resolved at that point in therapy, her feelings of isolation in her cultural experience were significantly decreased, which had a noticeable effect on her mood. Within four sessions, she was able to make decisions and problem-solve. The impact that the group had in such a short time was surprising. It seemed that the group intervention may have been more powerful than individual therapy in helping her cope with the cultural marginalization in that short a time.

MARKETING

Another consideration for therapists in forming the group is how they will market it to Latinos in their area. When therapists are trying to form a group with Latinos, they have to deal with the size of the Latino population in their area. Depending on where they want to form this group, they may have a smaller pool from which to draw upon than if they were running a group for the majority culture, and this can influence whether they will have the optimal number of members to form a group. Thus, marketing a group for Latinos can require extra effort.

The first impression that the client has of the group is through its marketing. Whether marketing is via a flyer, an e-mail, or a presentation, it needs to convey the spirit of the group. For example, for one of our groups, we created flyers that tried to convey that the group would not be a pathologizing environment. To this end, we included a list of difficulties clients could address in the group, such as feeling pulled between their family's values and the values of the mainstream culture, difficulties with relationships, and being a first-generation college student. We also advertised that the group would be conducted in a "laid back and supportive manner." Merely writing "support group for Latinos" wouldn't convey enough about the group and would leave it open for potential clients to project what the group might or might not be. Given the greater likelihood of negative preconceived notions about therapy, that may not be a worthwhile risk to take.

SYSTEMIC FLEXIBILITY

Sometimes the administrative system where therapy takes place needs to allow for flexibility when working with a minority population. The ways that a system can be restrictive can vary. It is important to examine if any part of a system may be negatively affecting a group's formation. For example, in our center there were restrictions regarding a required number of group members in order to run a group. Given all of the above obstacles to joining a group, it would be expected that

these groups would be smaller, and it became crucial that this requirement be flexed for several of the Latino groups in order to have them
run. Another systemic barrier to access can be the setting in which
groups are led. It can be hard for Latino clients to seek services at a
counseling center because it may expose them to other members of
their Latino community. Restricting services to such a setting could add
another barrier. For example, a Latino student shared that when there
were others in the elevator, he would become anxious when he pressed
the elevator button to the counseling center floor, because he was concerned they would know he was coming to counseling. Other group
members echoed his sentiment and elaborated on the shame it brought
up for them. This raises the question of whether we need to restrict
groups for these types of settings that carry a stigma, or if conducting
them in a setting that is not associated with "where the crazy people
go" may better match the clients' needs and increase their willingness
to access services. For example, having a group in a student union
building or in a center for cultural minorities may reduce the stigma
and increase access.

RECRUITING

The way that social workers relate to clients when inviting them to join
a group is a key aspect of making the group. It is important for social
workers to be well-versed in basic Latino values such as *familismo, personalismo,* and *respeto,* and to incorporate these values into the way
they relate to clients when inviting them to join a group. The therapist
can convey respect for the client's culture by going beyond simply
understanding its values and actually attempting to match them when
relating to the client. For example, in the pre-group interviews for our
Latino groups we conducted ourselves with *"personalismo."* We
engaged in relevant self-disclosure, usually along cultural dimensions,
such as: "I'm from Ecuador. I've been in this country for fifteen years";
"I've been to Peru, I took a trip there in 1997. Where in Peru are you
from?"; "You're from The Valley? I've never been there. I've gone as far
down as San Antonio. I've met a few people from The Valley, and they
say it's hard getting adjusted to Austin." We did not rush the interview
and allowed time for connection. We were real and transparent. In
addition, we conveyed a nonjudgmental attitude, trying not to intimidate the client with the authority ascribed to our role. This attitude of
personalismo (relatedness) conveys to the client a sense of what the
group will be like and how they may be treated as a person when they
join the group. This is particularly important when considering how
minorities have historically been pathologized in the mental health system (Miranda et al., 1996; Sue & Sue, 2003). Treating them with respect
and in a "related" fashion helps allay those fears.

MEMBERSHIP

There are three important membership considerations in the decision to develop a group for Latinos: (a) who will be included, (b) who will be excluded, and (c) how to make each member feel like they belong in the group. In order to decide who will be excluded, it is important to know the group's objective. Therapists can use the group's objective as their primary guide for the exclusion criteria; they exclude anyone who doesn't meet that goal. For example, if the group's goal is to address Latina women's issues, therapists can choose to exclude men. After that, therapists can be more invested in how inclusive they are of other member characteristics. In this women's group example, therapists can be inclusive of different levels of acculturation, language proficiency, age, and so on, since they already have a defined common factor in their goal to explore issues around being Latinas. In the Between Cultures group, we chose to include only those clients who acknowledged the experience of being pulled between cultures. Aside from that criterion, we opened the group to everybody. We had several Latinos, from the Caribbean, South America, and from the Rio Grande Valley, along with some Asian and Asian American members. Some were undergraduate students and some were graduate students. At the beginning of the group, we conducted activities and discussions that brought attention to the common theme of being "between cultures" in order to create cohesiveness. After the members were able to feel connected to each other, they were more open to explore their differences.

Members were usually very different from each other, and some had a history of being marginalized because they were different. In order for the group to feel cohesive, they needed to feel a sense of belonging from the start so as not to reproduce their experience of marginalization in the group. In groups for Latinos, one way to address this that can work especially well is by utilizing the concept of *familismo*. Latinos' identity can be intertwined with that of their family, so creating a sense of family within the therapeutic experience can be invaluable. Therapists can create a sense of an open, inclusive family in the group by modeling their acceptance of members' differences, and talking about the importance of respecting and welcoming differences, thus communicating the value of every member. In turn, members who feel respected and included usually convey that same respect and inclusion to other members, as different from them as they may be. This inclusiveness and feeling part of a family can be therapeutic in itself for a marginalized population.

THE THERAPEUTIC RELATIONSHIP

Latino values need to be at the core of the therapeutic relationship in a successful group for Latinos. Specifically, the values of *personalismo* and *respeto* need to be palpable to the members, regardless of the therapist's theoretical background. There are many ways to integrate these values into the therapeutic relationship throughout therapy. For example, in our group we related to the members of the group as people, not as cases. We were warm and engaged, rather than cold and detached. Too often Latinos in this country are faced with the cold, detached, and usually condescending face of prejudiced institutions where they have felt dehumanized; the last thing a therapist wants to do is to reproduce this experience. A warm, engaged way of relating creates a stronger personal connection with the client and disarms the traditional "doctor-patient" dynamic that can often pathologize minorities. Therapists also need to demonstrate that they are trustworthy. Because of a history of societal and institutional racism, Latinos may legitimately mistrust authority figures and helping professionals. The responsibility is on the therapists to demonstrate they can be trusted. One way that we accomplished this is by being genuine, emotionally present, and transparent with our clients. We have found that therapists whose presence is a "blank slate," may appear withholding, and it may be hard for group members to trust them. This is because, when faced with an ambiguous stimulus from a person with privilege and power, it would be adaptive for them, as members of a marginalized group, to assume that this person can't be trusted. Finally, we were respectful of and welcomed what the members brought to the group. When working with a marginalized population, empowerment of the group members is essential. Therefore, therapists need to allow group members to have input in how the group will work and give them ownership of the group. Furthermore, if issues related to culture are addressed in the group, therapists need to value the input from the members in order to respect individual differences in experiences and ways of coping.

READINESS FOR THERAPY

Therapists need to match their members' ability to fully engage in the therapeutic process. Lack of experience with therapy and skepticism about its benefits can be common among Latino clients, even after they have been accepted into the group. Many times, whether it is explicit or not, Latinos will join a group on a "trial" basis—to find out for themselves if group therapy works. Because of this, in the initial stages of group, therapists assume a more active leadership role and guide the members through the mechanics of group therapy until the therapist feels confident in group members' comfort and understanding of how the group will work. In so doing, therapists need to clearly convey what the members can expect to gain from the group, and help members feel hopeful and leave the initial groups with a sense that they have gained something from being there. Short of this, therapists run the risk that confusion about the purpose or usefulness of group early on results in unnecessary attrition. Clients who could otherwise benefit from the group may leave because they are genuinely confused as to their purpose in being there.

The specific techniques that therapists use to match the needs of their group members can vary and can be influenced by what the group is trying to accomplish. For example, in the En Español group, which aimed to provide general psychotherapy to Spanish speakers, therapists attempted to address cultural issues in working with Latino members by specifically altering the manner in which they usually conduct group at the beginning stages of the group. First, they explicitly conveyed what members could expect from the group. Second, they started the group with check-ins to provide limited structure. Third, the therapists were more active than they usually are in order to model for members how to keep up the flow of therapy.

In the Between Cultures group where the objective was to create community among marginalized minorities, maintaining a process format was less important. The objective was not to work on interpersonal process skills or to address deep-rooted conflicts, it was to provide support, validation, and a sense of belonging to members who were usually very unfamiliar with therapy. The group usually started with very active therapists, but, in addition, it used structured activities in the initial stages to help members interact around a topic relevant to a majority of the members. For instance, within the first two to three sessions, therapists conducted a drawing activity that illustrated the ways in which members were between cultures. Members were told that they would be sharing their drawings with each other along with a brief verbal explanation, but that they would mostly be answering questions about the drawings. This provided a very concrete task that tended to reduce client pressure to produce something appropriate to talk about. In addition to a clear explanation, therapists would participate and would be the first to present their drawings of how they are between cultures to the group, to clarify to the members how to present their drawings. Subsequently, the therapists took the lead in asking questions of other members after their presentations to show the members what kind of questions they can ask. This use of self-disclosure is an example of how *personalismo* is operationalized with Latinos, and different from practice with some other populations. Thus, in this group, because the objective was to create a community around cultural issues and because group members were so new to therapy, modeling and structured activities matched the members well and resulted in member retention and satisfaction.

The degree to which therapists need to take the lead and be more active in their groups also depends on the particular members of a group. After a few sessions in the Between Cultures groups, for example, the therapists would give the group the option to do an activity or to "talk." In some groups, especially those with therapy-savvy members, the activities quickly became obsolete, while in others the process of shifting to a self-directed discussion took much longer. Therapists need to walk the members through the motions of group until they are able to walk on their own.

TERMINATION

The way termination is done is an essential component of treatment in group therapy and can leave a lasting impression of the group for clients. Because of this, to be done effectively, it too needs to be infused with the values of the culture. For Latinos, the way of addressing endings can be different than for the majority culture. Rituals around endings can differ, and they can reflect the different ways in which endings are processed. The ultimate ending, death, is approached overall in a very different way culturally. In Mexico, for example, there is a holiday for the dead. On this day, it can be customary for relatives of the deceased to go to their graves, bring food, and eat together.

In our groups running on a semester system, our endings would come at the end of each semester. The first way we would address the ending was more like that of short-term models. That is, we would address the ending of the group from the moment the group began. Members were made aware of the ending date and were asked about their intention to leave or stay with the group early on. More important, we emphasized maintaining the value of the connections that the members had developed with both the other members and the therapists so that they could carry this with them. In the En Español group, a group that had become very close, the therapists decided to give each member a gift, a poem in Spanish that had a message relevant to the discussions of the group and adorned with symbolic artwork. Each item was individualized for each member. It was used as a transitional object for the members and a token of the value that the therapists had for the members. It also allowed the members to take something with them that acknowledged their progress. In addition, the members chose to bring some food to celebrate their accomplishments in the group. In these ways, both the therapists and the members acknowledged the significance of their relationships in the group in the ending.

FLEXIBILITY

Flexibility is at the core of effective group therapy with Latinos, and the message of this chapter is twofold: (a) it is the integration of Latino values into the structure of the group, not only by talking about cultural values but by incorporating them into the delivery of group therapy, that matters, and (b) it is crucial to evaluate how chosen interventions fit each group. For example, our suggestion to take value differences about time into account doesn't mean that for groups to be considered culturally competent, therapists are obliged to have their groups run late constantly. As tempting as it may be to want hard-and-fast rules, group practice with Latinos is never that simple. Rather than using a prescribed rule that ignores the particular group in front of them, social workers must step outside the box and question whether established rules still apply in the same way, if the rules are achieving their intended purpose, and if they are supporting the therapeutic aims of group participants.

The goal is to balance an integration of Latino values with the group's infrastructure, while still maintaining useful knowledge from established group theories. At times new social workers will err on the side of dismissing established theories, while at others times they will err by not incorporating enough of the cultural values into the infra-structure. No worker is perfect, but the goal is to strive to incorporate new and existing knowledge; to attain a flexible balance, a dynamic equilibrium between these two sides that evens out in the end.

A struggle with boundaries that took place in the En Español group illustrates the effort to maintain a dynamic equilibrium. This group started by being very flexible in their starting and ending time and allowing members to come late because of class conflicts. The idea was to incorporate the more flexible approach to time that is associated with Latino culture. At first, when the group was getting to know each other, this worked. After a few sessions, however, when the discussions started to get deeper, some members started complaining about member tardiness and erratic attendance. It became apparent that the inconsistency was starting to affect the safety of the members at this stage of the group. A decision was made to process this with the group and ask the members for an agreement around commitment. The result was that members committed to consistent attendance after realizing the issue was affecting their fellow group members. The therapists also agreed to have an informal check-in during the first ten minutes of each group that allowed for members arriving a little late and respected their difficulty leaving class; thus they were somewhat flexible in terms of timeliness. However, the therapists kept a firm ending time for the group, still retaining some aspects of the traditional group model. This solution proved successful and increased cohesion in the group and trust of the therapists. It was an appropriate solution for this stage of group, for these group members; and, in the way the decision was made and the need for flexibility in regard to starting time was respected, it allowed the therapists to integrate knowledge of traditional group theories with Latino values.

Conclusion

Leading groups for Latinos requires commitment and patience. Therapists need to invest extra energy in order to follow many of these guidelines. They have to deconstruct theory, be creative, know the culture, adapt established systems, and go against stigmatization, and there is much trial and error needed in maintaining a dynamic equilibrium. Though therapists may feel tired or lost at times and wonder if it is worth it, providing effective services to a group that is historically underserved and marginalized and witnessing the impact it has on Latino members can truly have a positive impact on the therapists and can be enough to make them want to do it again and again.

In this chapter, we explored many of the most salient variables that influence groups, and explored how they can be used in work with Latinos. One of the key factors in any service provided to Latinos is language. Language is a complex construct with implications for identity, the way services are received, and the availability of services. The next chapter presents an overview of the complex linguistic issues to which social workers must attend, regardless of the context of practice.

For Writing and Reflection

1. What might be some creative ways to recruit Latinos into your group?

2. What are ways in which you could help Latino group members who have had little experience
   with therapy stay in your group?

3. How would you integrate the Latino value of *personalismo* into the way that you relate to the members of your group?

4. How would you maintain a "dynamic equilibrium" between established group therapies and culturally sensitive interventions?

References

Arredondo, P., Toporek, R., Brown, S. P., Jones, J., Locke, D. C., & Sanchez, J. (1996). Operationalization of the multicultural counseling competencies. *Journal of Multicultural Counseling and Development, 24,* 42–78.

Census, U. (2000). Population Estimates Program, Population Division, U.S. Census Bureau, Washington, DC.

Díaz, M. L., Fuenmayor, M. J., & Piedrahita, S. (2007). En Español: Group psychotherapy with Latino/a clients. Symposium presented at the Annual Convention of the American Group Psychotherapy Association, Austin, Texas.

Díaz, M. L., Perez, M., & Craig, M. C. (2004). The curses and blessings of navigating between cultures: A group for Latinos/as and other minorities. Symposium presented at the National Latino Psychology Association, Scottsdale, Arizona.

Fenster, A. (1996, July). Group therapy as an effective treatment modality for people of color. *International Journal of Group Psychotherapy, 46*(3), 399–416.

Gutiérrez, L. M., & Ortega, R. (1991). Developing methods to empower Latinos: The importance of groups. *Social Work with Groups, 14*(2), 23–43.

McKinley, V. (1987). Group therapy as a treatment modality of special value for Hispanic patients. *International Journal of Group Psychotherapy, 37*(2), 255–268.

Miranda, J., Azocar, F., Organista, K. C., Munoz, R. F., & Lieberman, A. (1996). Recruiting and retaining low-income Latinos in psychotherapy research. *Journal of Consulting and Clinical Psychology, 64*(5), 868–874.

Olarte, S. W., & Masnik, R. (1985). Benefits of long-term group therapy for disadvantaged Hispanic outpatients. *Hospital and Community Psychiatry, 36*(10), 1093–1097.

Organista, K. (2000). Latinos. In J. R. White & A. S. Freeman (Eds.), *Cognitive-behavioral group therapy: For specific problems and populations* (pp. 281–303). Washington, DC: American Psychological Association.

Ormont, L. R. (1992). *The group therapy experience.* New York: St. Martin's Press.

Sue, D. W., & Sue, D. (2003). *Counseling the culturally diverse: Theory and practice* (4th ed.). Hoboken, NJ: John Wiley & Sons.

Torres-Rivera, E., Wilbur, M., Roberts-Wilbur, J., & Phan, L. (1999, December). Group work with Latino clients: A psychoeducational model. *Journal for Specialists in Group Work, 24*(4), 383–404.

Vasquez, M. J. T., & Han A. L. (1995). Group interventions and treatment with ethnic minorities. In J. F. Aponte, R.Y. Rivers, & J. Wohl (Eds.), *Psychological Intervention & Cultural Diversity* (pp. 109–127). Boston: Allyn & Bacon.

Yalom, I. (1995). *The theory and practice of group psychotherapy* (4th ed.). New York: Basic Books.

CHAPTER SIXTEEN

Latinos and Spanish

The Awkwardness of Language in Social Work Practice

Lissette Piedra

Introduction

"Do you speak Spanish?" the agency administrator inquired.

"Yes," declared the social worker on her first interview.

"We need a bilingual worker," the administrator sheepishly admitted.

"Okay." With that statement, the new social worker accepted her first social work position.

These four little sentences encapsulated my earliest lesson about the marketability of a bilingual social worker, even one who was fresh out of undergraduate education and had no real work (or life) experience. A competent bilingual social worker is a rare find, and neither my potential employer nor I (at least at that moment) was in any position to be choosy. As doubtless occurs in many similar instances, neither the supervisor nor the potential new hire had thought through what is meant by *bilingual*; often conversational ease with Spanish is confused with true bilingualism.

In an ideal world, this informational job interview would start with a discussion of language proficiency, which would include a determination of the level at which the potential new hire wrote, read, spoke, and understood Spanish and whether she or he had received any formal education in Spanish. This assessment would be followed by a discussion of the opportunities available for ongoing language training in professional terminology, how many limited English proficient (LEP) cases would be assigned, agency expectations for interpretation and translation outside of assigned cases, and, of course, the salary differential for being a bilingual worker. Inclusion of these topics would reflect a sophisticated understanding of what the agency and the clients need and expect from a bilingual worker and, equally important, of the service complexities that arise when addressing the needs of LEP clients (Engstrom & Min, 2004; Engstrom & Piedra, 2007).

Bilingual workers are diverse. Variations in verbal, reading, and writing skills affect language proficiency, as does proficiency in the professional terminology of a given field. Some bilingual social workers have conversational skills and can communicate verbally with clients, but are not able to write a business letter in Spanish. Heritage Spanish speakers may have verbal fluency but poor literacy skills: Heritage speakers are conversant in Spanish because they were exposed to the language by Spanish-speaking family members, but, because they received most of their formal education in English, they are English dominant (Engstrom & Min, 2004). True bilinguals are typically defined as possessing at least an eighth-grade fluency level in verbal, reading, and writing skills (Portes & Rumbaut, 2001). Even when a person is truly bilingual, there remains the question of familiarity with professional terminology, which constrains the types of encounters (administrative, medical, mental health) the bilingual worker can translate for (Moreno, Otero-Sabogal, & Newman, 2007).

Fifteen years have passed since my initial job interview, yet the need for bilingual social workers continues to outstrip the available pool of workers, creating serious service barriers for LEP clients and a host of dilemmas for agencies and their workers. What has changed is a growing awareness of the complexities involved in overcoming language barriers in health and mental health services (Lavizzo-Mourey, 2007; Partida, 2007; Schyve, 2007; Sentell, Shumway, & Snowden, 2007). Even so, a certain awkwardness underscores any discussion of Spanish-language competence in health and social services, usually stemming from tensions surrounding issues of rights, fairness, and feasibility. This chapter begins its discussion of language issues facing LEP Latinos by exploring the macro factors that shape and influence the language-assisted services environment. Understanding these macro factors is particularly important because of the political meanings associated with language and the resulting policy context framing these services. The second half of the chapter is dedicated to an overview of practice issues, including the challenges of working with interpreters. In many ways, this chapter reflects what I wish I had known as a bilingual case worker fifteen years ago, and what I have learned during the journey to improve the quality of services for LEP Latinos.

Language Access and Civil Rights

In the past thirty years, the number of people in the United States who speak a language other than English has grown tremendously because of immigration. In 1980, the Census Bureau estimated that 23.1 million U.S. residents (11 percent) spoke a language other than English. By 2000, the number of people who spoke a language other than English at home had more than doubled, to an estimated 47 million people—nearly a fifth of the U.S. population. More than half of these 47 million people are Spanish speakers (28.1 million), making Spanish the non-English language most frequently spoken at home in the United States (Shin, 2003). Although just over half of these Spanish speakers report speaking English "very well," a sizeable portion of the population reported speaking English less than "very well" and were considered by the 2000 census to have difficulty with English (Shin, 2003).

The need for language assistance is most acutely felt, by those who speak English less than "very well," during interactions with institutions that provide English-dominant services. Quality of life is largely shaped by the role these institutions play in daily living (Klinenberg, 2002; Lamphere, 1992; Mettler, 1998). Interactions between new minority populations and the majority population and/or existing institutions represent an opportunity for further participation in larger society; they also hold the possibility of heightening tension and alienation (Blau, 1977). At its core, the language issue is really about institutional access. The incorporation into and well-being of immigrants and their children within the larger society is affected by how language diversity is managed and the way in which language barriers to health and social services are addressed (Piedra, 2006).

The importance of language assistance is reflected in our current legal framework, which mandates language access in health care settings. In a seminal article, Chen, Youdelman, and Brooks (2007) traced the development of the federal mandate requiring language-accessible health care services from Title VI of the 1964 Civil Rights Act, which states that:

> No person in the United States shall, on the ground of race, color, or national origin, be excluded from participation in, be denied the benefits of, or be subject to discrimination

under any program or activity receiving federal assistance.
(42 U.S.C. 2000d)

Later, in 1980, the Department of Health and Human Services (HHS) issued a notice linking service inaccessibility due to language to discrimination on the basis of national origin (Chen et al., 2007). Therefore, in a society in which equitable access to public institutions prevails, language assistance becomes a civil right.

However, language assistance requires a high level of skill and resources, and many institutions were (and still are) ill-equipped to provide that assistance. To further complicate the matter, increased immigration of non-English speakers created a greater need for language-assisted services. In response, President Clinton issued Executive Order (EO) 13166, "Improving Access to Services for Persons with Limited English Proficiency," which directed all federal agencies to ensure that their programs provide equal access to LEP persons. The Bush administration upheld EO 13166; it also revised the extensive accompanying Policy Guidance to balance federally mandated language-assistance requirements with undue burdens on small business, local governments, and small nonprofit organizations (Chen et al., 2007).

EO 13166 is an unfunded mandate, meaning that although all programs that receive federal funding (e.g., Medicare) are legally obligated to provide language assistance for clients who need it, no additional financial resources are allocated to help meet that obligation. In addition, Medicare and private insurers usually do not pay or reimburse for interpretation and related services (such as written translations or telephone language lines), significantly reducing the actual availability of the service (Ku & Flores, 2005). The lack of insurance reimbursement creates harmful disincentives, because the costs and burdens associated with language services, unlike other general costs of providing usual care, are not evenly distributed across providers (Ku & Flores, 2005). Communities with high immigrant concentrations will have a greater need for language assistance than communities with low levels of immigration. Also, some providers believe that offering language access would both constitute a financial drain and attract more LEP patients; special-interest groups such as the American Medical Association have raised concerns over the financial burden of providing interpretation services (Ku & Flores, 2005).

Although the revised Policy Guidance makes allowances for the size of the organization and the LEP population concentration, it also reflects the lack of a nationwide system to address language barriers. As a result, language assistance in health care settings varies depending on state, region, language, medical condition, and institution (Chen et al., 2007).

To further complicate the situation, many states are home to "new-growth" communities with small but rapidly growing Hispanic populations. Between 1996 and 2003, the total Hispanic population grew by about 10 million, spreading out evenly across the nation (Cunningham, Banker, Artiga, & Tolbert, 2006). However, in new-growth communities, the Hispanic population almost doubled. In some areas the growth was even more pronounced. For example, from 1980 to 2000, the Latino population in Raleigh, North Carolina, grew to 72,580—an increase of 1,180 percent (Suro & Singer, 2002). In Atlanta, Georgia, the Latino population grew to 268,851, an increase of 995 percent (Suro & Singer, 2002). Although the Latino populations remain small relative to the total state population (6 percent for North Carolina and 7 percent for Georgia), the increasing number of areas experiencing such rapid growth has consequences for service delivery systems. In comparison to providers in areas that traditionally have had large Hispanic populations, these new-growth areas tend to lack the infrastructure necessary to meet the needs of LEP Latinos/as (Arroyo, 2004).

In the context of high levels of immigration and these shifting settlement patterns, language issues in the provision of health and social services continue to garner local and national attention. Attention to language issues also reflects broader cultural changes (Partida, 2007). While our legal framework obligates an expansion of language-assisted services, many Americans are ambivalent about the cultural implications of an unequivocal response to the needs of linguistic minorities. Because service providers are frequently confronted by this ambivalence even among their family and colleagues, a heightened understanding of the sociocultural backdrop that underlies language concerns can help facilitate health and social services with LEP Latinos/as, far more than a mere reiteration of the need for culturally competent services and adherence to professional codes of ethics.

What It Means to "Speak American" in a Linguistically Diverse Nation

At the end of the Academy Award–winning film *Crash*, an African American woman is involved in an auto accident with a cab driver. She gets out of her car and marches over to the cabby. Taking one look at him and hearing his accented English, she knows he is an immigrant. Incensed, she yells at him to "speak American." This simple exchange dramatically demonstrates that language is more than just a conduit of communication. Language conveys cultural meanings and functions as a signifier of group membership.

The United States has a long history of accepting immigrants into the country, but attitudes toward immigrants have ranged from benign tolerance to overt hostility. Even when there are policies and signs of receptivity, there is still a strong expectation that immigrants will learn English. This expectation is a deeply American notion, rooted partly in American mythology and partly in the economic necessity to function in a society that is English dominant. The American myth is embodied in melting-pot imagery, in which immigrants who come to this land from other countries with foreign cultures and languages, once exposed to American culture, adopt its values and language and "become American." In this model (and assumption) of assimilation, the loss of native language and the acquisition of English are important milestones on the path of becoming American.

The fact is that assimilation is hardly linear and rarely absolute, as demonstrated by the descendants of the Irish, Polish, Italian, and German immigrants of the early twentieth century, who continue to ethnically identify into the third and fourth generations. Moreover, the United States has always been a multilingual society (Sollors, 1998). Through the nineteenth and early twentieth centuries, we had a vibrant foreign-language press. For example, the Chicago Foreign Language Press Survey (1942) translated and published selected news articles appearing in Chicago-area foreign-language newspapers from 1861 to 1938. Serving now as a window into the linguistic diversity of the late nineteenth- and early-twentieth-century Chicago-area immigrant communities, these selected news articles reflect twenty-two different foreign-language communities in Chicago, as they were drawn from Albanian, Czechoslovakian, Chinese, Croatian, Danish, Dutch, German, Greek, Hungarian, Italian, Jewish, Lithuanian, Norwegian, Polish, Russian, Serbian, Slovak, Slovene, Spanish, Swedish, and Ukrainian newspapers. The most recent census identified 380 single languages or language families spoken in the United States (Shin, 2003).

Despite the presence of multiple languages, English dominance prevails, with a corresponding national pride in the identity Americans have as an English-speaking people. Therefore, in a country where language and democratic ideals are seen as the primary unifying forces, English becomes synonymous with patriotic loyalty. Among many American citizens, the concern is not primarily about whether immigrants speak English, as many do. Rather, the concern is that immigrants who also retain their native language somehow will not become fully American nor fully invested in becoming American. To people holding this view, accented English serves as a declaration of continued loyalty to the country of origin.

The growing presence of non-English-speaking immigrants has fueled national concern about the preservation of "American culture"

(Huntington, 2004). The "English only" and "official English" move-ments are more accurately seen as reflecting a growing anxiety about demographic change and its implications for American society than as serious attempts to preserve English. The fact is that most people who speak another language also speak English; many speak English "very well." When those who speak only English are combined with those who both speak a language other than English and speak English "very well," we find that an overwhelming majority of the U.S. population (92 percent) has no problem communicating in English (Shin, 2003). Language protection is hardly necessary in a country in which more than 90 percent of the population speaks English.

However, as a society, we are impatient with and mistrust those who do not speak English. Deeply rooted in our sociopolitical history is the notion that we are a democratic people and that our democratic ideals are expressed through a unified polity that speaks one language: namely, English. Many still believe that those who speak their native language in addition to English are not fully American.

Given this climate, many health and social services for Spanish-speaking immigrants are delivered within a larger social context that expresses mixed feelings about the legitimacy of bilingual services and use of resources to provide those services. In addition, service providers may also have mixed feelings about bilingual services. Most service pro-viders understand the importance of bilingual services, but some may wonder privately, "Why don't these clients just learn English? Why are they here if they don't know English and need so much help?"

The importance of learning English is not lost on immigrants. In one survey of immigrant opinion, social scientist Farkas and colleagues found that nearly nine out of ten adult immigrants (87 percent) said it is extremely important for immigrants to speak and understand English (Farkas, Duffett, & Johnson, 2003). Sixty-five percent of immigrants reported that the United States should expect all immigrants to learn English. These sentiments are tied to perceived employment opportu-nities for English speakers: 85 percent of immigrants who mentioned having difficulty with English reported that it was hard to get a job.

In a society where income determines quality of housing, neighbor-hood, and educational and health care resources, learning English takes on a whole new meaning—and a decided urgency. English proficiency enables greater earning potential and provides other social benefits as well. Immigrants' belief in the importance of learning English is under-scored by immigrant parents' strong belief that public schools should teach English to their children (Farkas et al., 2003).

Whereas macro issues shape the environmental context in which language-assisted services are delivered, practice issues emerge through individual interactions with other persons and with institutions. The second half of this discussion focuses on the ways in which language complicates practice issues in the health and social service sectors and what social workers can do to enhance services for LEP clients.

Language and Practice Issues in
Health and Social Services

An English-dominant society like the United States produces health and social service professionals who for the most part speak only English. Therefore, it can be difficult to appreciate the contextual variations of language proficiency and how that variability affects the clinical encounter. Moreover, even though health and social service providers find language-assistance services to be critical to the well-being of their patients and clients, access to those services is highly variable, depending on location and the availability of bilingual providers and interpreters.

The Kaiser Commission on Medicaid and the Uninsured assessed factors affecting health care for immigrants in four major cities (Los Angeles, New York City, Miami, and Houston). The commission found that, aside from financial factors, language access—in the form of bilingual providers and staff, translated materials, and interpreter services—was the most important factor in determining immigrants' access to health care (Ku & Freilich, 2001). Moreover, the commission found that although health care providers in each of the four cities studied made efforts to provide language capacity (in compliance with Title VI of the Civil Rights Act of 1964), language difficulties continued to pose a serious barrier to adequate medical care (Ku & Freilich, 2001). This was true even for Spanish-speaking patients, who tend to have greater access to bilingual health providers and interpreter services than other linguistic minorities; the commission found that many Spanish speakers could not communicate with their health care providers. The large numbers of Spanish-speaking patients needing interpretation or translation services overwhelmed existing resources. These problems are further compounded by the fact that many patients are poorly educated or even illiterate in their own languages, thus making translated materials (printed or online) useless.

The complexities involved in overcoming language barriers are best understood as the need to overcome the "triple threat" to service access and utilization confronting LEP clients (Schyve, 2007). Language issues compound existing service barriers in three ways: (1) service providers' underestimation of the difficulties in overcoming language barriers, even when a bilingual worker or an interpreter is used; (2)

differing cultural conceptualizations of health and illness; and (3) the presence of low health literacy, including low mental health literacy. Health and social services targeted at linguistic minorities must address this triple threat if they are to enhance service utilization and reduce disparities in access to mental health services. The following sections discuss how each of the three threats affects service utilization and how social workers can help lower communication barriers.

OVERCOMING THREAT #1: FOCUS ON COMMUNICATIVE COMPETENCE IN A TRIADIC RELATIONSHIP

As a profession, social work is committed to providing culturally competent services. This commitment emphasizes the knowledge, values, and skills needed to make services culturally relevant and effective (Marsiglia & Kulis, 2009). Communicative competence includes everything that is commonly referred to as *cultural competence,* but also extends to the linguistic transaction among the client, the interpreter, and the service worker. More specifically, communicative competence recognizes differences in the concepts behind words and in the contexts that shape the meanings of words (Gregg & Saha, 2007). Linguist John Gumperz explains:

> Whereas linguistic competence covers the speaker's ability to produce grammatically correct sentences, communicative competence describes his ability to select, from the totality of grammatically correct expressions available to him, forms which appropriately reflect the social norms governing behavior in specific encounters. (Gumperz, 1972)

This subtle distinction between linguistic competence and communicative competence is critical in managing language issues in a clinical encounter. Even when the worker is not bilingual and must use an interpreter, the way in which the worker engages the interpreter and client sends a powerful message to the client.

Straightforward language interpretation during a clinical encounter is necessary but not sufficient to overcome language-based barriers to care (Gregg & Saha, 2007). Language is a dynamic medium that includes much more than a system of words and grammatical rules. Linguists understand language to be composed of two systems: *langue* and *parole* (Gregg & Saha, 2007). *Langue* is a shared system of language based on a database of words and formal rules about the use of those words. *Parole* includes the *langue* and all the gestures, modes of delivery, and context that give the *langue* its full meaning in a given setting or situation. Language conveys meaning about the world and one's place in it, often signaling social status and group identity.

When language poses a communication barrier that must be overcome, the presence of an interpreter transforms a typically two-way
relationship into a triadic relationship, altering the dynamics of the
interaction (Sluzki, 1978). In language-concordant services, both the
service provider and the client use the dominant language as the common context of exchange. In a triadic relationship, all parties involved
in the interpretation—the client, the service provider, and the interpreter—must cooperate to create a common context of exchange and
to minimize translation error. Although the presence of an interpreter
inevitably alters the dynamics of an interaction, the reduction of language barriers, if handled sensitively, is an opportunity to draw upon
humanistic traditions that underlie the health and social service professions. Such an approach to the triadic relationship means recognizing
that each person is more than a conduit/receptor of language and that
engaged cooperation is required to produce a context suitable to
achieve communicative competence. Even so, before this cooperation
can exist, the interpreter must possess a level of linguistic competency
suited for the type of encounter being interpreted. Moreover, an assessment of the required skill level should occur even among bilinguals who
function as dual-role staff.

Dual-Role Staff

Dual-role staff are bilingual persons who function both as staff and as
interpreters. Although it is not uncommon to use dual-role staff to
address language barriers in health care (Elderkin-Thompson, Silver, &
Waitzkin, 2001; Moreno et al., 2007) and social service settings (Engstrom & Min, 2004; Engstrom, Piedra, & Min, in press), using dual-role
staff can have serious drawbacks for client care. Usually, such staff are
untrained in interpretation protocols, unfamiliar with medical or mental health terminology, or lack fluency in either English or the second
language (Engstrom et al., in press; Moreno et al., 2007).

The challenges associated with using dual-role staff are complex, and
usually relate to both linguistic and communicative competence. One
study conducted at a large health care organization found that one in
five dual-role staff had insufficient bilingual skills to serve as an interpreter in a medical encounter (Moreno et al., 2007). In this study, a
linguistic competency tool was used to measure comprehension, com-
pleteness, and vocabulary in both English and the second language,
through a written and oral assessment. There were three possible outcomes: not passing, passing at the basic interpreter level, and passing
at the medical interpreter level. Dual-role staff who passed at the basic
level showed a limited ability to read, write, and speak either English

or the second language. They were likely to make translation errors, including omissions and word confusion. A dual-role staff member who passed at the basic level could function as an interpreter in scheduling or conveying general information, but could not be used in a clinical encounter. Clinical encounters were more appropriately interpreted by staff whose language skills were at the medical interpreter level.

The study underscored the importance of assessing both English and second-language skills for those organizations that depend on dual-role staff. Interestingly, the study also conducted five focus groups, all of which revealed a general acceptance of the exam process and feelings of increased validation for the interpreter role (Moreno et al., 2007), reflecting dual-role staff's recognition that language assessment is needed and the importance of setting standards for interpretation.

Aside from issues of linguistic competence, communicative competence requires attention to a different set of complexities and requires a team approach to linguistic interpretation. Regardless of where one falls in the continuum of linguistic competence, knowing how to work with interpreters is important for anyone who works with LEP clients, because there are communication principles that will increase accuracy.

The social service or health care provider can also play a critical role in enhancing communicative competence. Elderkin-Thompson and colleagues (2001) examined interpretation error when bilingual nurses were used as interpreters. They found that errors occurred in 50 percent of the interpretation encounters, but that these errors were not random. Interpretation errors reflected systematic biases in the triadic transaction among the health care provider, the dual-role staff member, and the patient. In cases where errors occurred, interpretations coincided with the nurse's clinical expectations but did not match what the patient had actually said. Also, when errors occurred, the nurse-interpreters tended to slant their interpretations unfavorably against the patients, undermining their credibility. Interestingly, in those cases where inaccuracies occurred, physicians resisted reconceptualizing the problem when contradictory information was present. The LEP patients also contributed to the problem by explaining the symptoms with cultural metaphors that were incompatible with Western nosology. Therefore, all three partners in the triad relationship contributed to interpretation inaccuracies by not helping each other to understand.

However, successful interpretations also showed discernible patterns. Elderkin-Thompson and colleagues (2001) found that successful interpretations occurred when nurse-interpreters translated the data as completely as possible and allowed the physician to extract relevant clinical information. In addition, in successful encounters the physician summarized his or her perception of the problem to be interpreted back to the patient, creating an opportunity for verification and correction by the patient. Simple sentences were used and presented in a slow, systematic way, and patients were encouraged to give additional information. The nurse-interpreter and the physician also established rapport through nonverbal communication cues such as eye contact, smiling, nodding, and the like.

Clearly, accurate interpretation involves more than linguistic competence. The triadic relationship requires an engaged cooperation by each person (and maybe a bit of coaching) to ensure that the service provider and the client are able to accurately convey their meanings. Given the power dynamics among the service provider, the interpreter, and client, it is important that the service provider and the interpreter collaborate in establishing a context of care that will yield a high level of communicative competence.

Social workers who act as service providers or interpreters in health care and social service settings can play an important role as cultural brokers among the three partners by recognizing that communicative competence encompasses more than linguistic competence. The attention paid to the dynamics of a triadic relationship will facilitate the type of engaged cooperation among all three partners that enhances communicative competence.

OVERCOMING THREAT #2: CULTURAL DIFFERENCES IN CONCEPTUAL EXPLANATORY MODELS

Another major hurdle in service provision involves understanding the serious threat that cultural differences among service providers, interpreters, and clients pose to communicative competence. Part of the problem rests in our understanding of culture, which is generally conceived of as group-specific along racial and ethnic boundaries (Lakes, Lopez, & Garro, 2006). When culture is defined solely in terms of group membership, culturally sensitive interventions are reduced to addressing group stereotypes, rather than recognizing the ways in which culture shapes and constrains everyday life at the individual level (Lakes et al., 2006). Such static definitions of culture can be limiting.

Another part of the problem rests in the almost invisible way our beliefs about health, illness, and healing may conflict with our clients' belief systems. Everyone has belief systems that influence the interpretation of everyday life experiences and that guide behaviors. However, English-dominant providers and interpreters are trained using a Western medical model that generates ideas of health and illness that may be very different from those of their clients. Mental health treatment providers who are trained in a Western biopsychosocial model tend to see mental health problems as *conditions* that require formal treatment rather than as *situational stressors,* whereas research has found that ethnic minorities and individuals of lower socioeconomic status tend to view mental health problems almost exclusively as the result of situational stressors (Karasz, 2005; Karasz, Sacajiu, & Garcia, 2003; Karasz & Watkins, 2006).

Medical anthropology has long recognized that notions of health and illness can reflect "a culturally elaborated healing system that interacts with other sectors of a society's overall health care system" (Kleinman, 1980, as cited in Csordas, 1994, p. 284 n. 3). *Conceptual explanatory models* (CEMs) are those belief systems, held by individuals, that underlie conceptualizations of health and illness, influencing notions of healing and cure (Karasz et al., 2003; Karasz & Watkins, 2006; Kaufert, 1990; Kleinman, 1980). These CEMs have been found to be highly organized and useful in understanding patients' preferences regarding mental health treatment in primary care (Karasz et al., 2003). For example, one study of 121 Latino/a patients with depression identified therapy/counseling (88%) and talking to their primary doctor (75%) as helpful, compared to the 65 percent of patients who perceived medication as useful (Karasz & Watkins, 2006). Those who reported thinking that psychotherapy would be helpful thought so because it would provide support (72%), opportunities to vent (64%), and advice (52%). Among those who preferred to talk to their primary physician, approximately half did so because of the possibility of getting advice or guidance.

Interestingly, patients' responses also reflected that they conceived of their depression in different terms than their treatment providers did. Many treatment models seek to achieve a type of personal change in response to mental health problems. However, the patients' emphasis on using therapy or talking to a doctor to garner support, advice, and catharsis (e.g., common curative factors in psychotherapy; Drisko, 2004), rather than on seeking interpersonal, behavioral, or cognitive change, reflects the way in which different CEMs influence treatment choices. Therefore, it is important for social workers to listen for and discover how the CEMs of patients differ from the CEMs of the treatment providers. In addition, negotiating those differences may mean that the problem is reformulated and the treatment plan is adjusted to take into account *both* provider and patient CEMs.

OVERCOMING THREAT #3: SIMPLIFY HEALTH AND SOCIAL SERVICES AND INCREASE HEALTH LITERACY

The third threat that confronts linguistic minorities is shared by many English-speaking Americans: low levels of health literacy and an accompanying association with adverse health outcomes (DeWalt, Berkman, Sheridan, Lohr, & Pignone, 2004). An estimated 90 million adults (almost half of all American adults) have low levels of *health literacy*, which is defined as the "capacity to obtain, process, and understand basic health information and services needed to make appropriate health decisions" (Institute of Medicine, 2004). Problems associated with limited health literacy are prevalent in the medical literature and are consistently associated with age, ethnicity, and level of education (Paasche-Orlow, Parker, Gazmararian, Nielsen-Bohlman, & Rudd, 2005).

The United States health care system is highly complex and assumes that the individual will activate the system when needed and will take responsibility for self-care (Ratzan, 2001). Because of these built-in assumptions, those without access or the means to adhere to treatment are decisively disadvantaged. For non-English-speaking immigrants, lack of familiarity with the language and the culture creates a particular vulnerability to increased marginalization (feeling misunderstood or like they are being treated as outsiders), leading to behaviors that engender poor health (e.g., leaving the clinic) (Kimbrough, 2007).

It is important for social workers to know about health literacy practices that have been found useful. A recent study by the Commonwealth Fund and Kaiser Permanente identified five health literacy practices that staff considered especially valuable to patients and are applicable to other clinics: (1) a team effort that begins at the front desk; (2) the use of standardized communication tools; (3) the use of plain language, face-to-face communications, pictorials, and educational materials; (4) clinicians partnering with patients to achieve goals; and (5) an organizational commitment to create an environment in which health literacy is not assumed (Barrett, Puryear, & Westpheling, 2008). Any one of these practices will help with health literacy needs, even if a facility or agency cannot readily institute all of them all at once.

Health literacy difficulties are not isolated to the health care sector. Mental health services are used less by LEP clients, contributing to disparities in mental health care (Sentell et al., 2007). *Mental health literacy* has been defined as "knowledge and beliefs about mental disorders which aid in their recognition, management, or prevention" (Jorm et al., 2006). The stigma associated with a mental diagnosis also contributes to the limited access that LEP Latinos/as have to mental health care (Levin, 2007). Therefore, cultivating trust and respect as a way to overcome stigma are important strategies for social workers to use, in conjunction with compensating for limited literacy.

Understanding the Inner World of the LEP Client

LEP clients are on an acculturative pathway, and their experience with English is dynamic and ongoing. Imberti (2007) notes that to understand the person behind the new language, the social worker needs to be aware of the ways in which the foreign tongue can conceal the true self. She underscores two critical aspects of language that have a direct effect on engagement: (1) the emotional superficiality of the second language and (2) the significance of language as a cultural frame of reference.

A client may choose to speak in Spanish when discussing emotionally laden issues even when she or he has some command of English. An example is Maggie, a twenty-four-year-old Mexican woman who came to the United States when she was fourteen years old. Although she understands, reads, and writes in English, she speaks it with an accent. In daily life, Maggie communicates in English at work and in other public spaces. At home, she communicates in Spanish. When she sees her doctor, she prefers to communicate in Spanish, especially about any physical concerns. When asked to explain her preference, she refers to the intimacy of the content as an important factor: talking about one's body is different from talking about work.

It is easy to mistake the LEP client's desire to speak in Spanish as resistance or laziness. However, building a trusting relationship means seeing the world from the client's point of view. When language is an issue, conveying the desire to understand that point of view is essential, even if an interpreter is used. Imberti makes a distinction between linguistic competence and communicative competence when she states that "if a worker is invested in the practice of exploration and understanding of the immigrant client's foreign language experience, there is no need to be competent in the client's specific language." In social work, what is most relevant is the creation of a relationship context in which the process of being understood is given first priority.

The act of being understood is metalingual and preverbal: it is a feeling that someone values what you are conveying. The worker's emphasis on understanding the literal and symbolic meaning of a non-English speaker's communication facilitates the relationship by building trust through a process of communication, however imperfect. This process of understanding can be further enhanced by using simple language, avoiding the use of metaphors, and regularly checking for accuracy in interpretation (if an interpreter is used) or meaning (if the worker is bilingual).

In addition to understanding the emotional embeddedness of language, it is useful to appreciate the significance of language as a cultural frame of reference. Language shapes how we think about the world and our place in that world. One of the challenges of working with LEP clients is that once concrete needs have been met, it is difficult to separate ongoing adjustment difficulties from what Imberti suggests are suppressed reactions to distress that have no verbal outlet:

> Lacking the language used in the mainstream culture to communicate feelings in a way that makes sense to others, it is possible that symptoms become the only way for people to manifest suppressed reactions to discontent and distress when they are unable to articulate those feelings in a familiar, nonpathologic way. (Imberti, 2007, p. 71)

For clients who have strong Spanish-language preferences, it is important always to be mindful that underneath the communication of any symptom or complaint is a fear of being misunderstood. The cultural significance of events and corresponding emotions may not translate very well. For example, one bilingual social work student had a difficult time communicating with her Spanish-speaking mother after her first year away at college. She asked, "How do I explain that I learned to do an assessment?" Her mother would only ask, "What is an assessment?" The bilingual student did not have the words to explain a psychosocial assessment to her mother or the words to express the corresponding joy that comes with developing professional competence. Although both the mother and the daughter spoke Spanish, the educational experiences involved in becoming a social worker were sufficiently different that cultural gaps were created and exacerbated by language.

Conclusion

An old joke about language and American culture begins by asking, "What do you call someone who speaks three languages?" The answer is "Trilingual." A subsequent question asks, "What do you call someone who speaks two languages?" The logical answer is "Bilingual." The final question asks, "What do you call someone who speaks only one language?" The punch line is, of course, "American."

Because English dominates the linguistic landscape of the United States, despite the presence of other languages, there exists an acute need for heightened sensitivity to the language issues that emerge as new non-English-speaking immigrants adapt to a technologically and institutionally complex society. Despite the barriers and difficulties that language barriers pose in the health care and social service systems, these problems are not insurmountable. The resolution of language barriers requires thoughtful service planning, including language assessments for all workers who serve as interpreters; teamwork focused on enhancing communicative competence; and attention to the effect of low levels of health literacy on existing communication barriers.

In this chapter, we have presented an exploration of language, which cuts across all practice domains. Issues of language and its acceptance and rejection lie at the heart of social justice issues. In the final chapter of this book, the author explores the importance of macro practice to working with Latinos. Her integrated approach weaves together direct and indirect practice, with personal and community empowerment and social transformation being primary aims.

For Writing and Reflection

1. Limited English proficiency is often seen as a barrier to overcome. However, knowledge of another language could potentially be a source of strength. In what ways could having multiple cultural frames of reference be an asset? How would you reframe the situation for your client?

2. We live in a monolingual society in which the majority of citizens speak only English. In this context, it is difficult for monolingual workers to understand the service complexities in caring for LEP clients. How can social workers assist their agencies and colleagues to increase their awareness of language issues?

References

Arroyo, L. E. (2004). The health of Latino communities in the South: Challenges and opportunities [electronic version]. Retrieved April 2, 2008, from http://www.nclr.org/content/publications/download/26898

Barrett, S. E., Puryear, J. S., & Westpheling, K. (January 2008). *Health literacy in primary health care settings: Examples from the field.* Retrieved May 01, 2008, from http://www.commonwealthfund.org.

Blau, P. M. (1977). *Inequality and heterogeneity: A primitive theory of social structure* (pp. 19–44). New York: Free Press.

Chen, A. H., Youdelman, M. K., & Brooks, J. (2007). The legal framework for language access in health care settings: Title VI and beyond. *Journal of General Internal Medicine, 22*(Suppl. 2), 362–367.

Chicago Foreign Language Press Survey. (1942). *Chicago Public Library omnibus project of the Work Projects Administration of Illinois.* Special Collections Research Center, University of Chicago Library. See also the University of Illinois at Urbana-Champaign Internet archives. Retrieved May 4, 2008, from http://www.library.uiuc.edu/blog/digitizedbotw/2008/01/chicago_foreign_language_press_1.html

Csordas, T. J. (1994). *The sacred self: A cultural phenomenology of charismatic healing.* Berkeley & Los Angeles: University of California Press.

Cunningham, P., Banker, M., Artiga, S., & Tolbert, J. (2006). *Health coverage and access to care for Hispanics in "new growth communities" and "major Hispanic centers."* Washington, DC: Henry J. Kaiser Family Foundation.

DeWalt, D. A., Berkman, N. D., Sheridan, S., Lohr, K. N., & Pignone, M. P. (2004). Literacy and health outcomes: A systematic review of the literature. *Journal of General Internal Medicine, 19*, 1228–1239.

Drisko, J. W. (2004). Common factors in psychotherapy outcome: Meta-analytic findings and their implications for practice and research. *Families in Society: The Journal of Contemporary Human Services, 85*(1), 81–90.

Elderkin-Thompson, V., Silver, R. C., & Waitzkin, H. (2001). When nurses double as interpreters: A study of Spanish-speaking patients in a US primary care setting. *Social Science & Medicine, 52*, 1343–1358.

Engstrom, D. W., & Min, J. W. (2004). Perspectives of bilingual social workers: "You just have to do a lot more for them." *Journal of Ethnic & Cultural Diversity in Social Work, 13*(1), 59–82.

Engstrom, D. W., & Piedra, L. M. (Eds.). (2007). *Our diverse society: Race and ethnicity—Implications for 21st century American society*. Washington, DC: NASW Press.

Engstrom, D. W., Piedra, L. M., & Min, J. W. (in press). Bilingual social workers: Language and service complexities. *Administration in Social Work*.

Farkas, S., Duffett, A., & Johnson, J. (2003). Now that I'm here: What America's immigrants have to say about life in the U.S. today. Retrieved April 4, 2006, from http://www.publicagenda.org/research/research_reports_details.cfm?list=12

Gregg, J., & Saha, S. (2007). Communicative competence: A framework for understanding language barriers in health care. *Journal of General Internal Medicine, 22*(Suppl. 2), 368–370.

Gumperz, J. (1972). Sociolinguistics and communication in small groups. In J. B. Pride & J. Holmes (Eds.), *Sociolinguistics* (pp. 203–224). Harmondsworth, UK: Penguin Books.

Huntington, S. P. (2004, March/April). The Hispanic challenge. *Foreign Policy, 141*, 30–45.

Imberti, P. (2007). Who resides behind the words? Exploring and understanding the language experience of the non-English-speaking immigrant. *Families in Society, 88*(1), 67–73.

Institute of Medicine. (2004). *Health literacy: A prescription to end confusion*. Washington, DC: National Academies Press.

Jorm, A. F., Barney, L. J., Christensen, H., Highet, N. J., Kelly, C. M., & Kitchener, B. (2006). Research on mental health literacy: What we know and what we still need to know. *Australian and New Zealand Journal of Psychiatry, 40*, 3–5.

Karasz, A. (2005). Cultural differences in conceptual models of depression. *Social Science & Medicine, 60*(7), 1625–1635.

Karasz, A., Sacajiu, G., & Garcia, N. (2003). Conceptual models of psychological distress among low-income patients in an inner-city primary care clinic. *Journal of General Internal Medicine, 18*(6), 475–477.

Karasz, A., & Watkins, L. (2006). Conceptual models of treatment in depressed Hispanic patients. *Annals of Family Medicine, 4*(6), 527–533.

Kaufert, J. M. (1990). Sociological and anthropological perspectives on the impact of interpreters on clinician/client communication. *Sante Culture Health, 7I*(2 & 3), 208–235.

Kimbrough, J. B. (2007). Health literacy as a contributor to immigrant health disparities. *Journal of Health Disparities Research and Practice, 1*(2), 93–106.

Kleinman, A. (1980). *Patients and healers in the context of culture: An exploration of the borderland between anthropology, medicine, and psychiatry.* Berkeley, CA: University of California Press.

Klinenberg, E. (2002). *Heatwave: A social autopsy of disaster in Chicago.* Chicago: University of Chicago Press.

Ku, L., & Flores, G. (2005). Pay now or pay later: Providing interpreter services in health care. *Health Affairs, 24*(2), 435–444.

Ku, L., & Freilich, A. (2001). *Caring for immigrants: Health care safety nets in Los Angeles, New York, Miami, and Houston.* Washington, DC: Henry J. Kaiser Family Foundation.

Lakes, K., Lopez, S. R., & Garro, L. C. (2006). Cultural competence and psychotherapy: Applying anthropologically informed conceptions of culture. *Psychotherapy: Theory, Research, Practice, Training, 43,* 380–396.

Lamphere, L. (Ed.). (1992). *Structuring diversity: Ethnographic perspectives on the new immigration.* Chicago: University of Chicago Press.

Lavizzo-Mourey, R. (2007). Improving quality of US health care hinges on improving language services. *Journal of General Internal Medicine, 22*(Suppl. 2), 279–280.

Levin, A. (2007). Cultural beliefs keep many Hispanics from getting mental health care. *Psychiatry News, 42*(23), 8.

Marsiglia, F. F., & Kulis, S. (2009). *Diversity, oppression, and change.* Chicago: Lyceum Books.

Mettler, S. (1998). *Dividing citizens: Gender and federalism in new deal public policy.* Ithaca, NY: Cornell University Press.

Moreno, M. R., Otero-Sabogal, R., & Newman, J. (2007). Assessing dual-role staff-interpreter linguistic competency in an integrated health system. *Journal of General Internal Medicine, 22*(Suppl. 2), 331–335.

Paasche-Orlow, M. K., Parker, R. M., Gazmararian, J. A., Nielsen-Bohlman, L. T., & Rudd, R. R. (2005). The prevalence of limited health literacy. *Journal of General Internal Medicine, 20*(2), 175–184.

Partida, Y. (2007). Addressing language barriers: Building response capacity for a changing nation. *Journal of General Internal Medicine, 22*(Suppl. 2), 347–349.

Piedra, L. M. (2006). Revisiting the language question. In D. W. Engstrom & L. M. Piedra (Eds.), *Our diverse society: Race and ethnicity—Implications for 21st century American society* (pp. 67–87). Washington, DC: NASW Press.

Portes, A., & Rumbaut, R. G. (2001a). *Legacies: The story of the immigrant second generation.* Berkeley & Los Angeles: University of California Press.

Ratzan, S. C. (2001). Health literacy: Communication for the public good. *Health Promotion International, 16*(2), 207–214.

Schyve, P. M. (2007). Language differences as a barrier to quality and safety in health care: The joint commission perspective. *Journal of General Internal Medicine, 22*(Suppl. 2), 360–361.

Sentell, T., Shumway, M., & Snowden, L. (2007). Access to mental health treatment by English language proficiency and race/ethnicity. *Journal of General Internal Medicine, 22*(Suppl. 2), 289–293.

Shin, H. B. (2003). Language use and the English-speaking ability: 2000. *Census 2000 brief.* Retrieved April 5, 2006, from http://www.census.gov/prod/2003pubs/c2kbr-29.pdf

Sluzki, C. E. (1978). The patient-provider-translator triad: A note for providers. *Family Systems Medicine* (currently *Family Systems and Health*), 2(4), 379–400.

Sollors, W. (Ed.). (1998). *Multilingual America: Transnationalism, ethnicity, and the languages of American literature.* New York: New York University Press.

Suro, R., & Singer, A. (2002). *Latino growth in metropolitan America: Changing patterns, new locations.* Washington, DC: The Brookings Institution, Center on Urban & Metropolitan Policy, & the Pew Hispanic Center.

CHAPTER SEVENTEEN

"Solidaridad Y Justicia"

Latinas, Community Organizing, and Empowerment

Dawn Belkin-Martinez

Introduction

Social work has a long and proud history of assisting Latinos and other marginalized people adjust to life in the United States. While all immigrants face a host of challenges as they confront life in a new and different environment, Latino immigrants' adjustment to U.S. society and culture is made even more difficult because they face additional barriers to their successful integration into the nation. Some of these have been explored in depth in previous chapters, and include: ethnic and racial discrimination; language barriers; inadequate housing; limited employment opportunities; and inadequate education and job training. (Smart & Smart, 1995; Monat & Lazarus, 1991; Hovey, 2000a; Perez-Foster, 2001).

All of these barriers give rise to forms of stress that accompany the complex processes through which newcomers become integrated into a new society. These stresses often result in physical and mental illnesses and can limit Latino immigrants' self-esteem, efficacy, and sense of causal importance—critical characteristics of psychological empowerment essential for successful adaptation to a new society. They can also significantly reduce immigrants' life choices and options in their adopted country, placing them in situations where few alternatives are available to them. This renders them "objects" being acted on by government and social service agencies rather than active "subjects" making a difference in their own lives (Freire, 1996).

Given this context, community organizing and community social work should be an essential component of our work with Latino clients. Numerous studies have demonstrated that participation in grassroots community organizing appears to be effective in assisting immigrants to confront and overcome prejudice, discrimination, and other forms of marginalization they experience (Kieffer, 1984). The social work code of ethics notes that the "primary mission of social work is to help meet the basic human needs of all people with particular attention to the needs and empowerment of people who are vulnerable, oppressed and living in poverty" (National Association of Social Workers, 2000, p.1). Fundamental to social work is attention to the environmental forces that create and contribute to problems in living. Social workers need to be actively involved in those community efforts to alleviate these "problems in living."

To one degree or another, all immigrants experience problems with adjusting to life in a new country. Collectively, these problems are usually conceptualized as *acculturative stress*. Acculturative stress describes the stress that directly results from the rules and roles of behavior characteristic of the new country in which they find themselves, or stress that originates from the processes whereby individuals and groups of immigrants learn about and adjust to their new home (Smart & Smart, 1995).

If all immigrants experience some degree of such stress, in the American experience, new arrivals from Africa, Asia, and Latin America, whose ethnic or national origins are disfavored in the United States, face particular and more daunting challenges (Shibutani & Kwan, 1965). Specifically, many Latinos immigrate to the United States with few economic resources. Once here, they face the discrimination and prejudice that is accorded to darker-skinned people in this country. They generally earn less than their native-born counterparts, are limited to low-end jobs with few if any benefits, and experience little job security and even less chance of advancement. They often lack access to health services, adequate housing, and quality education for their children (U.S. Census Bureau, 2001).

Statistics confirm this assessment. A recent study found that Latino immigrants are overrepresented in the two most dangerous fields of employment: construction and agriculture (Greenhouse, 2001). The on-the-job death rate for Latinos is 20 percent higher than for whites and blacks, and the occupational death rate for Latino immigrants is even higher. Over 30 percent of all Latinos have no access to health insurance, with close to 50 percent of all Latino immigrants being uninsured.

Latinos have the highest high school drop-out rate (30 percent of Latinos drop out of high school compared to 12.6 percent of African Americans and 7.7 percent of Anglos). Finally, 28 percent of all Latinos live in poverty, with the percentage for Latino immigrants being even higher.

Confronted with this complex web of adverse factors and barriers to social and economic advancement, it is no accident that Latino immigrants suffer acculturative stress and discrimination and have trouble adjusting to life in the United States. In the Brazilian educator Paulo Freire's seminal book, *Pedagogy of the Oppressed*, he writes that oppressed groups of people often experience life as objects being acted upon, rather than as subjects in their own lives (Freire, 1968). This situation of powerlessness can cause mental and psychological stress and unhappiness. Freire's analysis is relevant to the lives of many Latino immigrants. As a result of experiencing this powerlessness in their new country, many Latino immigrants suffer from depression or other psychological disorders, or have higher rates of suicide, alcoholism, and drug abuse than other immigrants or people born in the United States (Hovey & King, 1997; Hovey, 2000a; Hovey, 2000b). Many suffer from physical ailments that go untreated because of poverty and a lack of adequate health insurance, thereby straining health service systems and governmental social safety nets. Finding appropriate strategies to address the serious range of problems experienced by growing numbers of Latino immigrants in this country is a major issue for society, the government, and the social work community.

Implications for Social Work Practice and Policy

Social work today often employs a "medical model" of service delivery when working with Latino immigrants. This model's primary focus is on addressing a client's individual physical and mental health needs in isolation from the social context in which the person is situated. Immigrants are frequently viewed as "fish out of water," persons disoriented and poorly equipped for the challenges facing them. The responsibility of the social worker is to provide them with coping skills and mental health services to ease their adaptation to and adoption of the dominant cultural characteristics of U.S. society (Westermeyer, 1989). The "culturally sensitive" model of social work practice with immigrants arose in reaction to inadequacies of the medical model (Hewitt, 1999). This alternative is still a basic service delivery model of practice, but one that attempts to more effectively understand and work with clients by becoming more attuned to them culturally and linguistically. It seeks to understand and work with individuals in the context of their cultural and ethnic values, traditions, and patterns of behavior and to take these into account in treatment.

For these reasons, the "culturally sensitive" practice model was certainly an improvement on the service delivery model that preceded it. What it lacked, however, were two key components: a broader context within which the issues and problems of immigrants could be situated, and a recognition of the critical importance of client empowerment in this process.

Over the last several decades, a new practice model has begun to emerge. Based on empowerment theory and participation in community organizing, it is one of the most promising theories and practices for assisting poor, oppressed, and neglected sections of U.S. society to marshal their resources and develop the skills necessary to overcome stress and the social and personal obstacles they face. This empowerment-based practice model looks at the strategies and methods that oppressed communities and individuals in our society develop to successfully access personal and social power (Gutierrez & Ortega, 1991). Collective empowerment through community organizing is one of the few activities available to Latino immigrants where they can enhance their psychological empowerment by developing self-esteem, causal importance, and efficacy through their own experiences. Empowerment through community activism provides a successful model that addresses both of the components missing from the dominant medical model employed by social work in working with Latino immigrants.

Community Social Work Practice: A Conceptual Model and Framework

"All oppression is destructive of life and should be challenged by social workers and clients" (Lee, 1994, p. 12). The obligation to challenge oppression is an existential, operational, and moral imperative, and not just for social workers. As long as society allows the oppression of one or more of its constituent groups, no other constituency is free from the threat of oppression. In other words, social work is, or should be, about empowerment. And social work practice is, or should be, about clients' involvement and participation in activities that work to transform them from passive objects being acted upon by others into active subjects playing a critical role in determining their own futures.

Paulo Freire (1968) was an important writer on empowerment practice in the context of community change. Central to his work are a number of themes concerning struggle, objectification, and the proper relationship between advocacy and empowerment. For clinicians who have adopted his approach, social work practice, like education, is essentially about struggle, from the struggle to transform the conditions that oppress and exploit clients, to ones that will enhance their lives and enable them to develop their full potential. At the same time, social work practice is about active client involvement and participation in activities that work to transform them from (in Freire's words) objects into subjects. That is to say from categories (e.g., "Latino immigrant") defined for them in which they are acted upon by government and policy makers, into self-defined subjects who know and act on their own behalf. For Freire, and the social workers who use his work, these two processes exist in dialectical relationship to one another. To put it another way, changes in the objective world can only come about from changes in individual subjectivities, and changes in people's consciousness derive from their participation in changing the conditions of their own lives (Rose & Black, 1985). Loosely, there are three steps in the conceptual framework: (1) seeing the problem or situation lived/experienced by the client, (2) analyzing the personal, cultural, and institutional factors that contribute to the problem, and (3) acting to change the problem or situation (Belkin-Martinez, 2004).

From Theory to Practice

As noted above, the first step in applying this community social work practice framework is to identify the problems as experienced by the clients. To facilitate this process, clients and providers usually engage in some sort of participatory research about the clients' problem(s). Social workers need to get to know their clients outside of the immediate problem(s) as well. This includes getting to know about the clients' work life, school life, and the issues the clients face on an ongoing basis. As they did in the settlement houses of the last century, social workers need to become intimately familiar with their clients' community. Social workers, along with their clients, for example, may conduct a community needs assessment or engage in participatory group activities, where the community comes together to express those shared aspects of their life felt to be unsatisfactory. Fundamental to this approach is working with common sense, popular culture, and popular wisdom. After the client, family, or community has come together to identify the problem(s), they are asked to produce a material representation of them, or as Freire might say, a code or generative theme. Clients can create a drawing, video, or audiotape that represents the issues at hand and are asked to make the link between themselves and the problem(s).

The next step is for the clients and social workers to analyze a problem by asking themselves: (1) What are the individual/personal factors that contribute to the problem? (2) What are the cultural factors that contribute to the problem? and (3) What are the institutional/political factors that contribute to the problem? The social worker can use a triangle as a visual representation to demonstrate how the three different factors interface with each other and "drive" the problem; or the worker can create a "problem tree," identifying the leaves as the outcome of the problem and the root as the causes of the problem. This is often the most challenging piece of work, as many of us are not taught to think critically and instead accept taken-for-granted assumptions about the world as "facts." This approach requires that, along with our clients, social workers question the dominant messages we receive from society and existing social situations. To survive oppression, most people accustom themselves to material conditions of life to the point where they come to think of these conditions as the "natural way to live." To help people become aware of situations and facts heretofore unknown to them, a community social worker engages in consciousness-raising, helping clients to question taken-for-granted assumptions about the world and deconstructing who these "facts" benefit. (Belkin-Martinez, 2004).

The final step involves clients discussing an action plan. Social workers and clients can produce a "planning the action" chart. The chart consists of several categories: (1) identification of the problem, (2) what needs to change, (3) long range vision, and (4) immediate plans. This is a dynamic process that involves reflection, adjustment, and the production of new knowledge.

CASE STUDY

Two social workers in a community mental health center decided to organize a support group for Latina mothers. The group consisted of eight mothers who had been referred to the counseling department by medical providers because of concerns around depression. The group initially contracted to meet weekly for three months. All of the clients acknowledged that they were indeed "depressed" and that their depression was affecting their relationships with their children and the larger community.

As the social workers and the Latina mothers worked together to identify the problem, there was almost unanimous agreement that depression was a primary problem affecting each and every one of them. The group created a drawing that visually demonstrated their many worries, the most prominent being steep housing rent increases for four of the group members. Through their shared participatory research, the social workers learned that half of the group members lived in the same housing project, which had contracted with the federal government program for subsidized housing. For the past thirty years, their landlord had received a voucher from the federal government to charge "market rate" rents in a neighborhood that was not "desirable" for market rate tenants. In other words, the landlord received thousands of dollars every month from the government in order to receive market rate rent for his building. Although the women had been paying below market rate rent, for over thirty years the landlord had been paid extra money by the government to compensate for this. At this point in time, however, the neighborhood had changed significantly, with many newcomers being more affluent and willing to pay higher rents. As a result, the landlord had decided not to renew his government voucher and announced to the tenants that he was planning to double their rents by the end of the year. Being unable to pay the new amount, these women feared that they would be evicted.

In the problem-analysis stage of their group process, the women drew a triangle with depression as the identified problem and were asked to talk about the personal, cultural, and institutional factors that they saw contributing to it. While all of the women acknowledged some history of loss and trauma, they were also able to discuss the cultural and institutional factors that contributed to their depression. They spoke at length about the lack of solidarity and community in the United States and how the culture of individualism puts forth the myth that "everyone needs to do everything on their own." They talked about how it was impossible to raise a family on poverty wages (all of the women worked outside of the home) when housing, medical care, transportation, and food were so expensive. Through problem posing and problem analysis, they were able to see that their depression was directly related to larger institutional injustices and societal cultural norms and values such as individualism and competition.

When talking about an action plan, the social workers brought up the idea of trying to resist the upcoming rent increase and to explore ways for the mothers to stay in their homes. Initially, the clients did not believe they had the right to fight for this. Wasn't it the landlord's right to do as he pleased? If it was his building, couldn't he charge whatever he wanted to? What right did they, mere tenants, have to ask him to renew his housing voucher with the federal government?

The social workers asked a local tenants' rights organization to meet with the group. Alongside their clients, the workers learned more about the federal housing program, and deconstructed dominant worldview assumptions about private institutions and who was actually receiving a subsidy. As noted above, the owner of the building had received hundreds of thousands of dollars over the last thirty years in "handouts" from the federal government, money from hard-earned tax dollars. As one of the mothers noted during a group session: "All of these years, I thought he was doing me a favor by keeping the rent affordable, but now I have learned that I have been paying him double [through her taxes] to stay there!" The women also discussed the racist/classist implications of the landlord's decision to not renew the voucher with the federal government. One said, "Before any of these rich people wanted to live in our neighborhood, he had no problem taking our money, getting money from the Feds, and renting to us, but now that these rich white people want to move to our neighborhood, all of a sudden we aren't good enough?" The mother's "knowledge" about the situation had been transformed; they were ready to take action to change the situation.

The group members initially wrote a letter to the landlord requesting that he renew the housing voucher. When he did not respond to their request, they sent him, the mayor, and members of the city council a petition, signed by thousands of individuals, again requesting he renew the housing voucher. Outreach to community members about the situation and rallies outside of the landlord's office fell on deaf ears. The deadline for the rent increases was approaching.

After an evaluation of the action plan, the women agreed that they needed to take the protest to another level; they needed to demonstrate, in a dramatic way, just how unreasonable the landlord was. The social workers suggested going to the landlord's office and refusing to leave until he agreed to meet with the tenants and discuss recommitting to the housing voucher program. The clients thought this was a great idea, but shared their concerns that the police would be called and everyone would be arrested. Many of the women were single mothers with inflexible jobs; they could not afford to be arrested.

After additional problem posing, the group developed a new action plan: the women, along with their supporters, would enter the building and when the police arrived, they would leave the building and hold a rally outside. Supporters of the group would refuse to leave the office, and they would be arrested in solidarity with the demand: recommit to the housing voucher program. Deconstructing the culture of individualism was an important component of the work; initially many of the women didn't think it was "fair" for the social workers to get arrested when "it's not really their problem." As one client noted: "I really had my worldview changed from these conversations in so many ways, first, about the actual housing situation, but, more important, about what community really means. It's not just my problem when an injustice like this happens; we are all responsible to act to change the situation and we all should do our part. That's the kind of world that I and all of the people in this struggle want to live in."

In the end, the mothers won! The police did arrive and indeed arrested about twenty supporters of the women (including many social workers!), and the mothers held a powerful rally outside the building attended by several city council members. The rally and subsequent arrests led to a great deal of press coverage. The following day, the mayor issued a call for the landlord to renew his housing voucher, and the daily newspaper ran an editorial supporting the demand for continuation of the voucher. The women's new "knowledge" about race, class, and power had become part of a larger community discussion.

Conclusion

The above clinical situation was a success in many ways: the women were able to generate tremendous political pressure on the landlord, who eventually recommitted to continue the housing voucher. More importantly, however, the women had become active subjects in the process; they not only changed their internal worlds—reporting reduced symptoms of depression—but they significantly changed their external world and had a profound impact on policy and politics for hundreds of families. The initial small group of eight women grew to include over fifty neighborhood woman, many of them who did not live in the project that had been the target of the intervention. As several mothers commented during the problem-analysis stage, "Even though I am not directly affected by this, I want to be part of the community response. I am not just going to lie back and take it anymore when bad things happen; fighting back gives me energy and makes me feel better." Several of the mothers have since gone on to volunteer with the housing organization that assisted them and are now leaders in the Latina community. This clinical example demonstrates Kieffer's (1984) assumptions that community organizing was a powerful intervention in helping the women increase their self-confidence, causal importance, and self-efficacy.

If we, as social workers embrace the core values of our profession, if we agree with Jerome Wakefield's assessment that social justice is the "key organizing value of social work" (1988), then we have no choice but to commit ourselves to utilizing community social work models in our work with Latino clients. We are not just trying to get our clients to adjust to an oppressive system of injustice; our work must include efforts to transform the system in order to meet the liberation needs of all. ¡Si, Se Puede!

For Writing and Reflection

1. How can social workers move from "case to cause" in our clinical work?

2. How do we deconstruct dominant worldview assumptions and raise awareness about cultural and institutional factors while "meeting the clients where they are at"?

3. Many social workers see a clear distinction between clinical work and macro work. The social workers involved in the case study clearly believed that clinical and macro work are all part of the same work and that the role of the clinician includes addressing all three factors in the

conceptual framework of an empowerment-based practice model. What are your thoughts about this?

References

Belkin-Martinez, D. (2004). Therapy for liberation. Retrieved September 6, 2006, from http://liberationhealth.org/documents/freiresummarysimmons.pdf

Freire, P. (1968). *Pedagogy of the oppressed.* New York: The Seabury Press.

Freire, P. (1996). *Pedagogy of the city.* New York: Continuum Publishing Company.

Greenhouse, S. (2001, July 16). Hispanic workers die at higher rate: More likely than others to do the dangerous low-end jobs. *New York Times,* p. A11.

Gutierrez, L. M., & Ortega, R. (1991). Developing methods to empower Latinos: The importance of groups. *Social Work with Groups, 14*(2) 23–44.

Hewitt, J. (1999). *Culturally sensitive social work practice.* Retrieved July, 6, 2001, from http//his.com/jhewitt/sj/sensitive.html

Hovey, J. D. (2000a). Acculturative stress, depression, suicidal ideation among Central American immigrants. *Suicide and Life Threatening Behavior, 30,* 125–139.

Hovey, J. D. (2000b). Psychosocial predictors of acculturative stress in Mexican immigrants. *The Journal of Psychology, 134*(5), 490–502.

Hovey, J. D., & King, C. A.(1997). Suicidality among acculturating Mexican Americans: Current knowledge and directions for research. *Suicide and Life Threatening Behavior, 27,* 92–103.

Kieffer, C. (1984). Citizen empowerment: A developmental perspective. In J. Rappaport, C. Swift, & R. Hess (Eds.), *Studies in empowerment: Steps toward understanding and action* (pp. 9–36). New York: Haworth Press.

Lazarus, R. S., & Folkman, S. (1984). *Stress, appraisal and coping.* New York: Springer Publishing Company.

Lee, J. (1994). *The empowerment approach to social work practice.* New York: Columbia University Press.

Monat, A., & Lazarus, R. S. (1991). Stress and coping: An anthology. New York: Columbia University Press.

National Association of Social Workers. (2000). *Code of ethics.* Retrieved January 17, 2005, from www.socialworkers.org/pubs/code/code.asp

Perez-Foster, R. (2001). When immigration is trauma: Guidelines for individual and family clinicians. *American Journal of Orthopsychiatry, 71*(2), 153–169.

Rose, S. M., & Black, B. L. (1985). *Advocacy and empowerment.* Boston: Routledge & Kegan Paul.

Shibutani, T., & Kwan, K.(1965). *Ethnic stratification.* New York: Macmillan.

Smart, J. F,.& Smart, D. W. (1995). Acculturative stress of Hispanics: Loss and challenge. *Journal of Counseling and Development, 73*(4), 390–405.

U.S. Census Bureau (2001). *The Hispanic population: Census 2000 brief.* (USC Publication No. C2KBR/01–3). Washington, DC: Betsy Guzman.

Wakefield, J. C. (1988). Psychotherapy, distributive justice, and social work, part 2. *Social Service Review, 62,* 353–382.

Westermeyer, J. (1989). *Psychiatric care of migrants: A clinical guide.* Washington, DC: American Psychiatric Press.

Index